Third-Party Risk Management: Driving Enterprise Value

Third-Party Risk Management: Driving Enterprise Value

Linda Tuck Chapman

rma
THE RISK MANAGEMENT ASSOCIATION

RMA is a member-driven professional association whose sole purpose is to advance sound risk management principles in the financial services industry.

RMA helps our members use sound risk management principles to improve institutional performance and financial stability, and enhance the risk management competency of individuals through information, peer sharing, and networking.

Edited by Frank Devlin

Cover design by Arielle Morris

Text design and composition by Stephen Druding

Front cover photo by Shutterstock, Inc.

RMA Product Number: 641215

ISBN: 978-1-57070-349-2

Library of Congress Control Number: 2018934606

Printed in the United States of America.

For my friend Krystelle Bilodeau.
Thank you for the thought-provoking conversations,
your enthusiasm, knowledge and insight,
and your gift of valuable feedback.

Contents

Foreword

The financial services industry is no stranger to utilizing third parties to achieve business objectives. Historically, third parties have provided significant benefits to allow financial institutions to conduct business in an efficient, and profitable, manner. This is especially true for community banks that required additional technical expertise, but could not financially support the staffing requirements such expertise would entail.

Until recent events, the primary focus on third-party relationship risk management (I refer to it as TPRM) in the financial services industry was on technology service providers. When I say recent, I mean over the past 10 years. As a regulator involved in community bank examinations, I have seen much reliance placed on third parties to provide key control functions such as internal audit, loan review, and compliance monitoring. I will admit my primary concerns about third-party providers regarded their level of expertise, extent of coverage, and accuracy of findings. Regulatory guidance regarding the supervision of third-party relationship risk management did exist; however, the Federal Financial Institutions Examination Council (FFIEC) was at the forefront. This was not surprising considering the FFIEC's responsibility to provide regulatory oversight of technology service providers.

The crisis provided the wake-up call for the financial services industry and the regulatory agencies regarding TPRM. We, collectively, became starkly aware of the increased reliance on third parties in all facets of a financial institution's business and the immediate need for the industry to strengthen TPRM practices. Financial institution management became fully aware that while it was acceptable to delegate specified activities, it could not delegate its responsibilities.

Developing a TPRM framework did not come with ease; significant changes were needed from several perspectives. Everyone had to understand the risk involved with third-party relationships, from the board to the front-line staff. Two framework components are worth noting: the needs to adopt a defined lifecycle and to determine the risk exposure for each relationship.

In this book, Linda provides beneficial detail about these components that will help you enhance your practical experience. I was fortunate to have the opportunity to meet and interact with Linda during my travels as a regulator to inform the industry of the regulatory perspective on TPRM. I became impressed with her understanding of TPRM's challenges to the financial industry and her passion about TPRM and the need to drive continued enhancements to TPRM industry practices.

I think you will find value in how Linda provides best practices from various financial industry representatives as well as from her own professional experience. There are aspects of TPRM we still do not know, which is one of Linda's "windows." You will understand what I mean by that as you enjoy your journey through her book.

John Eckert
Director of Governance and Operational Risk Policy
Office of the Comptroller of the Currency, Retired

SECTION

Driving Total Alignment

1 Third-Party Management: Asset Management or Compliance Exercise?

It came as a surprise when an executive responsible for sourcing, procurement, and vendor management at a large bank recently told me that the institution's efforts to create a third-party risk management function were pointless. He said that procurement had always performed due diligence on vendors, and there was no need for change.

Procurement's efforts and processes are a good start when addressing third-party risk, but procurement is only involved in larger deals, only with "vendor" third parties, and only for new relationships and some renewals. What about the rest of the third-party relationships—the business-led ones, for example?

Here are some important questions to ask at your institution: Have due diligence processes, controls, and monitoring changed to deal with the changing threat landscape? Can the small, innovative companies that have been brought on meet the bank's requirements and risk-tolerance thresholds? What happens after the contract is signed? Are bank and customer data protected after third-party relationships end? And can procurement help the business create opportunities for deeper, more strategic relationships with the bank's third parties? So many questions, and so few answers.

Third-party relationships are complicated. The critical ones and the activities they support are mini operational and cultural ecosystems unto themselves. Each is an assemblage of your institution; one or more third parties; multiple fourth parties; and the environments, geographies, and markets they operate in.

The uniqueness of each critical-activity mini ecosystem is intensified by its unique operations and your institution's high reliance on:

- Critical third and fourth parties for new technologies such as mobile apps.
- Technology infrastructure and applications that power operations and services.
- Customer transaction-processing and records management.
- HR and payroll services for employees.
- Market utility services to settle trades and clear checks.
- Contact or call centers for sales, customer care, and technical support.

And the list goes on.

Hundreds, thousands, or tens of thousands of third-party relationships power your institution every minute of every day, in every market and geography where you operate, for every product and service. Effective and efficient third-party lifecycle and risk management are also necessary for institutional safety and soundness.

Done well, third-party relationships deliver what you contracted for while bringing more opportunities to innovate. They help develop new and competitive products and services and help you find new markets and exit unprofitable old ones. They provide access to their specialized top talent, processes, and technology; share their expertise in automating, streamlining, eliminating, and improving processes; show you how to manage or reduce operating costs; and contribute to significant increases in the value of the enterprise, in many dimensions.

Despite all this, until recently third-party management simply wasn't on the radar for senior management and boards, except when material outsourcing was occurring or a new budget line hit certain limits. But regulatory guidance for third-party relationships has long been a focus, one that escalated following the financial crisis of 2007-2008. Instability across the system was a sharp reminder to regulators that a safe and sound financial system is dependent on many factors.

For a safe and sound system, financial institutions and the complex ecosystems of critical third-party relationships they operate within must also be safe and sound. Regulators know that critical third-party relationships have the potential to introduce instability and high levels of operational risk into the system. They also know that, historically, third-party lifecycle and risk management have been inconsistent, incomplete, and under-invested—and lacked attention from senior management and boards of directors.

In 2013, the U.S. Office of the Comptroller of the Currency (OCC) substantially raised the stakes, setting a new standard with *Bulletin 2013-29 Third Party Relationships - Risk Management Guidance*. Other financial services regulators were close behind.

The OCC defines a third-party relationship as "any business arrangement between a bank and another entity, by contract or otherwise." Although other U.S. regulators have

What is a Third Party?

An entity, including an affiliate, that has a business relationship with the institution or its customers, and is not itself a customer. Third-party relationships include both vendors and non-vendors.

Non-vendor third-party relationships are typically acquired by a business line/segment directly, not through a sourcing/procurement function. Financial remuneration, if applicable, is typically rendered outside of accounts payable processes. These third-party relationships may be managed solely by a business line/segment, or in conjunction with a corporate third-party risk management function.

Vendor third parties are service providers/vendors that provide a product or service to the institution. These relationships are typically sourced through a sourcing/procurement process. Payment is typically rendered by accounts payable.

Source: Third-Party Risk Management Round Table www.rmahq.org

not been as prescriptive about the scope of third-party relationships, their examinations and guidance have followed suit. In Canada, The Office of the Superintendent of Financial Institutions (OSFI) remains primarily focused on outsourcing (vendor) relationships.

For greater clarity, third parties are vendors, suppliers, outsourcers, and "nonvendors" such as financial market utilities, indirect lenders, correspondent banks, and many other function-specific relations. Unless specifically approved as a "carve out"—third-party relationships such as tax authorities, employee expense reimbursement, and charitable donations—third-party relationships are in scope regardless of whether they are sourced through a procurement or business-led process.

Critical Third-Party Relationships: A New Class of Assets?

Despite how essential these relationships are to the success of every financial institution—*affecting customers, market competitiveness, and revenues*—few, if any, business leaders think about their critical third-party relationships as intangible assets.

What could cause you and your institution to change your thinking and manage critical third-party relationships as assets, some of which may have tangible market value? Granted, you can't sell or trade the relationships like loans, investments, or financial instruments. But the success, failure, and suboptimization of critical third-party relationships affects your institution's reputation, operations, and financials—and ultimately can create or destroy value.

Should financial institutions think of the substantial direct costs; "sweat equity"; and the implementation, management, and governance costs related to third-party spending as investments in intangible assets, thereby creating or increasing value?

You can't value third-party relationships as tangible or intangible assets on your balance sheet, of course.

But here is evidence to make the case for change: The Financial Accounting Standards Board (FASB) says the long-term value of "...intangible assets that have indefinite useful lives will not be amortized but rather will be tested at least annually for impairment. Intangible assets that have finite useful lives will continue to be amortized over their useful lives."[1]

According to the Chartered Global Management Accountant organization, "Intangible assets (intangibles) are long-lived assets used in the production of goods and services. They lack physical properties and represent legal rights or competitive advantages (a bundle of rights) developed or acquired by an owner. To have value, intangible assets should generate some measurable amount of economic benefit to the owner, such as incremental turnover or earnings (pricing, volume, and better delivery, amongst others), cost savings (process economies and marketing cost savings), and increased market share or visibility."[2]

Sounds like a third-party relationship, no?

---

[1]FASB Summary of Statement 142 (2014) Goodwill and Other Intangible Assets http://www.fasb.org/summary/stsum142.shtml

[2]CGMA Tools: Three Approaches to Valuing Intangible Assets (Jan. 2012) https://www.cgma.org/content/dam/cgma/resources/tools/downloadabledocuments/valuing-intangible-assets.pdf

Consider the pharmaceutical industry. Its ability to bring new drugs to market is highly dependent on strategic third parties for the development and testing of drugs. Or the telecom sector, which relies on strategic relationships with smartphone manufacturers to deliver the latest advances that drive revenues and market share. Or the financial services sector, which is highly reliant on third parties for the development and delivery of digital strategies and products.

If your institution valued its most strategic, innovative, and essential third-party relationships as intangible assets, FASB rules say they would have to be tested annually to determine whether their value had increased or decreased. Is this a viable path to valuing these relationships for what they really are—strategic assets?

You may want to consider what it would take at your institution to sharpen the focus on creating, increasing, and protecting the value of your most critical third-party relationships. How would this change your third-party lifecycle and risk management practices?

Expect More Consumer Demand for Risk Visibility

Think of the rapid-fire disclaimers that often accompany ads on television and radio. What if the legal system and regulators required all financial institutions to make consumers fully aware of the actual scope of rights and obligations that they can successfully pursue or enforce?

Imagine if financial institutions ended every commercial with an extensive list of risks the consumer will be exposed to when doing business with them, the way that drug companies do.

Imagine every commercial ending with a disclaimer that the third parties they rely on to deliver services "may fail to safeguard your personal data," "may commit fraud," "may enable terrorist financing," "may make serious processing errors," or "may be unsure where your personal information is stored in the cloud."

Specific disclosure about material and potential third-party risk is not (yet) required. Further, only the fallout from failures that noticeably affect an institution's customers are disclosed—and usually only when that failure becomes a matter of public record. Such disclosures are usually limited to a serious service outage, when customers' personal information has been compromised, or as required by financial reporting rules. These are serious events. These incidents and issues have a potential to inflict severe damage on the firm's reputation.

What if some financial institutions could assure you that your money, investments, and personal information are safe regardless of which third parties they rely on? Would you prefer to do business with them, or those that couldn't?

The primary business of financial institutions is to manage risk for a profit. To do this, they must selectively acquire risk by relying on a complex set of criteria that enable fact-based decision making, powering operations with the right investments in technology, people, and processes.

Despite occasional crises, many of which have been caused by deviating from finely honed risk management practices, the financial services sector has a long and enviable history of effectively and profitably managing risk.

Most financial institutions have a venerable history of managing their capital, equity, and liquidity by applying fine-tuned risk management and decision-making capabilities. But over the past 20 to 30 years there have been dramatic changes to the way financial institutions operate. Complex, intertwined, co-dependent outsourcing; strategic alliances; and joint ventures have become the norm. Fact-based decision-making processes for operational risk management have not kept pace.

One area that is substantially underdeveloped includes the practices, processes, skills, and experience related to the hundreds or thousands of third parties that each financial institution relies on, and an institution's ability to generate sufficient insight and information to make informed, fact-based decisions. Such decisions include which services should be delivered with internal resources; which third parties should be contracted; the scope of services; the ability to manage complex relationships; the type and quantity of risk; the ability to respond to issues and failures; the ability to learn and grow within the third-party relationship; and the impact on customers when critical third-party relationships are entered, changed, or exited.

Before third-party risk management evolved into a programmatic approach, the expertise across risk domains was not applied in an integrated way regarding an institution's third-party relationships. Instead the relationships were treated as separate operational fields of management, only coming together to respond to serious incidents and issues. This has changed, and the sector is still trying to get it right. The rewards are not understood mostly because this is a new discipline with limited historical data and virtually no systematic analysis and response to the data that is available.

There are consequences for getting it wrong; some are easy to quantify and others are not.

Risk-Adjusted Cost of Capital: A Consequence of Exceeding Risk Appetite?

Some business leaders are more than willing to assume risks that exceed the institution's and/or their function's risk appetite. In many financial institutions, the decision to proceed is entirely in the hands of the business owner, and an "independent challenge" may be considered a career-limiting move by lower-level risk specialists. As a result, little or nothing stands in the business leader's way.

If a model is created to calculate the risk-adjusted cost of capital, then charged to business units accordingly, would this influence decisions about how much risk individual business leaders are willing to accept? And how would implementing a risk-adjusted cost of capital affect the risk culture of the institution?

Applying Existing Portfolio-Management Capabilities to Third Parties

Despite enormous depth and breadth in acquiring and managing significant portfolios of investments, loans, and financial instruments, critical third parties are not managed as portfolios—certainly not as portfolios of business assets or risks.

Looking at how loans are managed in a bank, in 1998 the OCC proposed that, "To manage their portfolios, bankers must understand not only the risk posed by each credit but also how the risks of individual loans and portfolios are interrelated. These interrelationships can multiply risk many times beyond what it would be if the risks were not related."

"Until recently, few banks used modern portfolio-management concepts to control credit risk. Now, many banks view the loan portfolio in segments as well as a whole, and consider the relationships among portfolio segments as well as among loans. These practices provide management with a more complete picture of the bank's credit risk profile and with more tools to analyze and control the risk."[3]

Isn't third-party risk segmentation, by risk rating, by critical activity, by service category, or by risk level and risk control function the foundation for portfolio management? A well-designed program, supported by enabling technology, enables risk identification, risk-adjusted work effort and controls, risk visibility, stress testing, and oversight. It enables a complete picture of the institution's third-party risk profile, and the tools to analyze and control risk.

Sound familiar?

Is It Just About Risk Management?

According to Ernst & Young's 2016 financial services third-party risk management survey, "Shifting Toward Maturity,"[4] the sector is making progress but still has a long way to go before third-party risk management practices are seamlessly woven into business practices.

- Thirty-nine percent of respondents said that all of their third parties fall within the scope of their third-party risk management program.
- Roughly a quarter of organizations said they can run on-demand risk scorecards.
- Thirty percent said that they are unable to report on contracts with incentive compensation structures.
- Eleven percent said they have fully integrated reporting tools.

Until programs and practices are more mature, it is hard for them to add value. But third-party management shouldn't be simply about managing risk and minimizing and avoiding loss events. It would be shortsighted to focus on risk management at the expense of investing in healthy relationships, innovation, performance, and cost management.

Third-party relationships are very good for your institution, its reputation, revenues, and resilience. That's why this book is about third-party lifecycle *and* risk management, not just risk management.

---

[3]OCC A-LPM (April 1998) Loan Portfolio Management Comptrollers Handbook https://www.occ.gov/publications/publications-by-type/comptrollers-handbook/lpm.pdf

[4]EY: Shifting Toward Maturity, 2016 financial services third-party risk management survey http://www.ey.com/us/en/services/advisory/ey-2016-financial-services-shifting-toward-maturity

What to Expect

This book is presented in three distinct sections. The first section describes the management environment by examining how the "tone at the top," the three lines of defense, operating and governance frameworks, tools, and processes come together. The second section examines several risk drivers. Some are the most common risk exposures: reputation, information and cyber, and business continuity. The others are risks that are often missing from third-party management programs: Bank Secrecy Act/anti-money laundering (BSA/AML) and model risk. The final section is about monitoring, governance, and the impact of a changing workforce on third-party management.

For the most part, the background information, concepts, and insights are presented in a consistent manner:

- Context
- What You Should Know
- What Your Institution Should Do

Executives and subject-matter experts from across the sector loaned their voices to the book, generously sharing their expertise and experiences. They also made a valuable contribution when they reviewed the concepts, information, and ideas presented, increasing my confidence that they are feasible and reasonable. Thank you!

I hope you enjoy reading it as much as I did writing it!

2 Building a Strong Risk Culture

When Greg Carmichael, president and CEO at Fifth Third Bank took the helm in late 2015, he powered Fifth Third's risk management practices on a journey of transformation.

In Carmichael's words, the years of "go-go growth at any cost are well behind us." Leaders everywhere are recalibrating the direction of their institution and the sector. Coming out of the financial crisis Carmichael saw many banks struggling. Some didn't survive insurmountable shortfalls in capital and liquidity. Of those that did survive, some won't survive in the long run. The predominant reason is misalignment between their business model and the current environment.

"Senior leadership needs to have a mindset of being strong through every cycle," Carmichael says, "strong in good times, and strong under adverse economic conditions."

Regulations are intended to ensure that all financial institutions are strong through every cycle, continuously operating in a manner that is consistent with the principles of safety and soundness. To achieve this, the regulatory burden is a heavy and expensive one, fed by a vast network of interconnected financial services regulations in force today.

A 2014 study conducted by the Federal Reserve Bank of St. Louis revealed that "governance practices may not be as critically dependent on direct expenditures as they are on the ability of management, boards, audit committees, and internal auditors to work together to properly focus oversight attention, and larger banks have an edge in focusing that attention more efficiently." These practices are referred to as "tone at the top."

The phrase was coined in an American Accounting Association research report on the behavior of entry-level auditors.[5] It has been widely adopted by the financial services sector to describe appropriate business behaviors that align with a strong risk management culture, demonstrated in the behavior of senior management and by the rewards and consequences throughout the organization.

Compliance and risk management are not interchangeable terms, and investments in compliance-related activities and processes may not translate into sound risk man-

[5]American Accounting Association Behavioural Research in Accounting (BRIA) http://www.aaajournals.org/loi/bria

agement practices. Compliance with regulations and laws should not be the end game. Effective risk management is reliant on a strong risk culture, communicated through the tone at the top and good corporate governance.

At Fifth Third Bank, "tone at the top" is supported by the North Star program. North Star is a set of interconnected strategic initiatives to strengthen competitiveness while de-risking the bank. Embedded in every North Star initiative is a strong regulatory core. This ensures decisions are aligned with tone at the top and the bank's risk appetite. Every employee knows what's important and where the bank is going.

Consistent communication across a large, dispersed population of employees is difficult to achieve. To address this risk, Carmichael expanded Fifth Third's Operating Committee to the bank's "Top 100". The Top 100 meets in person every quarter, and returns to their offices armed with a complete communication toolbox, consisting of talking points for local town hall meetings, prepared communication, and a corporate video. This ensures that bank employees are informed and remain aligned with the bank's tone at the top, strategic initiatives, goals, and progress.

To deliver the bank's strategic three-year plan, Fifth Third made significant investments in people, processes, and tools to strengthen the bank's tone at the top, risk culture, and risk management practices.

According to the Office of the Comptroller of the Currency, "Among the elements of a strong culture and an effective tone at the top are:

- a strictly enforced code of ethics that applies to everyone;
- open and candid communications throughout the organization;
- clear lines of authority and responsibility;
- transparency; and
- strong internal controls."[6]

Effective third-party risk management can only be achieved when there is a risk-centric "tone at the top" corporate culture combined with sufficient investment in expertise, processes, and tools; experienced people who work well together; and sufficient time invested by senior management and the board in governance activities.

"Effective governance is based on a partnership, with clearly defined roles, between the board and management," the OCC says. "The board has three key roles: strategy, people, and oversight ... while management's job is to manage. These roles are separated by a line-in-the-sand which can shift based on the circumstances. Frequent, open, and honest communication helps the partnership work."[7]

In practical terms, while smaller institutions are particularly challenged by the widening scope of regulations they must comply with, they may have a slight advantage over larger institutions because their board members are typically deeply engaged in many aspects of the bank's operations, including risk management.

As the scope of regulations has expanded, the size of quarterly board packages has become excessive—mostly due to regulatory guidelines that hold board members account-

---

[6]OCC: Corporate Governance and the Community Bank: A Regulatory Perspective (June 2005) https://www.occ.gov/static/past-conferences-and-seminars/cgts-final-exec-summary.pdf
[7]Ibid.

able for what were once management decisions. At Fifth Third, quarterly board packages can consist of thousands of pages of material. Audit committee members may also be required to consume two more thick binders of material.

Boards of directors in every financial institution can be hamstrung by the sheer volume of information they need to digest. But they must stay sufficiently informed and have the expertise to exercise their challenge responsibilities, which must be recorded in the board minutes. Their roles also make them liable for the actions of the bank.

Many would say that regulator involvement in a vast number of activities, at a detail level, impedes the board's ability to effectively govern the bank.

Regulatory Intervention in Third-Party Risk Management

In 2013, the OCC, Federal Reserve Board (FRB), Consumer Financial Protection Bureau (CFPB), and Federal Financial Institutions Examination Council (FFIEC) updated their guidance for the management of third-party risk, reinforcing and introducing increasingly intense expectations. Other regulators, such as the Securities and Exchange Commission (SEC), Federal Deposit Insurance Corporation (FDIC), and Canada's Office of the Superintendent of Financial Institutions (OSFI) have increased the expectations and rigor of examinations.

The consequences for failure to meet regulatory expectations are severe. Institutions of all sizes have received one or a series of matters requiring attention (MRAs) or findings for their third-party risk management practices because expectations are high—and they continue to rise. Institutions that don't respond to MRAs with sufficient rigor find those MRAs escalated to matters requiring immediate attention (MRIAs), and eventually to consent orders.

Without effective execution and appropriate action when issues, incidents, and deficiencies are identified, risk management is a strictly academic exercise. Carmichael recommends analyzing the effectiveness of prevention and detection practices and their effect on loss events and realized losses over time. The insight gained from trend analysis should be incorporated into risk management practices to strengthen or decrease controls in alignment with their effectiveness and cost/benefits.

Carmichael believes assessing the results of each institution's risk management practices, rather than focusing on comparative practices and how they are documented in peer institutions, is the best way for examiners to determine an institution's safety and soundness.

The Third-Party Risk Management Lifecycle

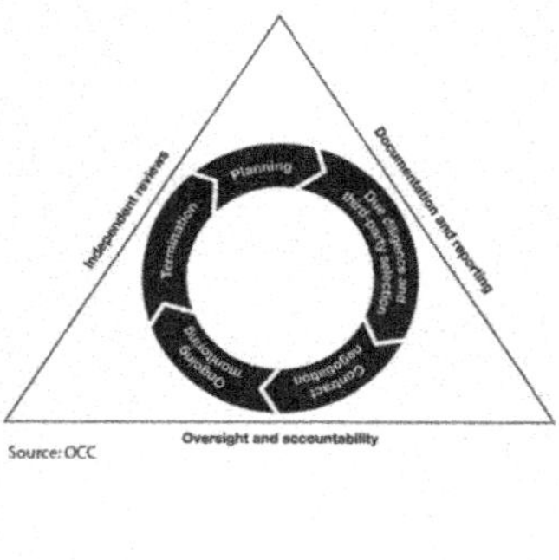

Source: OCC

Significant barriers to entry, widely adopted technologies, or highly specialized expertise means that many financial institutions across the sector rely on a core group of third parties to deliver critical services, domestically and internationally. This creates institution-specific and systemic concentration risk.

Because of concerns about systemic concentration risk, larger fintech companies are also subject to regulatory reviews. Many have been found to have significant deficiencies in their control environment.

Regulatory reports are available to the financial institution customers, and regulators expect their financial institution customers to support remediation activities and track deficiencies to closure. This results in an extra layer of oversight for the fintechs and activities intended to reduce systemic risk.

Financial institutions buy and sell services to each other and rely on financial market utilities, intermediaries, and many of the same third parties. The financial crisis was the perfect storm, highlighting systemic weaknesses of pervasive third-party relationships and the need for deliberately intentional detection and prevention activities.

Adding more pressure to the financial services ecosystem, the CFPB and the Department of Justice (DOJ) continue to issue enforcement orders and levy multi-million dollar fines for violations committed by financial institutions' third parties. In some cases, companies sidestep conviction but enter into sizeable financial settlements with regulators, including some third parties in common use across the financial services sector. For example, Akamai Technologies[8] and SAP SE were found to have "deficient internal controls"[9] that enabled bribery. In 2014, Hewlett-Packard paid a $108 million settlement to the SEC in a Foreign Corrupt Practices Act case, and was later convicted by DOJ. [10]

Although it is an executive agency and not a regulator, the CFPB has tremendous power. One hundred percent of cases reported by the CFPB in fiscal year 2015 were resolved in favor of the CFPB through litigation, settlements, issuance of default judgments, or other means. And there is no Court of Appeals. Five years into Dodd-Frank, as of the end of fiscal 2015, the CFPB said its enforcements had garnered more than $11 billion covering 25 million consumers.

Meanwhile, the subjects of CFPB supervisory actions had paid out more than $248 million to nearly 2 million consumers."[11] Do the math: The CFPB has a lot of money to invest in almost 700 examiners and enforcement attorneys. The combination of total accountability for internal and third-party compliance and financial institutions' deep pockets has proven extremely expensive for the sector. (As I wrote this book, how the CFPB's powers might be curtailed and the impact of other possible deregulation under the Trump Administration was far from clear.)

Theoretically, a financial institution should and would discontinue a business relationship with any third party with a high potential to harm the institution's reputation or expose it to risk simply by association. But realistically, even when an institution is aware of a third party's fines and convictions, it may not be reasonable or feasible to discontinue the business relationship. The Canadian government found this out firsthand. Contrary to the government's own directive, HP was not banned from doing business with the Canadian federal government for 10 years following an FCPA conviction.

At Fifth Third, senior management took a hard look at the risk/return of customer and third-party relationships and the bank's accountability for any fraud, regulatory violation, or sub-standard documentation. "In this environment, the bank is 100% accountable for the actions of its third parties, including fraud, regulatory violations, and quality

[8]SEC Enforcement Actions: FCPA Cases https://www.sec.gov/spotlight/fcpa/fcpa-cases.shtml

[9]SEC Press Release: SEC Charges Software Company with FCPA Violations (Feb 16) https://www.sec.gov/news/pressrelease/2016-17.html

[10]SEC Enforcement Actions: FCPA Cases https://www.sec.gov/spotlight/fcpa/fcpa-cases.shtml

[11]Financial report of the Consumer Financial Protection Bureau Fiscal Year 2015 http://files.consumerfinance.gov/f/201511_cfpb_report_fiscal-year-2015.pdf

of documentation," Carmichael says. "My job is to protect the bank, in good times and in bad, ensuring it is strong at all points in the cycle."

Despite causing a substantial hit to revenue, Carmichael and his team determined that some third-party relationships exceeded the bank's risk appetite, and Fifth Third exited all third-party consumer mortgage broker/dealer relationships.

Alignment of risk management practices between your institution and its critical third parties starts with alignment of "tone at the top" between the two organizations. Alignment is the start of business value because third-party risk management, done well, has the potential to deliver more benefits than regulatory compliance. Relationships with third parties that have sound risk management practices, a clean legal slate, and no reportable findings during regulatory exams are far less likely to expose your institution to risks—risks that consume valuable resources to address.

Because third-party relationships exist in almost every aspect of a financial institution's operations, third-party risk management practices are within the scope of virtually every regulatory exam. In addition to line-of-business exams within the third-party risk management program office, examiners review documentary evidence of compliance, completeness, lifecycle management for critical activities and relationships, compensating controls, issue and incident management, and actions taken to mitigate or compensate for known risks. Effective risk management in your institution cascades throughout your institution from its "tone at the top."

What You Should Know

Tone at the Top Starts and Ends with Senior Management and Board Engagement

The Federal Reserve describes what are typically understood to be the responsibilities of the board of directors and senior management for effective governance and management of third-party risk.[12] *OCC Bulletin 2013-29, Risk Management Guidance for Third-Party Relationships*, specifies that the strategies, activities, and contracts (referred to as "relationships") that involve critical third parties require board approval, including a review of a summary of due diligence results and management's recommendations.[13] This is a significant departure from the historical role of the board of directors, particularly in larger banks.

Because the use of third parties does not diminish the responsibility of an institution's board and senior management to ensure that the activity is performed in a safe and sound manner and in compliance with applicable laws, many third-party risk management programs have established a senior level third-party governance committee. Many institutions position this as a committee of the board, a subcommittee of the audit committee of the board, or a subcommittee of the enterprise risk management or operational risk committee.

[12]For additional information, refer to FRB Supervisory Letter SR 13-19 Guidance on Managing Outsourcing Risk https://www.federalreserve.gov/bankinforeg/srletters/sr1319a1.pdf

[13]OCC Bulletin 2013-29 Risk Management Guidance for Third Party Relationships https://www.occ.gov/news-issuances/bulletins/2013/bulletin-2013-29.html

Three Lines of Defense

The three-lines-of-defense (LOD) framework will be familiar to those in senior management, risk management functions, and internal audit because it is in everyday use across the financial services sector. It is a simple but comprehensive framework that helps to define and describe overall accountabilities for risk management across the enterprise. The framework has also been endorsed by regulators globally. "Appropriate accountability for the management of operational risk is essential. A 'three lines of defense' structure is one way to achieve such accountability," says OSFI.[14]

The three-lines-of-defense framework shapes risk management practices, roles, and responsibilities. Despite implementation practices that seem to refute this, it is not an organization structure. It is a framework or model that is intended to describe and structure risk management activities in the context of overarching responsibilities. It is also used to define the tasks and activities associated with effective risk management to ensure there are no gaps.

The UK's three-lines-of-defense framework was adapted by the Institute of Internal Auditors to clarify the scope of responsibilities in the second line of defense—home of those in specialized risk control functions.

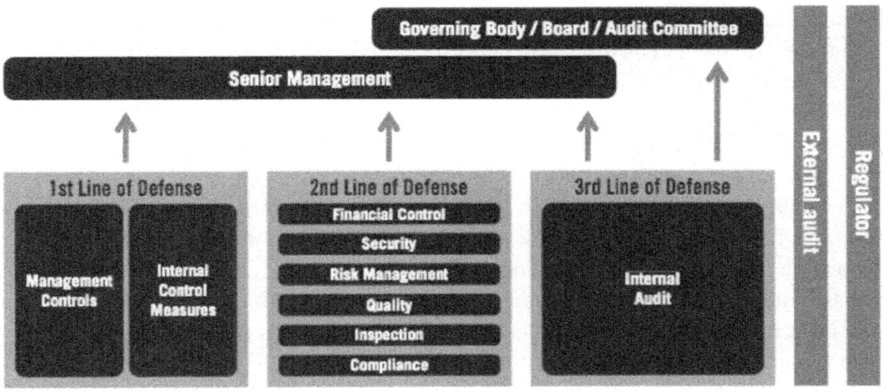

Source: IIA Position Paper on the Three Lines of Defense in Effective Risk Management and Control (January 2013)

Adapted from ECIIA/FERMA Guidance on the 8th EU Company Law Directive, article 41

With the increasing sophistication in all risk management practices, the responsibilities of the board of directors, senior management, responsible business leaders, risk management functions, and audit have expanded accordingly. The board and senior management set the tone at the top, and business leaders, risk management, and audit communicate the "what, how, when, and how often" to translate tone at the top into risk management activities and controls.

In the three-lines-of-defense framework, each institution has an external defensive perimeter. Think of the first line of defense as your institution's officers and soldiers who

[14]OSFI Operational Risk Management Guideline E-21: Sound Business and Financial Practices (Jun 2016) http://www.osfi-bsif.gc.ca/Eng/fi-if/rg-ro/gdn-ort/gl-ld/Pages/e21.aspx

are charged with protecting your institution's exterior defenses and keeping the bad guys out. Their responsibilities are clear and they are armed with skills, training, and external fortifications that have been implemented by the company's second line of defense, your military strategists and engineers.

The second line of defense has established a strong perimeter by designing the fortifications and tools that the first line uses to protect the perimeter and vital resources such as the treasury, vulnerable components, and the senior leadership team. The second line's toolkit consists of their skills and expertise in specific areas of risk management, and their constant vigilance that determines the effectiveness of the tools, training, and fortifications they designed. They need to conduct higher level testing, lead the response to incidents, periodically assess the strength of the fortifications and the appropriateness of risk management tools, and respond to weaknesses or changes to the threat landscape.

The first and second lines of defense have separate responsibilities but joint accountability for third-party risk management. The first line plays a dominant role in the processes for identifying, assessing, managing, and controlling risks. According to how each institution functions, it either leads execution processes or collaborates with risk control specialists.

At Fifth Third, the first line "is 100% accountable for risk," Carmichael says. To ensure it has sufficient resources to get this right, since 2016 Carmichael has approved more than 600 new risk management hires, the majority in the first line. This freed up the second line, transforming its role from "policing" to governance, process oversight, and compliance monitoring.

Because the first line of defense experiences third-party performance and risk events on the front line, it is closest to operational outcomes, issues, and incidents. It provides valuable insight to the second line of defense by recommending changes that will strengthen risk identification, or by proposing mitigation strategies and management controls. The second line can combine the experiences of the first line and its own skills, expertise, and experiences to strengthen lifecycle management and governance practices. Formal risk management in the first line is relatively new, so an entire chapter of this book has been dedicated to that topic.

The third line of defense is a small contingent of independent experts who represent the senior leadership team and the board. They test and verify that what is reported by the first and second lines is factual, and that everyone is doing their job according to policies, standards, and best practices. The third line often has access to qualified external sources and expertise, and therefore may be able to independently assess the effectiveness of the design and execution of third-party risk management.

While senior management and governing bodies like the board and the audit committee of the board are not formally within the lines of defense, they are ultimately responsible for the tone at the top, risk management strategies, policies, and practices. They provide a senior level of governance and oversight for risk management activities and events in a manner that no other function can.

What Your Institution Should Do

Tone at the Top

Senior management and risk specialists should keep their finger on the risk culture pulse at your institution. Here are a few "elevator" questions that can provide insight:

1. What does a strong risk culture mean to you?
2. How do we measure it?
3. How are individual risk management capabilities embedded in performance metrics and compensation?
4. What are the consequences for "bad risk behavior"?

Find a way to capture what is learned, and who is responsible for taking action. You may need to make some changes!

'Purpose-Built' Third-Party Risk Oversight Committees

A 2015 Risk Management Association survey on third-party risk management practices found that two-thirds "of responding institutions have specific risk oversight committees in place, formed specifically to oversee third-party risks." It also found that "risk oversight is increasingly at a senior level. In 22% of responding institutions, this committee reports to the board of directors. Thirty-five percent of responding institutions report that this risk oversight committee reports to the risk, operational risk, or audit committee of the board. This is dramatically different than in 2014, when institutions were still trying to determine whether they needed third-party risk oversight."[15]

Many institutions still resist the idea that third-party risk management governance committees should be populated with senior executives or select members of the board. Because this is still a relatively new discipline, your risk-oversight committee may consist of people without the experience or authority to make decisions about challenges, specific risk exposures, and systemic issues. Regardless of composition, your institution's third-party risk oversight function must have delegated authority from senior management and the board. It's hard to say "no" to a relationship or risk exposure that one of your senior executives is willing to accept, even when it's not in the best interests of the institution.

Some conversations and decisions that third-party risk management governance committees deal with require senior level insight and decision making. For example, business leaders may be tempted to take on undue third-party risk; risk control functions may not step up to their responsibilities; risk control functions may impose due diligence and risk control requirements that are unduly onerous with few or no commensurate benefits; keeping auditable minutes may be considered a waste of resources; or powerful senior executives may arbitrarily override risk specialists, removing whole categories of relationships from scrutiny. (The most common category of excluded third-party relationships is law firms.)

[15]The Power of Collaboration (Linda Tuck Chapman), The RMA Journal (July 2016)

If its members are not senior enough, or haven't been provided with sufficient information, your institution's risk oversight committee will not be well-suited to deal with these situations and to guide evolution of your third-party risk management program. They may simply be referees, or passive reviewers of reports to enterprise risk or operational risk functions. If this is the case, they are not providing effective or efficient third-party risk management oversight. This is a deficiency that should be remedied.

Regardless of the path your institution takes to get there, your board must be involved in third-party risk management oversight. To make this clear, in January 2017 the OCC published "Supplemental Examination Procedures for Risk Management of Third-Party Relationships." This document explicitly states that examiners should validate that there is evidence confirming that "the board [is to] approve[s] all critical third-party contracts" and that examiners must verify that "board minutes indicate that the board reviews and approves the following:

1. The methodology for determining critical activities.
2. Management's plans for using third parties involved in critical activities.
3. Summary of due diligence results.
4. Contracts with third parties involved in critical activities.
5. Results of management's ongoing monitoring of third parties involved in critical activities.
6. Results of periodic internal audit or independent third-party reviews of the bank's third-party risk management process."[16]

The examination procedures for other primary regulators were sure to follow.

One could argue that effective third-party management is simply good business. Consider that third parties are involved with every aspect of your institution's operations and can have a significant impact on your customers, employees, markets, expenses, revenues, safety and soundness exam, and compliance with regulations and laws. Doesn't third-party management deserve commensurate senior management risk oversight?

Risk Management Frameworks in Alignment

RMA defines enterprise risk management (ERM) as "the capability of an organization to understand, control, and articulate the nature and level of the risks taken in pursuit of a risk-adjusted return."

In banks, the enterprise risk management function is typically segmented into credit, market, and operational risk to oversee a broad spectrum of risks. Insurance companies typically have a fourth segment of risk oversight: insurance risk. Its purpose is to manage risks associated with "pricing/underwriting, reserving, catastrophe, claims, policyholder behavior, and new products."

Your operational risk management framework (ORMF) should be clearly aligned with your enterprise risk management framework (ERMF). RMA's Operational Risk

[16]OCC Supplemental Examination Procedures for Risk Management of Third-Party (January 2017) https://www.occ.gov/publications/publications-by-type/comptrollers-handbook/pub-third-party-exam-supplemental-procedures.pdf

Council has developed an operational risk framework designed to be scalable regardless of the size, scale, or complexity of the institution.

If your institution does not have an ORMF in place today, RMA's framework can be used to guide its development.

OPERATIONAL RISK MANAGEMENT FRAMEWORK

Moving to the next tranche of risk management frameworks, your institution should have a documented third-party risk management framework (TPRMF). This framework should clearly align with the operational risk management framework, which should be aligned with the enterprise risk management framework. This consistency makes it easier for internal users to understand and comply, and alignment is expected by regulatory examiners.

To distinguish the third-party risk management framework from other operational risk management sub-frameworks, such as the frameworks developed for information security, anti-money laundering, or business continuity management, it's common practice to be explicit about the policies, tools, and technologies that have been developed and deployed to specifically support the third-party risk management program. While not explicitly included in RMA's operational risk management framework, some institutions also include change management and training in their ORMF and operational risk sub-frameworks.

How Much Does Third-Party Risk Management Cost?

Do you know whether and how your institution is getting value for money, value beyond compliance? A trio of questions that deserve a thoughtful response are 1) what are the potential benefits?, 2) what is the best way to achieve them?, and 3) how much are we spending on third-party management?

You may want to have someone build an annual cost model for third-party management. Because costs are widely distributed, they can be opaque, particularly in larger institutions. Let's do the math in this plausible scenario:

Cost Drivers	Estimate ($$ thousands)			
Technology	$	50	-	150
3PRM office	$	350	-	5,000
Risk specialists	$	1,000	-	10,000
Legal services	$	700	-	6,000
Compliance/Ops Risk	$	900	-	4,000
Relationship Mgrs	$	1,250	-	7,000
Accountable Execs	$	200	-	500
Sr. Mgmt oversight	$	100	-	300
Board involvement	$	300	-	300
Risk Oversight	$	200	-	200
Issue Management	$	150	-	1,000
Regulatory & Reporting	$	50	-	150

©2018 Linda Tuck Chapman

Some people reasonably argue that the cost of third-party management should also include 100% of your sourcing/procurement function's annual operating costs, plus the costs associated with internal and external legal counsel for third-party contracts; site visits; the costs of cross-functional teams when responding to third-party issues and incidents; and a portion of your finance team's operating costs. Excluding these ancillary costs, the annual operating cost of third-party management ranges from a conservative estimate of $5 million in smaller institutions to $35 million in a large, systemically important financial institution (SIFI).

You decide what to capture in your cost model, but expect a big price tag. On a cost basis alone, you may decide that it makes sense to look beyond compliance with regulatory guidance, instead focusing on harvesting the highest value possible.

Procurement is a Risk Control Function

Most financial institutions have implemented standard sourcing and procurement processes. In all but the smallest institutions, procurement is a discrete function. Until recently, the primary mandate for procurement has been cost reduction, which has been achieved by introducing professional procurement practices and consolidating the population of approved vendors.

Procurement processes have historically included due diligence; negotiating pricing, terms, and conditions; defining controls; and reporting. While not recognized as such, procurement has always been a risk control function, and is more so in the current environment. What's different now is the scope of due diligence, and the amount of rigor and risk-adjusted processes. "Regular assessments and evaluations are the key to an effective risk management program. This is best done before problems emerge," the OCC advises.[17] Holding procurement responsible for specific aspects of third-party risk management, including managing activities and workflow; producing quality documentary evidence; and designing actionable service level agreements will strengthen your program.

[17]OCC: Corporate Governance and the Community Bank: A Regulatory Perspective (June 2005) https://www.occ.gov/static/past-conferences-and-seminars/cgts-final-exec-summary.pdf

With the right leadership, sophisticated procurement organizations may have the competencies necessary to effectively integrate procurement and third-party risk management. In this case, they own the TPRMF—policy, processes, and execution.

In virtually all financial institutions, responsibility for third-party risk oversight is the responsibility of operational risk management. Operational risk management should ensure that third-party risk management processes throughout their lifecycle are tightly integrated with other risk control groups and management practices in the first line of defense.

In the past couple years, many institutions have transferred ownership of the third-party risk management framework, policies, standards, processes, and controls to operational risk. Procurement and other risk control functions retain responsibility for execution. This is usually for one of two reasons: 1) procurement failed to get it done, and 2) expansion of scope from just the vendor population to all third-party relationships moved it beyond the scope of procurement.

Regardless of how the work gets done, the threat landscape, the speed of business, and regulatory requirements are bringing third-party and other operational risk management functions closer together than ever. Misalignment between risk control functions will frustrate the business, while creating gaps, overlaps, and missed opportunities.

For a stronger program, each risk control function should take the time to acquire a good working knowledge about the professional disciplines embedded in other risk control functions.

Reporting Can Inform or Distract

There is a notable difference between the criticality of a third-party relationship and the risks third-party relationships present to your institution throughout their lifecycle. Naturally, highly critical relationships should get more attention than those that are less critical, particularly if they have a higher level of risk because of deficiencies in the third party's risk controls. In those cases, there is a high probability they could harm your institution's operations and reputation.

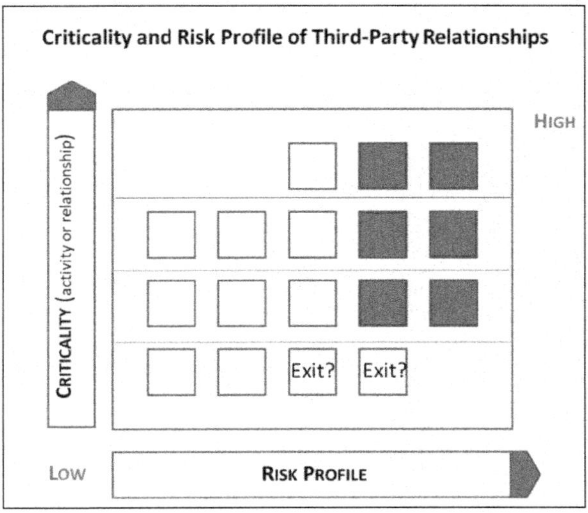

Senior management, risk committees, and the board of directors need timely and accurate information about critical relationships and activities, tier I and high risk relationships, risk exposure, and incidents. Senior management should understand why third-party relationships are designated as critical and/or high risk, and how risk tiering takes both factors into account. Further, it's important to know whether highly critical and higher-risk relationships are performing according to contractual obligations and management's expectations. Unlike with non-performing loans, in most financial institutions the processes for managing highly critical, high-risk, and non-performing third-party relationships are substantially immature.

At a minimum, management reporting should provide insight into significant changes to the risk profile of the entire portfolio of critical third party relationships embedded in critical activities; the performance history of most critical third parties; material changes or serious issues associated with critical third-party relationships and activities; and information and insight into trends—preferably by critical relations and activities and by key risk driver/risk factor.

Third-Party Risk Management Technologies

Unless your institution invests in purpose-built, third-party risk management software and a searchable repository, it will take a small army to stay on top of the volume of activities, data, and documentary evidence. In the absence of a software platform, actionable reporting will take a lot of time to produce and trend analysis will be virtually impossible.

Most institutions provide internal stakeholders across the first, second, and third lines of defense access to the third-party management software platform. Access can be controlled by automated permissions according to role and ownership of specific third-party relationships and engagements. Automated access and workflow helps to appropriately share the workload and timing of risk management activities, and increases the probability that required activities will be completed.

Many institutions also provide their regulatory examiners with unsupervised access.

Establish a Senior Level, Third-Party Risk Management Oversight Committee

As much as your management team may wish to avoid striking another steering committee, now's the time for third-party risk management. This discipline is a very long way from maturity, and it will take senior-level experience to guide the ship and make the best decisions. "Senior level" means senior enough to have the experience and authority to make decisions on behalf of the institution, and to be able to say "no" to powerful business leaders. In some institutions, this is a committee of the board—a subset of the risk committee. In others, it is a senior executive committee. And some institutions have or are considering adding an independent "ex-officio" third-party expert.

Your team is working hard to build, implement, and manage your institution's third-party relationships, but they may not entirely understand what's important. And in these relatively early days there will be several formal or informal challenges. One way to get this right is to make the tone at the top heard by offering visible support in the form of a senior executive oversight committee, and ensuring there are consequences for bad behavior. On a more granular level, deploy key risk indicators in the context of risk appetite, risk thresholds, and risk tolerance.

A quick primer:

Risk appetite is a statement about how much and which risks your institution is willing to take on.

Risk thresholds draw the boundaries for acceptable levels of risk.

Risk tolerance is the amount of risk your institution and businesses have "tolerated" or taken on.

Key risk indicators (KRIs) are metrics used to determine which risks will be measured, how they will be measured, and the frequency.

Naturally, every KRI will have a risk threshold. Third-party risk management KRIs should be few in number. In fact, many institutions have fewer than 10 third-party risk KRIs. Meanwhile, risk thresholds should be in obvious alignment with your institution's risk appetite.

KRI reporting is typically in the form of "red, yellow, green" and should focus on critical relationships that are "yellow" or "red" and portfolio-level KRIs that are close to or exceeding their risk threshold.

Surprisingly, many institutions haven't implemented third-party risk management KRIs. In others, these indicators are "works in progress." Very few institutions can confidently say they have implemented the right KRIs, with optimal risk thresholds. As institutions collect information about their third parties' issues, incidents, and performance, the quality of information will improve. Combined with guidance from senior management and risk oversight committees, KRIs will improve over time.

In the absence of specific key risk indicators, it's hard to know what to measure. But KRIs that separate clear "signals" from all the "noise" are hard to design. Because of this, it would be very helpful to provide your institution's third-party risk management leadership team with some guidance so they can understand what's most useful and relevant. This guidance should come from senior managers and risk control specialists, particularly about how to meet the needs and expectations of your board.

Because of the low level of maturity of KRIs, in February 2017 the RMA Third-Party Risk Management Round Table's Steering Committee (Deborah Manos-McHenry, SVP and Chief Sourcing Officer, Huntington National Bank; John Klapmust, SVP and head of Third Party Risk, Bank of the West; Linda Quong, SVP Vendor Management, Charles Schwab & Co. Inc; and myself) commissioned a special task force to build a KRI library. Here is a sample set of KRIs that address concentration risk:

KRI Name	Elements	Details/Scope	Risk Threshold Limit(s) *	Controls (examples)	Notes
CONCENTRATION RISK Geographic	The number of critical 3rd and 4th parties supporting critical business activities located within a 75-mile radius of any single geographic area	High-criticality 3rd and 4th parties (e.g., data centers with >50k client records and/or transaction volumes; 3rd and 4th parties with a tier 1 RTO (e.g., <4 hours)	A maximum total of 9 critical 3rd and 4th parties that support critical business activities located within each defined geographic area	Business Continuity and Disaster Recovery Plans Hot backup site(s)	Exceptions: • Areas with severe physical threats and risks (e.g., earthquakes and tornadoes) FEMA may have specific guidance • Locations that include your institution's data center For easy reference, create geo-maps for each in-scope geography, noting the location of each in-scope 3rd and 4th party and our data center(s)

Over time, KRIs in the RMA library will be fine-tuned or substituted based on feedback from member institutions. The overarching goal of the library is to establish a reliable baseline for trend analysis at the institution and sector levels. Being better informed about what's been "tried and true" elsewhere, and where your institution stands relative to its peer group and the sector, can strengthen your institution's third-party risk management program.

Harvest Value from Your Investments

Today there's probably a fuzzy line of sight between specific loss events and your third-party risk management program. This makes it hard for third-party risk management professionals to articulate what value comes from investments made in third-party risk management activities. And some third-party risk management professionals may be so focused on task management that they don't think about generating value for money.

Here are some potential sources of value, beyond compliance:

1. **Detect and Prevent Known Risks**
   - Knowing the right questions to ask your third parties helps to reveal important control deficiencies and unexpected constraints.
   - Established processes increase the likelihood of selecting third parties with the best combination of services, corporate compatibility, financial impact, and risk management practices.
   - Proven expertise structuring deals, terms, and controls helps to avoid or mitigate known risks.
   - Internal experts can educate critical third parties about risk controls and what's important.
   - Organized, workflow-enabled processes minimize cycle time to conduct targeted due diligence and evaluate risks.
   - Internal capabilities, skills, and knowledge can build "strong fences" with common-sense, risk-adjusted controls; contract terms; and management practices.

- Crisp, concise service- and operating-level agreements measure the right things, at the right time, in the right way.
- Institutionalizing "black box" thinking ensures your institution learns from its experiences.
- Defined rights and responsibilities mean that your risk experts can challenge poor decisions that can introduce unnecessary risks.

2. **Avoid Nasty Surprises**
   - Standardized, risk-adjusted tools and defined accountability enable monitoring of third parties for significant changes in key officers, competitiveness, stability, and strategic direction.
   - Specific accountability and follow-up ensures proactive performance management.
   - Early warning signals embedded in processes can identify deterioration in performance and risk controls before they harm your institution.
   - Processes and tools coordinate and accelerate responses to systemic issues and serious incidents.
   - Knowledge about critical third parties' disaster recovery and business continuity management capabilities and plans can inform your institution's plans.
   - Early notification of third-party customer complaints means prompt response, including the potential to participate in or oversee remedial actions.
   - Early awareness enables an appropriate response to any third-party legal actions and regulatory findings.
   - Periodic access to independent control assessments creates insight to existing or new control deficiencies, remediation plans, and timing.
3. **Protect Your Institution's Reputation**
   - Effective third-party management enables risk-based, informed decision making… *which is good for your institution, and better for key stakeholders.*
   - Your institution can compensate for known risks…. *The best defense is a good offense.*
   - If your institution knows more about third-party risks than your competitors, it should be able to do a better job managing those risks.
   - Early warning means a quicker response … *likely faster than your competitors.*
   - Time spent dealing with issues and incidents is *time <u>not</u> spent taking advantage of opportunities.*

Encourage Collaboration with Peer Institutions and Risk Specialists

Many third-party management practitioners are revisiting their assumptions and strengthening processes and controls design, and clarifying activities, frequency, roles, and responsibilities. If you ask regulators about the level of maturity of third-party risk management across the sector, they'll tell you that it's still early days. In addition to effective risk management within individual institutions, they remain concerned about systemic and concentration risk.

Some institutions make the mistake of resting on their laurels after remediating their matters requiring attention (MRA) or going through a regulatory exam with no new MRA. This relatively new field is evolving very quickly and your program needs to remain current with regulatory expectations and institutions of comparable size and complexity.

Regulators encourage and expect collaboration on risk management practices. Active collaboration provides an opportunity to problem-solve together and share assessment and due diligence criteria, effective controls, and hard lessons learned. Networking and active participation in groups like the RMA Third-Party Risk Management Round Table can provide a good point of reference. Round tables periodically tackle "big hairy" problems by striking purpose-built task forces like the Common Assessment Task Force, co-chaired by round table members Rohan Ranadive, SVP and TPM Program Group Manager, BB&T, and Tammy Knies, first vice president, Purchasing & Vendor Management, People's United Bank.

A well-crafted program, commensurate with peer institutions, improves adoption and increases its effectiveness.

3 Lifecycle Management

Once the business strategy is set, the first step in any successful third-party relationship is to recognize that every relationship has a lifecycle.

Before regulators forced greater awareness of third-party risk management there were significant variations in lifecycle management practices by institution. *Some* aspects of lifecycle management, for *some* third-party relationships, were well executed by *some* functions or *some* individuals. Apart from enterprise-critical relationships, senior management oversight of third parties was often dim at best; management reporting was non-existent; and the board was rarely, if ever, made aware of critical relationships, which critical activities they were associated with, or problems.

In fact, until relatively recently it would be generous to say that any financial institution had implemented systematic lifecycle management and governance practices for critical third-party relationships and activities. In many cases, even complex services such as consumer mortgages had not been thoroughly mapped.

Because critical activities are often delivered by different internal functions, points of failure and vulnerabilities related to third-party relationships may be opaque. Without proper knowledge of a critical third-party relationship, the second line of defense—the risk control specialists—can't help. And the third line of defense—internal audit—can't evaluate the effectiveness of lifecycle management practices if unaware of critical third-party relationships.

Lifecycle management assumes that every third-party relationship has a beginning and an end, and may change over time. Each third-party relationship is part of your institution's operational, financial, and reputational ecosystem. Part of the rationale for investing in lifecycle management is to be aware that all parties in the relationship change over time. Your institution can influence the direction of the relationship, and will be affected by its changes.

Like any complex process, third-party lifecycle management involves a series of key activities.

A former head of third-party risk management at a large U.S. bank notes that because lifecycle management and risk controls can often change over the life of the contract, risk thresholds across the enterprise will also change. Therefore, it's advisable to create a mechanism to review standard and bespoke controls for your institution's critical relationships.

These controls may have been implemented at the outset of a five-year relationship with a critical third party. As such, they may have been appropriate for the first two years but now must be enhanced to meet current requirements and respond to changes in the internal or external environment. Rohan Ranadive, senior vice president and TPM Program Group Manager, BB&T, advises, "One should not wait until contract renewal to make important or necessary changes to third-party controls."

Regulators expect ongoing review of an institution's third-party program, Ranadive says, including design of controls and how the program aligns with the overall risk management framework.

The following lifecycle management model is a generic depiction of these activities, so it can be adopted for use in any institution.

Lifecycle Management Model

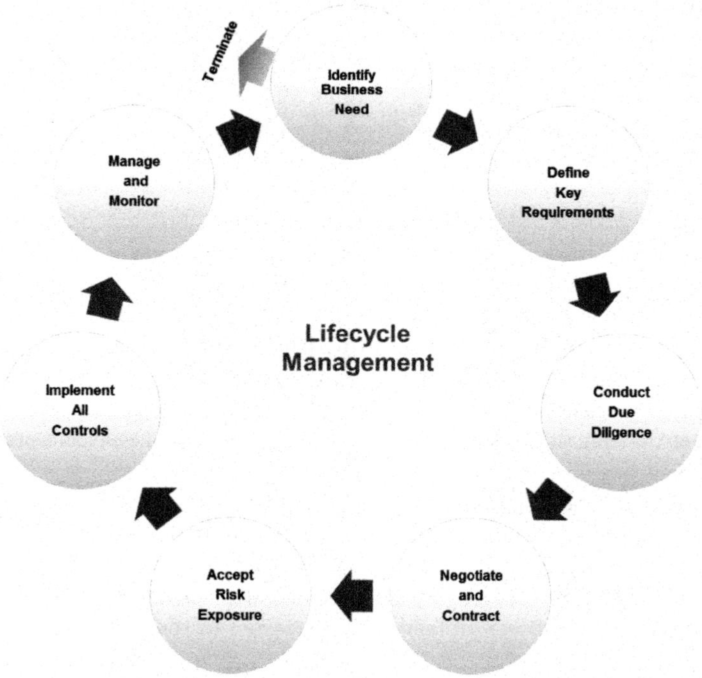

©2018 Linda Tuck Chapman

What You Should Know

Regulatory guidance for third-party risk management is similar across primary regulators. The Federal Financial Institutions Examinations Council (FFIEC) summarizes guidance from five regulatory bodies. The Securities and Exchange Commission (SEC) relies on its own guidance for high-level direction, and on U.S. Office of the Comptroller of the Currency (OCC) guidance for specifics.

Guidance is updated infrequently. The most significant changes appeared at the end of 2013, when the U.S. OCC and the Federal Reserve updated their guidance in OCC 2013-29 and SR 13-19, respectively, followed by the FFIEC's updates to *Appendix J (Business Resilience)* in 2015. The biggest challenge today is meeting the expectations of examiners, which have been on a sharply upward trajectory since updated guidance was published. But in fairness, at the time of the financial crisis, third-party management practices were inconsistent and many controls were inadequate.

To many, achieving a clean examination feels a bit like playing a game of "whack a mole." Examiners seem predisposed to expecting that every institution's practices related to every aspect of the complexities of third-party management be at the highest level of any institution they have examined.

One aspect of third-party risk management that has proven particularly problematic is the third party's use of subcontractors. The OCC's Supplemental Examination Procedures say examiners must:

- Determine whether any third-party relationships involve the use of subcontractors.
- Review the bank's methodology for determining whether third parties use subcontractors.
- Determine if the bank maintains a database or inventory that can distinguish all third parties that use subcontractors.[18]

This requirement is a tall order for "less critical" third parties. Many institutions report that examiners' expectations regarding subcontractors continue to evolve, and the expectation is to capture a growing number of subcontractors in programs, including fourth-, fifth-, and even sixth-party relationships.

Undoubtedly, tightly managing the risks and lifecycle of highly critical third parties is important. It can be debated whether it's a reasonable expectation, but regulators expect financial institutions to engage at similarly deep levels with their "highly critical" and "less critical" third parties, and their fourth parties and beyond. Does this go too far?

Your Third Party's Third Party: Understanding Your Exposure

Some third parties—a leading mortgage servicer, for example—service every major bank in the U.S. Because the mortgage servicer is a critical third party to financial institution customers, the critical third parties of the servicer are the financial institutions' material

[18] OCC - Supplemental Examination Procedures for Risk Management of Third-Party Relationships (Jan 17) https://www.occ.gov/publications/publications-by-type/comptrollers-handbook/pub-third-party-exam-supplemental-procedures.pdf

fourth parties. As a result, it is important that these major banks assess the controls of their third parties AND critical fourth parties.

In other cases, some of the mortgage servicer's critical third parties, such as its outsourced data center (the financial institutions' material fourth parties) also have direct relationships themselves as critical third parties to financial institutions. This is not an uncommon scenario. As a result, knowing your institution's critical third parties and their critical third parties (your fourth parties) is important to understanding your overall exposure.

A tabletop scenario: Your bank outsources its data center and infrastructure management to a third party in Chennai, India. Your critical third-party mortgage servicing company outsources its servicing platform and infrastructure to the same third party in Chennai. In other words, the bank has doubled its risk exposure for critical activities and relevant relationships. This could be a problem if a major cyclone and torrential rains hit Chennai.

Just knowing your institution's total third- and fourth-party risk exposure and integrating business continuity management plans will make a big difference to the speed of recovery from serious service failures.

Once you get past highly critical third parties and have insight into your institution's highest exposure to concentration risk, it's hard to understand the value of doing more if the third party was found to have sound operational and risk management practices. It also seems to contradict the principle that each institution will "adopt risk management processes commensurate with the level of risk and complexity of its third-party relationships."[19]

Governance experts deliberately exclude management responsibilities in their definition of good governance. Here is the Institute on Governance's definition: "*Governance determines who has power, who makes decisions, how other players make their voice heard, and how account is rendered.*"[20]

Just as boards of directors can't manage the institutions they govern, financial institutions can't manage the operations of third parties. Good governance of critical third parties, then, relies on sound lifecycle management processes, defined accountabilities, strong controls, and transparency.

Over time, as best practices settle into common use and financial institutions become more adept at managing third-party risk, regulators may similarly mature their thinking about the value of good governance and the impossibility of managing third-party operations.

Identifying the Business Need

Every third-party relationship starts and ends with a business need. Awareness that there is a business need can come from many sources. Some examples:

---

[19]OCC - Supplemental Examination Procedures for Risk Management of Third-Party Relationships (Jan 17) https://www.occ.gov/publications/publications-by-type/comptrollers-handbook/pub-third-party-exam-supplemental-procedures.pdf

[20]Institute on Governance http://iog.ca/defining-governance/

- An agreement for an existing relationship is at or nearing its expiry date.
- Business needs have changed, necessitating an amendment to an existing third-party relationship.
- A new business need creates a need for one or more new third-party relationships, or material changes to an existing one.
- The competitive market has changed, driving business needs in a different direction.
- Someone has a great idea for a new product, process, or services, and your institution wants to meet the competition or beat them to market.

Business Requirements

Business requirements for third-party relationships are hard to nail down. Despite a lengthy career as a chief procurement officer and management consultant, I've always found it much harder to define business requirements for my group than for those in corporate management roles and for my clients.

I've found that reusable frameworks, like my adaption of what is known as a Johari window, make the job of defining business requirements much easier.

The Johari Window

A Johari window is a useful tool to think through the "known" and the "unknown" that I've used over the years to help colleagues and clients define their business requirements. I ask questions to uncover expectations and surface hidden assumptions, then translate those expectations and assumptions into business requirements.

This is my version of a Johari window:

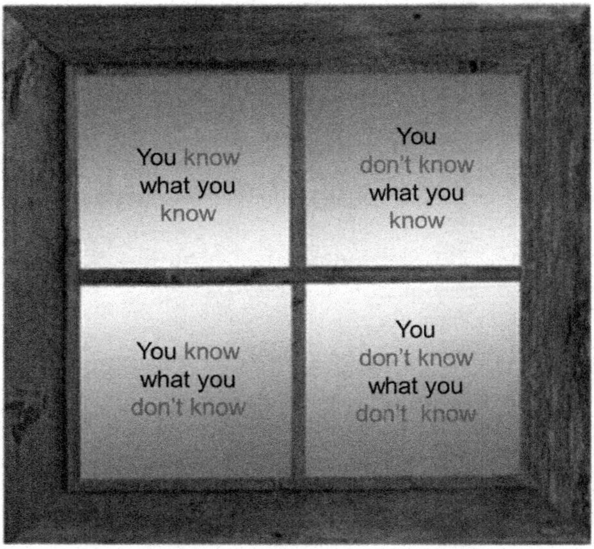

©2018 Linda Tuck Chapman

The first pane, "*You know what you know,*" can represent when an experienced sourcing professional or business analyst systematically documents "known" business needs and requirements.

The second (lower left) pane, "*You know what you don't know,*" takes a certain degree of self-awareness to be effective. Most business leaders are aware of gaps in their knowledge of the market, opportunities, processes, tools, and services that can be delivered by third parties. This self-awareness allows them to comfortably explore opportunities with intention. This pane of the Johari window can be used as a tool to clarify assumptions and expectations by increasing your level of knowledge about the topic at hand. This knowledge moves you back to the first pane, where "*You know what you know*" can be translated into specific business needs and requirements.

The downside is that third parties are often the source of this new knowledge, which they will shape to communicate needs and expectations that can be satisfied with their service or product. This is a slippery slope, and almost always influences buyers, deflecting their initial requirements and expectations. A skilled internal business partner with sourcing and/or appropriate business expertise can help business owners sidestep the temptation of allowing a third party to tell them what they want.

The third (upper right) pane in the Johari window is "*You don't know what you know.*" Spending too little time thinking about this means that you're quite likely to be disappointed when the third party fails to meet unspoken expectations. It takes a very skilled business analyst or sourcing professional to translate a business leader's ideas and assumptions into explicit requirements, and to surface unspoken expectations.

The last (lower right) window, "*You don't know what you don't know,*" is the most challenging. The best anyone can hope to achieve is to minimize what falls in this window through research, thoughtful analysis, and good questions.

In addition to using a Johari window and structured processes to define business requirements, you'll find more ideas and proven methodologies in the chapter about technology risk. As a thinking tool, a Johari window can help you ask better questions and reduce the risk that you've overlooked something important or risky.

I've used this framework as a thinking tool for most of my career. Many thanks to Corey Jack of the Schulich Executive Education Center for introducing me to it.

Due Diligence

The nature and depth of due diligence should be proportional with the criticality of third-party relationships and activities, and inherent risks that the relationships present to your institution. Inherent risk is the amount of risk that exists in the absence of controls. Once due diligence is completed, contractual terms have been agreed to, and internal controls are established, the level of residual risk can be determined.

Inherent and residual risk can be the same if the third party's internal controls are found to be substantially deficient. Inherent risk should be determined before starting third-party due diligence activities. Residual risk is usually lower than inherent risk because the relative strength of the third party's internal controls has been determined during due diligence.

The purpose of due diligence is to confirm facts and assess the third party's capabilities. North American regulators describe basic due diligence requirements in detail in their respective regulatory guidance. The FFIEC says, "Due diligence should serve as a verification and analysis tool, providing assurance that the service provider meets the institution's needs. Due diligence should confirm and assess the following information:

- Existence and corporate history;
- Qualifications, backgrounds, and reputations of company principals, including criminal background checks where appropriate;
- Other companies using similar services from the provider that may be contacted for reference;
- Financial status, including reviews of audited financial statements;
- Strategy and reputation;
- Service delivery capability, status, and effectiveness;
- Technology and systems architecture;
- Internal controls environment, security history, and audit coverage;
- Legal and regulatory compliance including any complaints, litigation, or regulatory actions;
- Reliance on and success in dealing with third-party service providers;
- Insurance coverage; and
- Ability to meet disaster recovery and business continuity requirements."[21]

In most third-party risk management programs, a flurry of due diligence questionnaires is sent to the incumbent and prospective third parties. Hundreds and even thou-

---

[21]FFIEC IT Examination Handbook InfoBase http://ithandbook.ffiec.gov/it-booklets/outsourcing-technology-services/risk-management/service-provider-selection/due-diligence.aspx

sands of questions are posed during the selection phase and again during the monitoring phase. Each question needs a thorough response, which is then analyzed by the financial institution's risk control specialists. Even with the questionnaires and workflow configured in third-party risk management software tools, this is an onerous process.

Now imagine you're a third party, expected to quickly respond to a growing avalanche of due diligence questionnaires. Each has comparable questions, but not the same questions. Many responses to many questions are bespoke.

Some third parties are pushing back. Some will not respond to RFPs unless they strongly believe they will win the business. Others charge their clients for responding to due diligence questionnaires. Others send standardized responses, ignoring the actual questions. This makes it harder for the financial institution to evaluate responses, and eliminates the possibility of automating any part of evaluation processes. Some third parties have "due diligence week." Others restrict access for site visits, sometimes until they have a critical mass of customers.

Vendors including Black Knight and many larger financial institutions subscribe to The Santa Fe Group's Shared Assessments Program.[22] The program was started in 2005 with six members of the financial services industry, the "Big 4" accounting firms, and several key industry service providers. The original goal was to create a more efficient way to share risk assessment data and leverage best practices to standardize procedures.

This is a "trust but verify" approach to due diligence that employs a Standardized Information Gathering (SIG) questionnaire that can be used to collect due diligence data, including controls for cybersecurity, data security, IT, privacy, and business resiliency. The questions have been mapped to relevant U.S. and international regulations. The AUP (Agreed Upon Procedures) can be used as a standardized approach to verifying the third party's response during an onsite review.

As third-party risk management practices mature, one or more for-profit services and/or industry utilities may gather and store information typically sought during due diligence and make it available to financial institution clients. (Third-party management has improved significantly in the past three to five years, and is still evolving. It will likely take another three to five years before best practices crystallize into a mature state.)

Several groups and enterprises are assessing ways to drive more efficiency into due diligence and monitoring processes. Deborah Manos-McHenry, SVP and chief sourcing officer at Huntington National Bank,[23] believes that "there will be an inflection point between regulatory pressure on institutions and the cost of compliance that will drive the sector and many of its third parties to a shared assessment model."

Catherine Allen, president and CEO at The Sante Fe Group, describes the Shared Assessments Program this way: "The Shared Assessments Program selectively coordinates 'collaborative assessments' between several financial institutions that share the same vendor. These assessments are agreed upon in advance. The assessments are completed by the vendor and the results are shared with the participating parties. This has been successful among large banks and the law firms that are in common use."

---

[22]The Sante Fe Group: Shared Assessments https://sharedassessments.org/

[23]Huntington National Bank www.huntington.com

Peter Hill of Black Knight is responsible for enhancing and executing on his company's strategic risk management plan, identifying existing or potential business risks, and developing solutions to mitigate or prevent them. [24]

As a subject-matter expert and the accountable executive, Hill notes:

> *Most financial institutions typically have a significant population of vendors that they rely on. All of these vendors will require assessments at a degree of detail relevant to that vendor. If your company is a vendor this means having to complete an ever-increasing number of risk assessment requests in a continual loop.*
>
> *Black Knight has actively participated in many different attempts, with a broad spectrum of industries and companies, to create a common assessment tool or questionnaire to standardize requests for information during due diligence and throughout the relationship, and enable sharing of completed assessments. This would significantly reduce the effort to develop and/or respond to multiple, similar assessments, and significantly streamline the due diligence process. Common assessments and a shared database of completed assessments would be a big benefit to vendors and their customers.*
>
> *While common assessments intuitively make a lot of sense, it remains very challenging to get agreement from financial institutions to adopt a common assessments model. Each institution wants to add its own suite of "special" questions which, of course, invalidates the principle of commonality. The person who solves this will be owed a mountain of gratitude, and in my opinion, deserves to become very wealthy.*
>
> *To provide some standardization in the risk assessment process, Black Knight has developed a secure Web portal that clients can log into for access to our standard suite of documents that are typically requested by our clients. This has helped to reduce the time invested in completing risk assessments from three to four days down to one to two days.*
>
> *There are other avenues that can augment or replace third-party risk assessments, such as SSAE 16, SOC 1, and SOC 2 reports. Unfortunately, while these have become a standard requirement for many institutions, they have not reached the level of adoption required to fully replace most questions asked in risk assessments.*
>
> *The ultimate responsibility for a risk event is with the company that engaged the third party. This is why third-party risk management is a mission-critical activity that must be effective in the identification and management of vendor risk, and adopted by every employee in the company.*

Regardless of the form and format of due diligence, it helps to be mindful of a few facts:

- Despite what third parties tell you, your institution is not the only one conducting due diligence on their operations and controls.
- SSAE16 and SOC2 audits cost money. If your institution wants one that is specific to the services it's receiving, you'll have to pay for it—either as a hidden or discrete cost. Audits take time and cost tens of thousands of dollars.
- Due diligence shouldn't be a fishing expedition. Risk control experts should request only information that's needed and can be evaluated.

[24]Black Knight Financial Services http://www.bkfs.com

RFPs can be a useful tool to guide due diligence, but they take time to prepare. The upside of using an RFP template is that it's a purpose-built tool for communicating business requirements and gathering pertinent information about third parties. RFPs are also a quick and fair way to disqualify third parties that can't meet qualification criteria. When they aren't used, due diligence embedded in the process—corporate profile, officers, being certain of risk management and HR practices, history of litigation, service delivery location, etc.—will need to be completed using alternate means, and the evidence stored in an accessible repository.

An RFP is not always practical or feasible. But FFIEC guidance assumes that financial institutions will issue an RFP, then perform due diligence. Innovation and the speed of business mean that formal RFPs with structured evaluations and sequential due diligence are being issued with decreasing frequency.

Most business leaders and many sourcing professionals have determined that a formal RFP shouldn't be the only option. In their place, many institutions acquire new services from third parties with whom they have pre-existing relationships, initiate third-party relationships as a "proof of concept," or replace RFPs with informal market scans. The form and format is far less important than conducting sufficient due diligence and storing the evidence.

A challenge your institution may face is meeting regulatory expectations regarding the depth and breadth of due diligence. Examiners and auditors prefer predictable, standardized processes that generate solid documentary evidence. Some examiners also expect financial institutions to conduct due diligence on "speculative RFPs" as a method of identifying alternative third parties for contingency planning.

If you're simply testing the market, there are better ways to go about this. Going to market when your institution has no intention of switching third parties is expensive and undermines the credibility of future sourcing efforts. It is not recommended.

Site Visits

Another aspect of due diligence is site visits. A site visit, prior to award, is recommended for the most critical activities, particularly when the third party is processing a high volume of transactions or has access to much confidential customer data. Some institutions rely instead on SSAE16 or SOC2 reports of the third party's internal controls.

Allen says, "The Shared Assessments Program created the 'trust but verify' model with the SIG and the AUP because it is one thing to have your service providers fill out a questionnaire or have an audit firm do it for them, but it is entirely another to send your people onsite to verify their controls."

"By segmenting vendors by level of risk," Allen adds, "some firms have created a methodology of using the SIG only for some vendors, periodically conducting onsite risk and control assessments with others, and sharing this information with others in the industry. The AUP process provides for verification of the controls reported in the SIG, but gives no 'opinion.'"

Ultimately, the decision of whether to conduct a site visit should rest with the business owner, subject to challenge by risk control experts in the second line of defense.

Expending scarce resources on a visit should increase the quality of due diligence flowing through to risk controls and performance management criteria. Many institutions don't conduct site visits because of the cost. And when they do, most don't have a structured guide to help plan the visit and systematically assess what they have seen. Many institutions send teams that include individuals who don't have defined responsibilities or expertise. These are all good ways to waste time and money.

Reference Checks

Surprisingly, not everyone checks references before making an award. References are most useful when the company providing the reference has acquired the same or very similar services from the third party. There is a lot of value in business leader-to-business leader discussions, particularly if the third party isn't part of the discussion. Most times, references are open and candid. What's discussed is confidential, and can reveal useful information that can inform decisions about the scope of services and management controls.

Compliance with Laws and Regulations

Broadly speaking, the processes designed by risk control functions and embedded within your institution's third-party risk management program should address risks and controls for laws and regulations that apply to many business segments and their third-party relationships. The relevant business segment and the compliance group are the most reliable sources of information about which laws and regulations specifically apply to critical activities and third-party relationships within their span of control.

Because your institution can't outsource its accountabilities, it's advisable to take the time to determine whether existing and new critical third parties have appropriate knowledge, practices, and controls to comply with laws and regulations. Third parties often have clients in many sectors. Many laws are common to all their clients, but regulations are often sector or service specific. Smaller companies and even larger corporations can have limited awareness of at least some of their clients' regulatory requirements.

It may be tempting to believe your institution can rely on "sweep" clauses in third-party agreements—clauses designed to hold the third party accountable for compliance to regulations and laws. This reliance may be misplaced, particularly if the third party doesn't fully understand what is required, doesn't have a process to stay current with changes to existing regulations or quickly deal with new ones, or feels forced to agree with your institution's terms and conditions due to competitive pressures.

Controls, and Compensating Controls

There are controls and then there are compensating controls. Controls are easy to define. Where a third party's risk management policies, practices, and controls meet or exceed a financial institution's requirements, they provide assurance about the third party's control environment. In this case, the financial institution will negotiate controls in the form of contractual terms to maintain that level of assurance.

Controls are designed to be:[25]

1. **Preventative** to prevent a risk from being realized—for example, the "input of an incorrect postcode preventing the user from continuing the transaction." This category of controls can also be called "before the event" or "ex ante" controls.
2. **Detective** to detect a risk that might happen or has happened—for example, "an exception report." This category may also be called "after the event" or "ex-post" controls.

Some examples of third-party controls include a contractual obligation to share results of the annual testing of disaster recovery plans or provide an SSAE-16 or SOC2 independent assessment of internal controls. These preventative controls are typically by contractual obligation. Other preventative controls may be included in specific sub-agreements like specifics in service- and operating-level agreements, or in transition plans.

Third-party controls complement commonly used internal controls such as management oversight, segregation of duties, policies and procedures, training, risk diversification, and performance and capacity management.

Compensating controls are one or more steps down from the institution's "ideal" controls. In this case, the compensating control goes as far as possible towards controlling a known risk, but not as far as the "ideal" control. The FFIEC's definition of a compensating control for information systems may not be entirely clear to individuals outside of the risk community. Here's the FFIEC's description: "A management, operational, and/or technical control (e.g., safeguard or countermeasure) employed by an organization in lieu of a recommended security control in the low, moderate, or high baselines that provides equivalent or comparable protection for an information system."[26]

To clarify, compensating controls are controls designed to offset or counteract deficiencies in the third party's existing control environment. In simple terms, when the third party's controls are deemed less than effective, compensating controls are negotiated with the third party or implemented by the business unit to mitigate or minimize risks associated with the third party. In many cases compensating controls don't provide "equivalent or comparable protection." Equivalent or comparable protection may not be feasible, so risk control specialists and compliance and legal experts design compensating controls that do the best possible job to protect their institution.

Controls including compensating controls are deemed effective (strong), partially effective (adequate), or ineffective (poor). "An evaluation of 'poor' could include an excessive control. Such an evaluation may make it easier to identify where there is a need to modify controls and help shape the subsequent action plans."[27] The effectiveness of controls is the foundation for rating discrete risk exposures to arrive at the residual risk. Remember, inherent risk is the institution's exposure to risk in the absence of controls. Residual risk is the institution's exposure to risk after assessing the effectiveness of controls.

---

[25]Institute of Operational Risk - Operational Risk Sound Practice Guidance - Risk Control Self Assessment (Mar 10) https://iorinstitute.org/public/100310RiskControlSelfAssessment.pdf

[26]FFIEC IT Examination Handbook InfoBase http://ithandbook.ffiec.gov/glossary/compensating-control.aspx

[27]Institute of Operational Risk - Operational Risk Sound Practice Guidance - Risk Control Self Assessment (Mar 10) https://iorinstitute.org/public/100310RiskControlSelfAssessment.pdf

Third-party controls should be included in the contract. They should periodically be retested throughout the lifecycle of the relationship according to criticality of the activities and the relationship, and the amount of risk the institution is exposed to.

Contracting

Effective contracting is vital for effective third-party risk management. The tremendous effort it takes to source, evaluate, assess risks, finalize scope and quality of services, and design appropriate risk controls must be captured in an agreement that reflects the spirit and intent of the relationship.

In collaboration, the legal department and risk control specialists in many institutions have developed a standard set of contractual clauses. Some address specific regulatory guidance, such as the Fed's requirements for incentive compensation or the FFIEC's audit requirements. Others deal with critical risk controls such as business continuity management plans or SOC2 reports. Institutions with more mature third-party risk management programs have taken this further by risk-adjusting contract controls and configuring their third-party risk management technology solution to tell their legal department and business owner which clauses should be negotiated into the third-party agreement.

No one ever gets everything they want, particularly when it comes to legal agreements. When the third party gets your institution to agree to differences in standard contractual clauses, a best practice is to rate "contract and compliance risk" based on the changes. New or different clauses either remain effective or are "partially effective" or "ineffective." This may give rise to a challenge or three. Regardless, business owners need to know the nature and level of risk they are accepting with new third parties, amendments, and renewals.

Manos-McHenry[28] describes the following best practice for contracting risk controls in third-party agreements:

> *Huntington has established procedures to draw attention and additional scrutiny to certain clauses in supplier contracts. Deviations from these 14 "critical" and seven "high importance" clauses require consultation with subject experts and escalation and approval within the bank prior to executing a contract. In some cases, deviation from approved clauses will result in a higher residual risk rating.*
>
> *Among Huntington's "mandatory" 21 legal provisions, the ones that are most heavily negotiated are:*
>
> 1) *Ownership of deliverables.*
> 2) *Indemnification against third-party claims.*
> 3) *Caps on the supplier's liability.*

Due diligence takes time, sometimes a lot of time. Many business leaders implement relationships without completing due diligence and without a contract. Sourcing, due diligence, and contracting processes need to get a lot faster before this will change. Sending a draft contract, key terms, or clauses to "finalist" third parties for review and comment can shorten the timeline to contract. Senior management and risk specialist involvement

[28]Huntington National Bank www.huntington.com

in contracts that are mired down ensures that problematic clauses have a chance of being resolved more quickly.

Risk Acceptance

After due diligence is completed and all controls, terms, and conditions have been negotiated, the nature and amount of risk the business segment or leader will absorb into the business requires documented acceptance.

Most financial institutions have implemented a tool—either in a purpose-built technology or on a spreadsheet—to assess the inherent risk of third-party relationships. During design or program enhancements, individual categories of risk—financial stability, business continuity management, fraud—can be assessed in terms of the strength of internal controls.

The overall relationship should also be risk rated. While most institutions currently rate inherent risk, many plan to implement a residual risk tool that will assess the level of risk after evaluating the strength of the third party's internal controls. Most institutions will eventually follow in their path as this relatively new risk management discipline evolves.

Risk can be accepted by the "wrong" business leader. A good question to ask is whether the contract owner is the business owner. In many institutions, technology and operations contracts are sourced, negotiated, managed, and "owned" by the CIO or head of operations, but the risk is to the business.

A best practice is to have the business unit—not the corporate function acting on its behalf—accept the risk. The ultimate business owner usually appreciates having the insight into all third-party risks that could impact business, and should be making the decision regarding which risks to accept and whether additional controls are warranted. The risk-acceptance process is an effortless way to get this information in front of the business owner.

At Huntington, Manos-McHenry says, "We all own risk. Once due diligence is complete and subject experts have assisted the business in assessing the controls environment of a supplier, the contract is routed for approval with controls-assessment ratings and deviations from critical clauses documented and captured in the contracts repository. Approvers include the business owner and the operations or IT function acting on its behalf."

Monitoring

Once the contract has been executed, transition is underway or complete, and controls have been established, it's time to move to the monitoring phase. This is a big topic, so it has been covered separately in Chapter 10.

McManos-Henry provides the following advice:

> *It's important that sourcing and procurement professionals in financial institutions understand that their roles have changed and are continuing to evolve. Traditional "category management" organization structures whereby vendors are managed according to broad categories of spend or services/commodities no longer work (and are definitely not efficient) in a first-, second-, and third-line-of-defense model. Financial services regulators expect the relationship manager within the business unit*

to understand and manage all aspects of the relationship. They frown upon efforts of centralized procurement teams to assume responsibilities that belong in the business.

Many procurement leaders at large financial institutions struggle with this shift in responsibilities while vendor costs are rising and chief risk officers are playing a larger role in sourcing and selection. The lowest-cost provider won't win your business because in many cases it hasn't invested in necessary controls.

In some institutions, the chief financial officer may be questioning the value of centralized sourcing/procurement departments. In others, the pendulum is starting to swing from centralized procurement into a federated sourcing team that combines third-party procurement and third-party risk management into a third-party management team. The scope and mandate for these reconstructed teams is third-party lifecycle and risk management.

Organizations that do not understand this fundamental shift will not succeed in the long run. They run the risk of having too heavy a staffing model. Compounding the inefficiency are duplicate or even triplicate responsibilities across centralized procurement, first-line-of-defense vendor managers, and third-party management organization leading to massive confusion, wasted resources, and regulatory issues. Several large financial institutions today suffer from this "duplicate effort" syndrome, but depending on who you talk to, you will get a different story. The most likely root cause is primarily because third-party management and third-party risk management organizations have been formed relatively quickly in an effort to address regulatory findings, including MRAs, and meet regulatory expectations.

If you are a chief financial officer, chief risk officer, or chief operating officer it may be helpful to ask yourself whether your institution has optimized the various departments and teams that manage risk and generate value from third-party relationships. In my experience, between 35% to 50% efficiencies can be gained by organizing effectively, leveraging the right tools and technologies, and reducing redundant management personnel.

As chief sourcing officer, Manos-McHenry is responsible for Huntington's sourcing, procurement, and third-party risk management program. Here is how she describes Huntington's "Gateway" process for acquisition and renewal for third-party relationships.

Led by the sourcing function, the process pulls together the appropriate stakeholders in decision making for high-risk deals and those over $1 million. The deal passes through three governance and oversight "Gates":

Gate 1: Prior to selection of the supplier or commencement of a structured negotiation to document the strategy in the planning / due diligence phase.

Gate 2: After selection when the business case is more refined.

Gate 3: Prior to contract signature when the results of due diligence questionnaires can be reviewed with the applicable subject experts and the business, together with a summary of the negotiated terms in comparison with Huntington's approved clauses for critical relationships.

There will be times when your institution sources a third party and legitimately bypasses standard processes. An example of a good rationale is the need to rapidly acquire a

What Your Institution Should Do

Due Diligence

The conflict between the "need for speed" and the need to comply with regulatory guidance is soluble. Here are some practical suggestions:

Leverage existing third-party relationships. Rely on existing due diligence and risk assessments when acquiring new products and services. The concept of "build once, use many" works elsewhere, why not for third-party risk management? An execution obstacle may be found in the existing workflow design. If so, introduce the "reusability" concept for different engagements with the same third party. "Age" existing due diligence and documentary evidence. Conduct due diligence only on the specific risk exposures that are different in the new product or service.

Regarding procurement, don't be the "sourcing police." Help the business define its requirements—need to have vs. nice to have. Make it easy for the business to undertake structured, unbiased market assessments before formally going to market. Streamline your processes; automate where possible; and educate the business on processes, workflow, deal structuring, and third-party risk management.

Implement or use existing procurement technologies, such as eRFX technologies, more broadly. eRFX technologies are relatively inexpensive and can be acquired "as a service." They are a quick and inexpensive way to acquire a substantial portion of information gathered during due diligence. And utilize eRFX technology for both vendor and "non vendor" third parties. There are many standalone, low-cost solutions on the market. It's a proven shortcut that works.

Automate as much due diligence as possible and consider selective outsourcing.

new software to help harden your perimeter after a serious DDoS (distributed-denial-of-service) attack.

Documentary evidence and approvals are important. It's in your institution's best interest to document the rationale when non-standard processes are used to source a third-party relationship. If it's a big departure from standard processes, it may be prudent to get approval from your third-party governance committee.

You may also want to archive any documentation and due diligence conducted on the "best alternative" third party to strengthen evidence of contingency planning for critical relationships and activities.

If you haven't already done so, now is a good time to buy a solution to manage the enormous volume of data and records generated by a robust third-party risk management program. Keep it actionable and up to date.

Site Visits

Outsourced site visits and assessment of the third party's internal controls are becoming more common, particularly where long distances drive up the cost of visiting in person. If your institution follows this path, the selection criteria, due diligence, and performance management of the outsourced third party visitor should be subject to the same rigor as any other third-party relationship. Expectations, requirements, prerequisite expertise and experience of the assessors, and cost of optional or exceptional services should be clear.

Be vigilant about assessing the quality of the site visit reports. Some outsourcers have been found to produce poor-quality assessments that include few or no findings.

Risk Acceptance

The risk-acceptance process or tool is a communication process for business leaders who own the relationship and the risk. It should include crisp and concise information about the third party and inherent and residual risks.

Templating the risk-acceptance process to capture the full picture of costs, risks, and other important considerations is useful. It can include a relationship profile with information such as if the third party winning or losing the business is a customer, if the third party is contributing to your institution's diversity or corporate social responsibility goals and incremental capital costs, changes from prior contract costs, savings, and its disposition.

The meaty topic of post-contract management and monitoring is covered in the chapter on monitoring.

Termination

In deciding whether to exit or diminish any third-party relationship, it is important to review the products and services provided by the third party. A material change to the scope of services will affect the ones that remain in force, whether through higher pricing, lower service levels, less management attention, and reduced investments in resources by the third party. In some cases, the third party may choose to terminate remaining services because the reduced scale of the relationship is not strategic, profitable, or both.

If a determination is made to terminate some or all of an agreement, it's important to have a controlled exit. It is rare that your institution will no longer require the services. It is more likely that some or all of the services will be delivered by a different third party. Cooperation between parties is not guaranteed.

The third party will begin to lose interest in your account, and will pull its best and most experienced people. Mitigation strategies including incentive compensation may be the best course of action.

Information management should be engaged, particularly if the third party has access to important or confidential information assets. As a former chief procurement officer, I've seen many contracts that did not specify termination controls. In some cases, the financial institution did not own the information assets and/or operating procedures. This may be costly or impossible to remedy at the time of exit.

Investing in a purpose-built third-party management technology means that exit notifications, controls, and processes can be built into workflow, reducing the potential for a disorderly exit.

Spotlight on Peter Hill, CRO, Black Knight Financial Services[29]

An important element of Peter Hill's responsibilities as chief risk officer at fintech Black Knight is risk management and governance of Black Knight's third parties—companies that, to Black Knight's financial institution clients, are fourth parties. Here is how he describes that process:

The global threat landscape continues to evolve exponentially with new vulnerabilities being identified at an alarming rate. There were more new vulnerabilities identified by June 2017 than were identified in all of 2016. Exploitation of these vulnerabilities is being made easier with the release of NSA hacking tools and greater sophistication and capabilities of the actors in the threat landscape.

A company's largest vulnerability could be from an external third party. Consider the Target and Home Depot breaches. To survive and thrive, companies globally must have robust risk and security management structures, including effective management of third parties.

In addition to effectively managing risk, vendors need to manage regulatory and client expectations, which include very clearly defined requirements for third-party management. A significant component of enterprise risk management (ERM) at Black Knight is the vendor risk management department. This department is the critical function that protects the company from undue exposure to risks from our vendors. We have a set of structured risk processes that manage the vendor risks from origination through termination of their services. These processes include:

- *Review of all requests for outsourcing of services and products across the company to determine if there is already a vendor with a similar product or service in place, or if there are any reasons we should not engage with the vendor.*
- *Performing risk assessments to evaluate the health and risk posture of the vendor, including:*
  - *Financial risk.*
  - *Security risk.*
  - *Reputation and business risk.*
  - *Country risk.*
  - *Legal risk.*
- *Risk assessments to determine the risk tier and risk rating of the vendor.*
- *Once the vendor is selected and onboarded, a scorecard is established with the divisional vendor relationship manager. The scorecard is used for monthly tracking of compliance to service level agreements (SLAs) and the vendor's overall ability to meet expectations.*
- *Ongoing risk assessments are performed based on a schedule that is determined by the vendor's risk tier. Should any of the assessments identify a deficiency from the original assessment, the division (line of business) is engaged and must take action.*
- *Monitoring alerts are set up and triggered by changes in any of the key risk drivers, such as the vendor's financial position, business risk, etc.*
- *Should a decision be made to terminate the relationship with the vendor, the risk management team facilitates the exit process.*

However, there's more to effectively managing third-party risk than just having a strong tone at the top and a robust vendor risk management process. You must ask:

[29]Black Knight Financial Services www.bkfs.com

- *How do you ensure compliance with the vendor risk policy, standard, and processes?*
- *How do you create and provide meaningful reporting at the detailed division level and summarize it at the executive and board of directors level?*
- *How do you keep on top of rapidly changing regulatory requirements and standards?*

These are all questions that keep your average chief risk officer—me—up at night.

While we're not building Rome, it takes some time to build a strong, robust vendor management program that is effective across the company. At Black Knight, we've done this through an unwavering commitment to build a structure that meets our client and regulator expectations, but more importantly, one that meets our high standards for effective risk management.

Some of the factors that contributed to effective risk management are:

- *Active involvement from employees throughout development of our vendor risk management policy and procedures. This enabled comprehensive identification of relevant requirements and actions regarding vendor risk management, as well as providing inherent buy-in from employees.*
- *Tying concerns identified through the vendor assessment process to the company's "risk findings" process to capture, track, and report all identified risks in the company.*
- *Relevant vendor risk reporting at the division level that drives action and is summarized for review at monthly executive risk committee meetings.*
- *Regular training and awareness sessions for all employees on the importance of vendor risk management and the actions expected of them.*
- *Close liaison with the legal division, which reviews all contracts for required risk and security language and also provides another mechanism to ensure the vendor risk management team is appropriately engaged.*
- *A feed from the accounts payable process to capture if there are payments to third parties that are not in the vendor repository.*
- *Use of an eGRC tool to capture, track, and manage all relevant vendor information as well as integrate with the other enterprise GRC modules to enable the company to have a holistic risk picture.*
- *Performing onsite reviews of vendors as required.*

Even with these processes enabling a robust vendor risk management program, there is no opportunity to put your feet up and relax. Your vendors must be monitored on a continual basis for any changes to their risk profile. This requires monitoring for changes to their financial position, legal exposure, business resiliency, security posture, and country risk.

SECTION 2

Key Drivers of Inherent Risk

This book focuses on many sources of inherent third-party risk. Most of the risks listed below are addressed in the book, and six of them warranted their own chapter. These appear in bold text in the list below.

1. Anti-Corruption/Anti-Bribery
2. **Anti-Money Laundering**
3. **Business Continuity Management/Resilience**
4. Cloud Computing
5. Company Officers and Corporate Viability
6. Contract
7. Financial Viability
8. Foreign Service Delivery Location
9. Human Resources
10. Incentive Compensation
11. **Information and Cybersecurity**
12. Insurance
13. **Model**
14. Performance
15. Privacy
16. Physical Security
17. Records
18. **Reputation**
19. SOX-Reportable Financial Loss
20. Subcontractor
21. **Technology**

4

Information Security, Cybersecurity, and Privacy

The media is filled with headlines and stories about privacy breaches and the resulting fines and lawsuits. Few things concern customers more than notification of unauthorized access or use of your institution's confidential customer information, particularly when it's theirs—and particularly when most breaches are the result of criminal activity and malicious attacks.

The financial services sector is built on the principles of safety and soundness. An information security or a privacy-related breach is a breach of that trust, making it one of the biggest threats to your reputation. Reputational damage takes a long time to repair, particularly where there are deficiencies in your institution's controls that are obvious even to ordinary consumers.

A data breach can be very expensive. A 2016 study conducted by the Ponemon Institute for IBM said, "The average cost for each stolen record [in the U.S.] containing sensitive and confidential information has risen from $217 to $221. The number of breached records per incident this year ranged from 5,125 to 101,520."[30] When an incident in the financial services industry involves a third party, the cost per record and incident are much higher.[31]

Information security and cybersecurity are recurring, weighty agenda items for the board, senior managers, risk committees, risk control experts, and business leaders. As a result, serious attacks, breaches, and incidents are now subject to issue and incident management processes, and may be escalated and tracked at the highest levels.

The overarching goal of information security and cybersecurity professionals and investments is to protect precious information assets from unauthorized or improper access, copy, or use; deliberate or inadvertent damage, disclosure, or changes; and accidental or deliberate destruction.

"Integrity" should be their motto:

- Integrity of data sent to, created by, transacted by, stored by, and managed by third parties.

[30] Ponemon Institute LLC (sponsored by IBM) 2016 Cost of Data Breach Study: United States, page 2
[31] Ibid.

- Integrity of the complex ecosystems that financial services companies operate within.
- Integrity of the management, systems, operations, and reputation of your third and fourth parties.
- Integrity of security within the Internet of Things, systems, application programming interfaces, and software tools.
- Integrity of the information that is available about your institution.
- Integrity of your people and management team.
- Integrity of the people, processes, and technologies at your third parties.
- Integrity of your institution's risk management practices.
- Integrity of your institution's risk appetite and thresholds, and willingness to stay within them.

Multiple incidents are likely to damage your reputation and erode confidence in your institution's safety and soundness. Customer information breaches are said to inflict the most damage to an institution's reputation, and may attract regulatory sanctions and fines. Discrete, short denial-of-service incidents may be mostly annoying and relatively inexpensive to remedy, but some are far more serious.

In 2017 hackers released highly sophisticated hacking tools stolen from the U.S. National Security Agency (NSA) "into the wild." Then, the number of global malware and ransomware incidents quickly rose. These hacking tools are available on the Internet, for free or as low-cost "as a service" software, including distributed-denial-of-service (DDoS), Zero Day, and ransomware tools.

Edward Snowden, "security leaker extraordinaire," said in an April 2017 tweet, "Quick review of the #ShadowBrokers leak of Top Secret NSA tools reveals it's nowhere near the full library. NSA is just an agency of just one government, there are many more nation states doing the same or similar things. Who knows what else will be unleashed?"

Because the issue is so complex, and the threat landscape, actors, and methods to combat risk change at dizzying speed, it's easy to lose perspective on what constitutes good information security and cybersecurity risk management "hygiene."

The terms "information security" and "cybersecurity" are often used interchangeably. They are closely related, but are not the same.

Information security is exactly that. It's the set of policies, processes, and tools your institution deploys to secure the quality, integrity, and accessibility of sensitive, confidential, and protected information or data and trade secrets. These assets may be in the form of electronic and paper records, or proprietary know-how, technologies, and processes. Because there is a physical aspect to information security, many organizations delegate responsibility for third-party records management and physical security to their information security risk control function.

Cybersecurity and cyber risk management are how these precious assets are protected from unauthorized electronic access, use, changes, or destruction. Financial assets, resaleable information, and intellectual property are the most attractive targets to criminals. Protecting them is increasingly difficult in the multi-sourced, global, cloud-based, complex third-party ecosystems where financial institutions and their third parties operate.

Here are a few more definitions to round out the discussion:

Cyberspace is "a global … interconnected network of information systems infrastructures including the Internet, telecommunications networks, computer systems, and embedded processors and controllers."[32] It's big, it's complicated, and it's very accessible by design regardless of intention.

Privacy is the reasonable expectation by individuals and corporations alike that their confidential, proprietary information is safeguarded. This expectation is enshrined in national and global laws and regulations, which are stringently applied.

Regardless of what you call these categories of risk, it's never a question of whether your institution will have information and cybersecurity problems. It's a matter of how bad they will be. Cybersecurity is impossible to achieve. That makes information security unattainable. It is understood that cyber risk "is not something that can be avoided; instead it must be managed."[33] Investments in information and cybersecurity are a significant and growing cost because they include protection of your institution's records, networks, systems, computers, applications, and data—whether onsite, in transit, available to or managed by a third party, or in storage. As a former chief procurement officer, I can recall instances where procurement and contracting to acquire purpose-built applications and tools was a 24-hour process, unlike a typical procurement process that may take weeks or months.

What You Should Know

Managing third-party information and cybersecurity risk means making good choices about who you do business with; hiring the right risk specialists; and making prudent investments in strong processes, tools, and technologies. Capable risk management professionals can effectively identify key risks; define requirements and risk controls for third parties; and build and maintain effective processes to assess, monitor, and control third-party information security, cybersecurity, and privacy practices.

The Target breach of December 2013 is synonymous with poor "hygiene" in information security and cybersecurity risk management. The retailer missed the boat on every dimension: people, process, and technology. Because of Target and other high-profile exploits, the prospect of banks becoming a "Target" may cause sleepless nights for risk specialists and senior managers alike.

Educating others about risks and putting the right processes and controls in place is the responsibility of risk specialists, supported by senior management and their "tone from the top." A good place to start the awareness journey is by developing a good working knowledge of key indicators of information, cyber, and privacy risk that result from critical third-party relationships.

Key risk indicators include:

- Onsite or remote third-party access to your institution's systems and networks.
- Access to data, regardless of whether the data is in transit or at rest (stored).

---

[32]NISTIR 7298 Revision 2, Glossary of Key Information Security Terms

[33]COSO in the Cyber Age (January 2015), page 2

- Use of cloud computing.
- Subcontractor access to the third party's or your institution's networks and/or data.

Mark Silver, CISSP, CTPRP, GISP, vice president Third-Party Risk, Hancock Whitney Bank[34]—and a former information security professional—advises that your institution should track both access to and custody of data. This means reviewing and requiring different controls for each because the impact of these different risk exposures can vary.

In past years, information security and cybersecurity risk specialists were asked to identify key third-party risks, recommend controls, then step aside. Theoretically the business or segment leaders made explicit decisions on whether to accept risks, which was usually their decision alone. In practice, leaders were often blind to or underinformed about the risks.

A common challenge is reluctance by many institutions' information and cyber risk specialists to make the call on whether it is safe to do business with a third party. They know that networks and information assets are never entirely safe.

Strengthening information and cyber risk management practices means that your people and processes need to change. Risk management is everyone's responsibility, and risk specialists are expected to assume greater responsibility and accountability over the risk landscape for third-party relationships than ever before. They need to act well beyond developing due diligence and requirements, assessing risk, conducting onsite inspections, and making recommendations.

Risk specialists, particularly information and cyber specialists, need to take a stand on what is and what is not an acceptable risk, and to exercise their authority.

Exercising their authority means they must say "no" or "not this way" to business leaders. In regulatory parlance, this is referred to as a "challenge." Comfortable habits are hard to break, so senior management will need to help—in the form of a carrot or a stick, depending on the situation.

According to Joyce Brocaglia, CEO of the Alta Associates[35] executive search firm and founder of the Executive Women's Forum on Information Security, Risk Management, and Privacy:[36]

> *Cybersecurity has become a board-level imperative. As corporations race to create competitive solutions through digitization and transformation, the complexities of securing the enterprise are magnified. As such, the role of the chief information security officer (CISO) has become more crucial. Selection of a uniquely qualified leader has become essential to the success of building a resilient corporation.*
>
> *CISOs must have the capability to engage with business and technology leaders to proactively evaluate third parties and new technologies, enhance their risk management capabilities, and mitigate risks. Selecting the right CISO and developing a world-class team will not only help secure your institution, it can protect your brand and stock price and provide a competitive advantage.*

---

[34]Mark Silver, Hancock Whitney Bank https://www.hancockwhitney.com/

[35]Alta Associates http://www.altaassociates.com/

[36]The core mission of the Executive Women's Forum is to engage, develop, and advance women leaders in information security, IT risk management and privacy www. http://www.ewf-usa.com/

In the world of people, process, and technology, there is a reason people come first. If you don't get the people part right, the rest doesn't matter. No tools or technologies can replace strategic information and cybersecurity leadership or diversely talented teams.

When it comes to risk controls, it's extremely difficult to stay current with the threat landscape, solutions, and best practices. Things change day-by-day and minute-by-minute. Criminals and malicious hackers can be backed up with big money and/or have access to large resource pools. Their sole purpose is to cause harm to your institution, for their benefit. Because of this, there will always be gaps in controls and processes designed to address a never-ending flood of new vulnerabilities and threats.

Some gaps are known and persist because of high costs to fix, inexperience, or it's not practical to try to close them. Information and cyber risk specialists need to make good, informed decisions on how to proceed. In the words of John Klapmust, senior vice president Third-Party Risk Management at Bank of the West, "Don't let perfection get in the way of good."

Speaking of "good," here are some good controls that you should be aware of:

1. **Contract-signing authorities** should be based on dollar thresholds and risk.
2. When a corporate function "owns" contracts on behalf of business segments, including business or segment leaders in the **risk-acceptance** process ensures they understand the third-party risks their business and the institution are taking.
3. Incidents are subject to escalation and reporting procedures. **Systemic issues are often an unmanaged opportunity**. Insights into cyber risks are opaque, buried in multiple databases, or exist only in people's heads. High employee turnover, particularly among millennials, means that those heads have likely moved on. The safest course of action is to establish a process to transform this knowledge and data into actionable information, acknowledging it may be incomplete.
4. Beware the "**Internet of Things**," devices with RFID tags or embedded chips that interact with one another and with people via Internet-based applications. Increased interconnectivity means a sharp increase in the number of points of entry into networks and systems. In turn, this means a sharp increase in cybersecurity threats. In July 2016 the National Institute of Standards and Technology (NIST)[37] published a report that can help inform your institution's risk controls for these and other connected devices. NIST refers to interconnected devices as "primitives," which "allow formalisms, reasoning, simulations, and reliability and security risk tradeoffs to be formulated and argued."[38]
5. If a third party has **access to your network or information assets**, or if your institution accesses a **third party's** services via its **Web portal**, consider implementing requirements for two-factor authentication[39] and strong passwords with pre-scheduled changes—and prohibit the use of free anti-virus and malware pro-

[37]NIST - National Institute for Science and Technology, U.S. Department of Commerce

[38]NIST Special Publication 800-183 Networks of 'Things' Computer Security http://nvlpubs.nist.gov/nistpubs/SpecialPublications/NIST.SP.800-183.pdf

[39]Two-factor authentication means that users must log in with a password AND enter information known only to the user. Most financial institutions now require two-factor authentication for online access by their customers.

tection. These are common vulnerabilities for smaller third parties. It only takes a single point of entry for hackers to get into a third party's network, and through theirs into yours. (This is how criminals installed malware in Target's network.)

Once they're in, they're in.

6. Leading up to **termination**, when the relationship comes to an end, third-party risk management programs need to adequately address the recovery or destruction of information assets. All institutions should have an up-to-date record of the data assets their third party has. Contractual terms should address how these records are returned to your institution in a useable format and the steps the third party must deploy to destroy records. Execution of these processes often involves the information security and business continuity management functions.
7. Educate your employees and leaders on the risks of going around IT to acquire **cloud-based services.** Have them acknowledge the rules during annual compliance training and implement consequences with some teeth. According to the Harvard Business Review Analytic Services report on cloud computing, 16% of respondents reported going around IT to acquire cloud-based services. Responding CIOs also confirmed that identity management, security, and compliance are much more difficult in the cloud.[40]

   A key finding in the BCI Institute HorizonScan 2017 research study, consisting of 729 organizations from 79 countries, identified a growing concern about dependency "on 'the cloud,' technology, important third-party applications, and

[40]Harvard Business Review Analytics Department: Cloud Computing Comes of Age (sponsored by Oracle) https://www.oracle.com/webfolder/s/delivery_production/docs/FY15h1/doc16/HBR-Oracle-Report-webview.pdf

infrastructure as it relates to our ability to react, strategize, and recover from any particular type of vital recipient application incident."[41]

Investments in **data-loss prevention controls and activities** have proven effective for reducing direct costs, indirect costs, and recovery time when a breach occurs. The following table shows the percentage of companies surveyed by the Ponemon Institute that deploy these controls and activities. Most companies use a combination of them.

	2010	2011	2012	2013	2014	2015	2016
Endpoint security solutions	36%	41%	42%	40%	53%	50%	48%
Training and awareness programs	67%	63%	53%	51%	51%	50%	52%
Expanded use of encryption	58%	61%	52%	57%	50%	52%	49%
Additional manual procedures and controls	58%	54%	49%	46%	43%	40%	41%
Data loss prevention (DLP) solutions	42%	43%	45%	49%	39%	39%	38%
Identity and access management solutions	49%	52%	47%	43%	39%	40%	41%
Security intelligence solutions	22%	21%	26%	28%	34%	37%	39%
Other system control practices	40%	43%	38%	34%	33%	32%	30%
Strengthening of perimeter controls	20%	22%	25%	23%	21%	19%	18%
Security certification or audit	33%	29%	19%	19%	20%	19%	21%

Source: Ponemon Institute LLC[42] (sponsored by IBM) 2016 Cost of Data Breach Study: United States[43]

Following its breach, Target made changes to improve information security and cybersecurity. Here are some changes that Target made public:[44]

- Monitoring and logging rules and alerts, centralized log feeds, and enabled additional logging capabilities.
- White listing point-of-sale systems, including all registers, point-of-sale servers, and white listing rules.
- Enhanced segmentation of point-of-sale management tools, network firewall rules, and firewall governance.
- Reviewing and limiting vendor access.
- Enhanced security for employee and contractor passwords and accounts.

It is *unlikely* that any but the largest, most sophisticated "unregulated" third parties have implemented risk management practices that resemble those found in your institution. And it is even more *unlikely* that they have been able to hire or retain information security and cybersecurity specialists, who work in a profession with high demand and short supply. Further, few invest in third-party risk management. If they have invested at

[41]BCI Institute HorizonScan 2017 http://www.bcifiles.com/HorizonScan2017.pdf

[42]Ponemon Institute https://www.ponemon.org/

[43]Ponemon Institute Research Report (sponsored by IBM) 2016 Cost of Data Breach Study: United States https://www.ibm.com/security/data-breach/

[44]Target website https://corporate.target.com/article/2014/04/updates-on-target-s-security-and-technology-enhanc

all, many treat third-party risk management like an inconvenient "customer compliance" exercise. Notable exceptions are those third parties that are exceptionally forward-looking, have experienced a serious breach themselves, or are subject to regulatory reviews.

The following example shows just how lax some third parties can be.

"Laptop Larry," A Mini Case Study

By Mark Silver, CISSP, CTPRP, GISP, Vice President Third-Party Risk Hancock Whitney Bank

A niche provider selected by a business unit was brought forward for risk assessment and contracting. The business unit's intent was to engage this firm for specialized advisory services related to some of our largest customers. Access and full custody of our customers' personally identifiable information (PII) data, our highest level of protected data, was integral to providing the service.

As soon as we began the vetting process, it quickly became clear that the firm did not have even a basic information security program. When asked where our customers' PII data would be stored, the answer was "Larry's laptop." They said that Larry has the software needed for the analysis, so everything needs to be stored there.

This firm and its team had the expertise needed for this niche engagement. However, they were completely unaware of even the most basic information security and cybersecurity standards and controls.

The days of contracting with a provider without the proper controls is over, regardless of expertise. It will come as no surprise that we selected a different provider who had appropriate controls, and have been happy with the results.

The best protection for your institution's information assets, networks, and systems is to engage only those third parties that meet your business requirements and take risk management as seriously as their customers do.

In May 2018 the EU General Data Protection Regulation (GDPR) comes into effect. An attempt to provide greater assurance to consumers about collection and use of their personal data, it places even more stringent requirements on companies. As I was writing this book, many were rushing to comply. In an increasingly global economy, companies and financial institutions can expect conflicts between regulations and legal requirements to rise, making it increasingly difficult and costly to comply.

When it comes to third-party information, cybersecurity, and privacy, the best defense is a good offense. Define expectations, contract for them, then inspect what you expect.

Easy to say, hard to do

The OCC's and other regulatory guidance describe taking a "lifecycle management" approach to information security and cybersecurity risk management, which have a direct correlation to your institution's ability to comply with privacy laws. As noted in an earlier chapter, third-party lifecycle management includes processes to identify, assess, manage, and control risks, and provides appropriate oversight throughout the life of the relationship—including when it reaches its end.

What You Should Know

The core purpose of information security and cybersecurity programs is to protect the privacy and rights of an institution's customers and itself. Executed well, that is what they deliver while complying with laws, guidance, and regulations. And there are many laws, guidance issuances, and regulations to lead the way, along with many examples of failures and their consequences.

Furthering the 1978 Right to Financial Privacy Act, in 1999 the U.S. Congress passed the Gramm-Leach-Bliley Act into law. The act "declares it is a violation of this act to obtain, disclose, or provide documents under false pretenses pertaining to customer information of a financial institution."[45] Federal bank acts also contain provisions regulating the use and disclosure of personal financial information. Canada, meanwhile, has the Personal Information Protection and Electronic Documents Act (PIPEDA), the federal private-sector privacy law. Some provinces have privacy legislation that has been deemed "substantially similar" to PIPEDA, which means that it is applied instead of PIPEDA in some cases.[46]

Translating legislation into guidance, the U.S. Office of the Comptroller of the Currency (OCC) says "a bank's information security program must be designed to ensure the security and confidentiality of customer information, protect against any anticipated threats or hazards to the security or integrity of such information, and protect against unauthorized access to or use of such information that would result in substantial harm or inconvenience to any customer."[47]

If this subject were to be examined in detail, this book would be longer than *War and Peace*. Instead of a technical or scare-tactic approach, this chapter is intended to inform and guide your thinking about what's important and common shortcomings in current practices—and to provoke your thinking about your information security, cybersecurity, and privacy practices for third-party relationships.

What Your Institution Should Do

Be "exam-ready" every day. It has been said that, "Regardless of their motives, cyber attackers are relentless, sophisticated, and patient."[48] Because of the potential for significant impact on customers and the high risk of loss, regulators and internal auditors subject information/cybersecurity programs, practices, controls, responses to incidents, and enhancement "roadmaps" to rigorous examination and audit. The scope of audits and examinations includes the institution's third-party management program and how risk management programs, processes, and evidence align and complement each another. Knowledgeable, sharp-eyed professionals are looking for consistency, strengths, inconsistencies, and gaps. Employee awareness is matchless. Employees

[45]Summary S.900 — 106th Congress (1999-2000) [GLBA] https://www.congress.gov/bill/106th-congress/senate-bill/900

[46]Office of the Privacy Commissioner of Canada https://www.priv.gc.ca/en/privacy-topics/privacy-laws-in-canada/02_05_d_15/

[47]OCC Bulletin 2001-8: Guidelines Establishing Standards for Safeguarding Customer Information, Page 1

[48]COSO in the Cyber Age. https://www.coso.org/documents/COSO%20in%20the%20Cyber%20Age_FULL_r11.pdf Page 12

are the real "first line of defense" when it comes to managing third-party information security and cybersecurity. Compliance training is sacrosanct: Don't cut the budgets for information security and cybersecurity training, regardless.

Silver recommends you consider "where the data meets the road."

"In the modern business environment," he says, "we must rely on third-party providers for niche skills or areas of expertise. Initial due diligence and third-party vetting have a great impact in making sure you have chosen the right partner. A word of caution: This is a point-in-time review. It is the day-to-day first line management and monitoring activities that will make the difference in the long term. Control environments change over time, so continuous monitoring and periodic updates of all due diligence information has become a new best practice."

Everyone is familiar with the "See Something, Say Something" campaign run by the New York City Transit Authority. This catchy slogan has been widely adopted to refer to security matters of all types, and financial institution employees are trained to take it seriously. Employees at all levels are more aware than ever of their role as informal members of their institutions' risk management team. This is what the Federal Financial Institutions Examination Council refers to as successfully creating a "security culture."

"An institution's security culture contributes to the effectiveness of the information security program," it says. "The information security program is more effective when security processes are deeply embedded in the institution's culture."[49]

Don't reinvent the wheel. Effective risk management is a team sport. In this case, all financial institutions are on the same side. Consider formalizing a collaboration framework and process with peer institutions. Regulators encourage collaboration on risk management practices, and your institution's resources may stretch further. Collaboration can strengthen internal practices, help tighten controls, and help to prevent or detect more vulnerabilities and threats than if your risk specialists are operating independently. When a threat or new vulnerability is detected, a peer network enables timely sharing of findings. When appropriate, the network can collaborate on prevention and detection strategies. Taking this a step further, individual specialists can become sub-networks, specializing in specific aspects of information, cyber, and privacy risk. This approach can reduce systemic risks, and improve response times across the sector when an incident occurs.

Leverage proven frameworks and methodologies. This is a different spin on "don't reinvent the wheel." Assessing third-party information, cyber, and privacy risks isn't new. The amount of rigor is. There is extensive regulatory guidance on information, cybersecurity, and privacy risk management, plus tips from not-for-profit organizations and professional associations and certifications.

The expectation for every financial institution is to implement repeatable processes to identify inherent risks and determine whether internal controls or changes to the structure of services delivered will mitigate or minimize risks. The third-party risk management program should include processes, workflow, and an accessible repository for relevant information requested from the third party. The third party should respond, provide the requested information and supporting

[49]FFIEC Information Technology Examination Handbook: Information Security 2016, page 6

evidence, and open its door for a site visit if one is needed. Risk specialists should assess the information and evidence provided to determine if additional controls are required and if residual risk is within the institution's risk tolerance.

The COSO Cube (below), developed by the Committee of Sponsoring Organizations of the Treadway Commission (COSO), provides a framework to test for completeness. Risk adjusting due diligence, controls, monitoring, and governance activities is essential for effective risk management, particularly information security and cybersecurity risk management. Trying to determine whether your institution's risk controls are effective, efficient, and risk adjusted is an ongoing challenge. Too much noise can drown out what's most important.

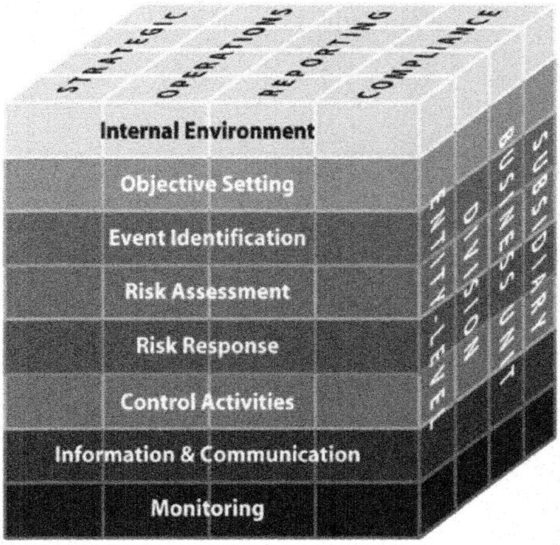

Source: COSO in the Cyber Age https://www.coso.org/documents/COSO%20in%20the%20Cyber%20Age_FULL_r11.pdf

Key activities during program execution include:

- Establishing the control environment.
- Risk assessment.
- Controls.
- Information and communication.
- Monitoring.

The COSO cube content and activities should look familiar. But when it comes to third parties, application is a little different than when it's applied internally. Lifecycle management activities are focused on how the third party manages risk within its operations, and the impact this will have on your institution's safety and security.

Don't waste precious time "fishing." During this long journey to third-party risk management program maturity, there are many institutions with a sizeable backlog of information security and cybersecurity risk assessments. Some still allow the business to start the contracting and implementation processes before risk evaluations are complete. Despite the backlog and unknown risk exposures, some risk specialists continue to ask third parties for information and documentary evidence that is not commensurate with the criticality of the activity or third-party relationship. If you ask them why, they'll likely tell you that they may uncover more risks. Resources should be used wisely. No third-party relationship is entirely safe.

5

Business Resilience Risk

Financial institutions and their third parties have an inseparable reliance on a complex, intertwined global network of suppliers, joint venture partners, channel relationships, processors, cloud-based services, and many other relationships to deliver services from the most basic to the most complex. Clearly, there are many places where these relationships can break down, creating a need for business continuity and disaster recovery planning. Linnea Solem, vice president and chief privacy officer, Deluxe Corporation,[50] says, "Business continuity and disaster recovery disciplines are distinct but interrelated. Business continuity plans help organizations continue operating when faced with a business interruption or disaster. Disaster recovery focuses on specific resumption of operations. Bringing the programs together is a focus of business continuity management."

Business continuity management (BCM) is the foundation of your institution's business resilience: the true purpose of identifying, assessing, and managing BCM risk. Choose your critical third parties wisely. The best business resilience strategy is to never need one.

[50]Deluxe Corporation https://www.deluxe.com/

Few financial institutions have mature processes to identify, assess, manage, and control third-party business resilience. Many limit their work effort to due diligence conducted during the selection process—which is often rudimentary—and infrequently monitoring critical third parties' business resilience throughout the lifecycle of relationships.

Investing in business continuity management is more than just "buying insurance" for your institution. Done well, it protects your biggest assets: customers, revenue, infrastructure, and reputation. Some perspective: The cost of acquiring a new customer is said to be anywhere from three to 30 times the cost of keeping one. Even the smallest interruption of service can erode customer confidence. And even minor incidents are inconvenient and irritating, and may cause your customers to move their business to a competitor.

The overarching goal of business reliance management practices is to prevent or minimize the impact on your institution's customers, employees, and operations resulting from issues, incidents, and serious failures by your third parties. These practices fall under the umbrella of business continuity management and disaster recovery (DR) risk management processes and practices.

Ten or 20 years ago, material third-party relationships were often confined to long-term, behemoth outsourcing contracts that provided the illusion of effective risk management. At that time, senior executives really liked the idea of having "one throat to choke."

Solem cautions, "Third-party service provider relationships today are less about a traditional, expansive data center agreement, and are more likely to be about a specific service or set of services, components, or a technology layer."

Today, contract terms are shorter, and institutions contract with multiple third parties to deliver complex, interconnected services. Compounding the complexity of financial institutions' operational ecosystems is "pass through" reliance—your critical third parties' reliance on their own critical third parties. In the world of third-party risk management, "pass through" third-party relationships are referred to as your material subcontractors or fourth parties. And it doesn't stop at fourth parties. The daisy chain of reliance on critical third parties is passed along, and passed along. For financial institutions, this complex ecosystem means that it can be very difficult to determine where potential points of failure exist. There is rarely ever only a single point of failure. This reliance on an opaque interconnected ecosystem is just one dimension of what is referred to as concentration risk, which is dealt with in more detail elsewhere in this book.

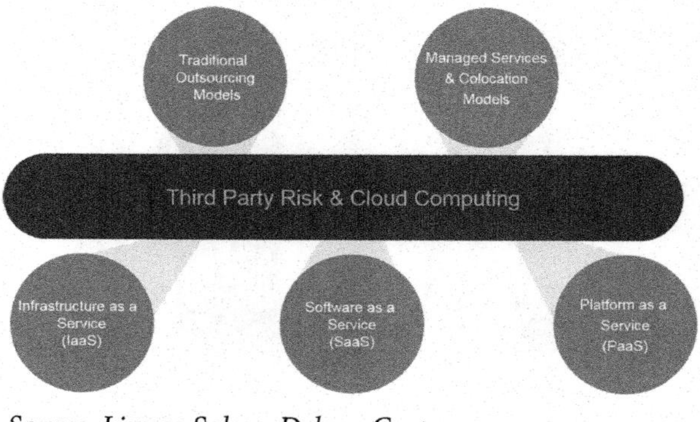

Source: Linnea Solem, Deluxe Corp

Understanding the nature of systemic concentration risk—*undiversifiable risk across the financial services sector*—should raise real questions about systemic business resilience and the bona fide capacity of institutions and the sector at large to recover from serious, concurrent failures of several fintech behemoths. Add the growing reliance on cloud-based services, the rise of the Internet of Things, and extensive use of low-cost providers in potentially unstable locations and you get a clear picture of how and why BCM risk is increasing.

Many internal experts have pushed responsibility for business resilience risk relating to third parties to the first line of defense, rationalizing that they are in the best position to understand their business resilience needs. Maybe so, but business leaders and segments are focused on their customers, the competition, and the bottom line. Their people have little or no expertise in what to assess, how to determine the strength of their third parties' internal controls, and how to monitor them.

Solem advises, "In today's ecosystem, organizations need to incorporate third-party management, third-party capacity, and operational and cyber resilience testing with their third-party service providers into their business resilience programs."

The Open Compliance and Ethics Group[51] has a useful business impact analysis playbook that can be downloaded at no cost at its website (https://www.oceg.org/resources/business-impact-analysis-playbook/).

In addition, updating guidance issued in 2003, the Federal Financial Institutions Examination Council (FFIEC) issued a new "Appendix J" to its *IT Examination Handbook*, "Strengthening the Resilience of Outsourced Technology Services," in early 2015. This guidance is much more prescriptive and is expected to significantly improve processes and practices across the sector over time.

Many BCM professionals are waking up to their responsibility and accountability to strengthen their institutions' business resilience. They are tightening up the processes, setting standards and risk thresholds, and establishing key risk indicators for BCM and DR related to critical third-party relationships.

Business continuity management risk is a measure of **business resilience**—your institution's ability to recover in the event of an interruption, disruption, or discontinuity of your institution's operations or services. In the context of third-party risk management, these are the result of one or more of your third parties' inadequate or failed disaster recovery and business resumption plans.

If disaster befalls one of your third parties, your institution needs to be prepared. Disasters can befall any company. Anywhere. Anytime. You can't predict when disaster will hit your third party, particularly if you know little about where it is delivering services from and its operations, locations, and preparations. If that's the case, it will be impossible to prepare for the impact of a disaster that your third party experiences. You'll be unprepared for the impact on your institution if a third party is plagued by strikes or widespread riots when a government changes, or is affected by a natural disaster like a debilitating hurricane or an ice storm.

No geography is immune from natural disasters, as the harrowing late summer and early fall of 2017 continued to demonstrate. Here is a list of countries most hit by natural disasters between 1995 and 2016. This includes earthquakes, typhoons, tsunamis,

[51]https://www.oceg.org/resources/business-impact-analysis-playbook/

landslides, and flash floods. The number of natural disasters is increasing and will likely increase due to climate change. Note that this research list does not include statistics for terrorist activities, which are also on the rise.

These disaster figures are a stark reminder that **all countries, geographies, and populations are vulnerable.**

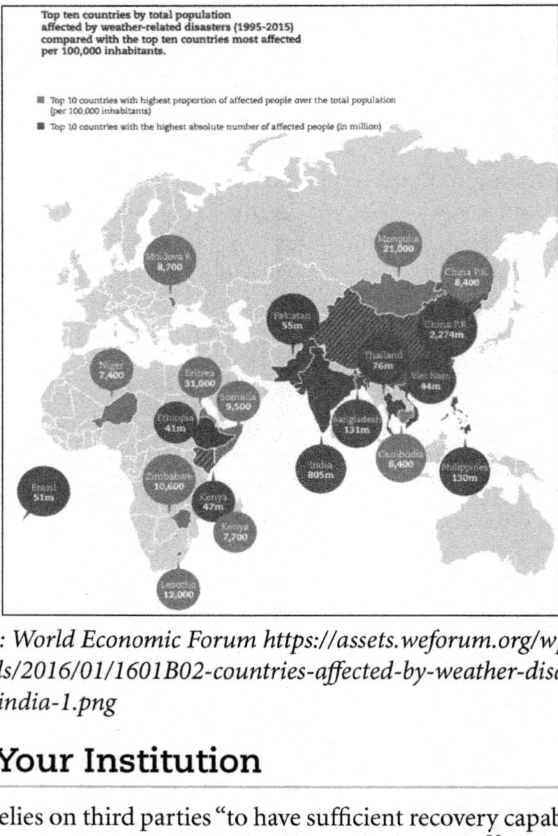

Source: World Economic Forum https://assets.weforum.org/wp-content/uploads/2016/01/1601B02-countries-affected-by-weather-disasters-china-india-1.png

Protecting Your Institution

Your institution relies on third parties "to have sufficient recovery capabilities for the specific services they perform on behalf of the financial institution."[52] Senior management in financial institutions therefore relies on internal BCM professionals and business leaders to provide assurance of the institution's business resilience.

Internal BCM professionals need to develop effective processes to identify, understand, and analyze inherent risks in third-party relationships, their likelihood of occurring, and the potential impact that severe disruptions or failures may have on their institution and business segments.

Hold these experts accountable for determining the most effective and efficient way to do this. They should be held accountable for testing BCM controls with the intention

[52]FFIEC IT Examination Handbook, Appendix J: Strengthening the Resilience of Outsourced Technology Services, page 2

of ensuring the institution avoids or minimizes serious business interruptions, and for guiding informed risk mitigation and response strategies that will protect the institution.

The effort expended on business continuity risk management should be commensurate with the criticality of the service or activity being performed by each third party relative to your institution's overall operations or those of the business segment.

What You Should Know

Business continuity risk is a key risk factor in most third-party relationships. Business interruptions can be minor—simply an inconvenience in terms of management time and effort to resolve—or they can be serious and all-consuming.

Any service delivery failure by a third party can be immediately apparent, and an interruption or serious failure can have a tremendous negative impact on your clients and reputation. Everyone experiences these: Service interruptions and failures are common and frequent. The following statistics were provided by The Business Continuity Institute:

Seventy-three percent of survey respondents experienced at least one serious disruption to their operations in the previous 12 months. Failure by a third party was one of the top three causes of disruption.

Thirty-nine percent of disruptions that were caused by a third party originated below the immediate third party. This means that the originator was the third party's provider, or the institution's subcontractor.

Fifty-two percent reported that the main cause of disruption was an IT or telecommunication outage; 48% reported the main cause was weather.

Key Risk Indicators

Higher levels of business continuity risk may be related to one or more of these key risk indicators:

1. The third party supports or provides services or applications where your institution has a recovery time objective (RTO) of less than 24 hours. There is usually a direct correlation between RTO and criticality of services.
2. A third party processes and/or stores large volumes of transactions and/or data.
3. Concentration risk arising from the use of third-party global data or processing centers. Outages in one location may disrupt business continuity on a much broader scale.
4. Unclear or unacceptable recovery point objectives (RPOs), where the age of files that will be recovered from backup storage post-failure can create unrecoverable data-integrity issues.
5. The third party doesn't have or is unwilling to provide details of BCM and DR policies and plans. This can include an unwillingness to provide the results of disaster recovery and business resumption tests. This requirement should be correlated to criticality of services or the relationship.

Business impact analysis (BIA) is the first step in determining the criticality of any third party to the institution, whether it's multiple business segments/units or a single business segment/unit. In keeping with the concept of "risk adjusting" your program, the amount of work invested in assessing and managing business continuity risk should be commensurate with the criticality of the third-party relationship and activity supported by the third party.

BIA is the first step in developing a business continuity plan. It should include:

- Identification of the potential impact of uncontrolled, non-specific events on the institution's business processes and its customers;
- Consideration of all departments and business functions, not just data processing; and
- Estimation of maximum allowable downtime and acceptable levels of data, operations, and financial losses.

Source: FFIEC IT Examination Handbook: Business Continuity Planning, page 6

For critical relationships and activities, the potential for a serious business interruption and its likely effect on business operations should be estimated by conducting a BIA. Particularly for highly critical third parties, where possible the BIA should include a methodology for quantifying the duration of disruption from multiple likely scenarios, their projected financial impact, and the impact on the institution's customers and reputation.

An emerging practice in financial institutions is scenario analysis, often in the form of structured table-top exercises to deal with serious failures of critical third-party relationships. The FFIEC proposes that "the parties can discuss scenarios of significant disruptions that may necessitate transitioning critical services to alternative TSPs."[53]

Scenario analysis could be incorporated into your institution's Risk Control Self Assessment (RCSA) activities. If you plan to undertake scenario analysis for highly critical third-party relationships—*a best practice*—you will likely choose to start with third-party relationships with high reliance on specific third parties to deliver critical services, or ones that have a high potential to cause significant financial losses or reputational damage.

The Institute of Operational Risk's guidance on RCSAs is a proven methodology that can be leveraged to thoughtfully develop or strengthen resilience. Business leaders and segments know which third-party relationships are critical. These should be included in their RCSA.

Provided the RCSA process is recognized as a useful tool by the institution's business leaders, "The findings from an RCSA can be used to formulate appropriate action plans to address identified control gaps, taking into account risk-reward (cost-benefit) considerations as part of the overall operational risk management approach."

"In this respect RCSA promotes analysis and monitoring of factors that affect the level of operational risk exposure. A further driving force behind the growth and emergence of RCSA is the fact that RCSA acts as a complementary audit and management tool, as

---

[53]*FFIEC IT Examination Handbook*, Appendix J: Strengthening the Resilience of Outsourced Technology Services, page 5

well as being the generally accepted means to satisfy corporate governance and regulatory requirements."[54]

"Firms should take the opportunity to create risk mitigation plans (RMPs) from RCSA outputs that are directly aligned to their strategic and business planning. That way, RCSA outputs will continue to maintain their relevance as they will always be a cross-reference to ongoing senior management strategic and operational activity."[55]

Further, realistic contingency plans and potential exit strategies should be developed to establish a course of action where serious deficiencies or material control weaknesses exist. Despite "switch costs" and "switch risks," these ultimately may be the best risk mitigation strategy available, particularly where the risk of failure is high.

Business continuity planning is the set of processes and procedures used to build a plan that ensures essential business functions can be quickly recovered in the event of a serious disruption, with the goal of ensuring they are operable during or immediately following all incidents. Business continuity plans are built on the results of the BIA and typically point to both contingency and disaster recovery plans to prevent or recover from catastrophic interruptions to business operations. The goal of business continuity planning is to minimize the disruption by quickly recovering, establishing procedures to seamlessly switch to a "hot backup" site, and/or invoking predefined "work arounds" that will be in place until the issue or incident is resolved.

In extreme cases, your institution may help a critical third party survive its own disaster, such as the loss of a facility or critical technical failure. This is entirely feasible, and may be the best course of action for recovery for a small company that is critical to your operations. The larger the company, the less feasible this is. The exception is where your institution has contracted to have your services intentionally "ring fenced" by the third party, and an execution plan is in place.

A conversation with a chief auditor at a U.S. bank about business continuity risk management for "mission critical" third parties took an interesting turn. The discussion turned to: How realistic is it to prepare a traditional business continuity or contingency plan when a smaller bank outsources its banking system backbone to a huge fintech, and the fintech fails? What if many other small banks use the same failed fintech?

This raises the specter of systemic concentration risk. A solution could be for a group of mutually reliant banks to be ready to take over a fintech and run it as a shared utility.

Business Continuity Management: *A Relatively New Profession*

Business continuity management has evolved into a professional discipline. This is good news. Proven methodologies and best practices have emerged and continue to, and they can be leveraged.

In 2004 the Singapore Economic Development Board (EDB), in collaboration with the Singapore Business Federation (SBF) and the Business Continuity Management

[54]Operational Risk Institute Operational Risk Sound Practice Guidance: Risk Control Self Assessment, page 5
[55]Operational Risk Institute Operational Risk Sound Practice Guidance: Risk Control Self Assessment, page 18

(BCM) Institute, developed the Singapore Standards 540 for Business Continuity Management.

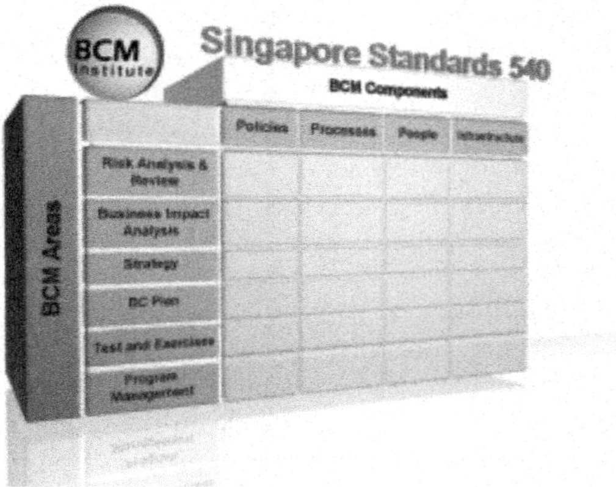

Source: BCM Institute and Singapore Standards (SS540)

Additionally, the International Standards Organization (ISO) created ISO 22301:2012 Societal Security – Business Continuity Management Systems. This standard "specifies requirements to plan, establish, implement, operate, monitor, review, maintain, and continually improve a documented management system to protect against, reduce the likelihood of occurrence, prepare for, respond to, and recover from disruptive incidents when they arise. Sixty-eight percent of 190 financial institutions participating in the BCI HorizonScan 2017 reported that they rely on ISO 22301 to guide their business continuity program."[56]

"The requirements specified in ISO 22301:2012 are generic and intended to be applicable to all organizations, or parts thereof, regardless of type, size, and nature of the organization. The extent of application of these requirements depends on the organization's operating environment and complexity."[57]

Although these standards for business continuity management were developed for internal use by corporations, they can be leveraged for third-party risk management. Applicable to large and small institutions, they can be a framework to develop requirements and conduct due diligence to test for strengths and gaps in your third party's business continuity management, disaster recovery, and business resilience policies, programs, and practices.

Some countries have created national standards, including Singapore, the UK, Canada, many member countries of the EU, Australia, New Zealand, Thailand, India, Malaysia, Japan, Hong Kong, and Indonesia. Some of these countries legislate business continuity management practices.

The U.S. does not have national standards. However, as mentioned earlier, in 2015 the FFIEC issued regulatory guidance in the *IT Examination Handbook's* Appendix J, "Strengthening the Resilience of Outsourced Technology Services."

---

[56]BCI Institute: HorizonScan 2017 http://www.bcifiles.com/HorizonScan2017.pdf

[57]ISO 22301:2012 Societal security – Business continuity management systems—Requirements

When your institution's critical third parties are delivering services from jurisdictions with national standards and/or they have adopted ISO 22301:2012, a copy of their (recent) certificate of compliance that covers services delivered to your institution could be an efficient and effective substitute for conducting your own due diligence.

Contingency Planning

In the event of a serious incident or failure, it is rarely feasible for the institution to recover on its own by delivering services internally. In extreme cases, it may not be possible for the third party to recover from a serious incident or disaster. The FFIEC proposes the following courses of action:

1. Partner with other financial institution clients to take over the third party's operations.
2. Perform the services yourself.
3. Contract with an alternative third party.

Appendix J states, "Given the increased concentration of providers in the TSP industry, a financial institution should ensure that it has identified, and potentially prearrange, a comprehensive set of alternative resources to provide full resilience of operations…" [58]

This sounds great in theory. But in many cases it simply isn't feasible to quickly move operations to a different third party or bring the function in-house. There are many scenarios where it is not possible for the institution or the business segment to continue to deliver reliant operations or services.

Lessons Learned

Linnea Solem

Vice President and Chief Privacy Officer, Deluxe Corp.

Context for Strengthening Business Continuity Management

The maturity of BCM is not based solely on updated guidance but is adapted from actual events that triggered both business continuity response plans and disaster recovery plans on a broad scale. Adapting programs and learnings from real recovery events instead of solely from test plans has enabled the sharing of lessons learned and best practices across the sector.

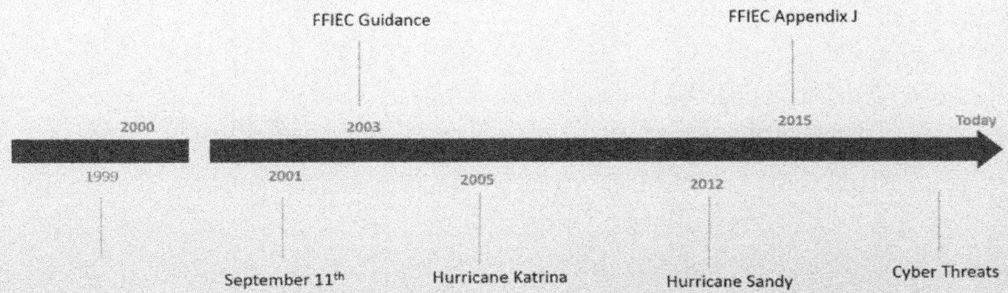

58*FFIEC IT Outsourcing Examination Handbook*: Appendix J: Strengthening the Resilience of Outsourced Technology Services, page 5

BCM and DR Testing with Critical Third-Party Technology Service Providers (TSPs)

Testing is a critical function for ongoing BCM, whether the service is conducted within the organization or outsourced. Defining a testing approach that blends internal tests with outreach and cooperation to critical third parties is essential. However, it is important to factor into the planning that many service providers cannot realistically conduct independent testing with each of their financial institution clients. Leveraging "table top" tests, integrated scenario planning, and proxy testing—and testing interdependencies—will bring greater maturity to the testing options within your BCM programs and improve business resilience.

What Your Institution Should Do

Once the criticality of a third-party relationship or activity has been determined, it stands to reason that business continuity management requirements are defined by the business and/or accountable executive(s). One of the most common challenges with this is that people in the business charged with defining requirements and assessing the strength of a third party's business continuity program typically don't have the prerequisite knowledge, expertise, and experience.

At smaller institutions and third parties this gap in expertise and knowledge may be compounded by the absence of a business continuity management function or lack of experience by a BCM professional when it comes to applying expertise to establishing frameworks and tools for use outside the institution.

"International standards specify requirements for setting up and managing an effective business continuity management system (BCMS). A BCMS, like any other management system, has the following key components:

- A policy;
- People with defined responsibilities;
- Management processes relating to
  - Policy,
  - Planning,
  - Implementation and operation,
  - Performance assessment,
  - Management review, and
  - Improvement;
- Documentation providing auditable evidence; and
- Any business continuity management processes relevant to the organization."[59]

[59]International Standards Organization: ISO 22301:2012 Societal security — Business continuity management systems — Requirements

The ISO "Plan Do Check Act" (PDCA) model applied to BCM processes

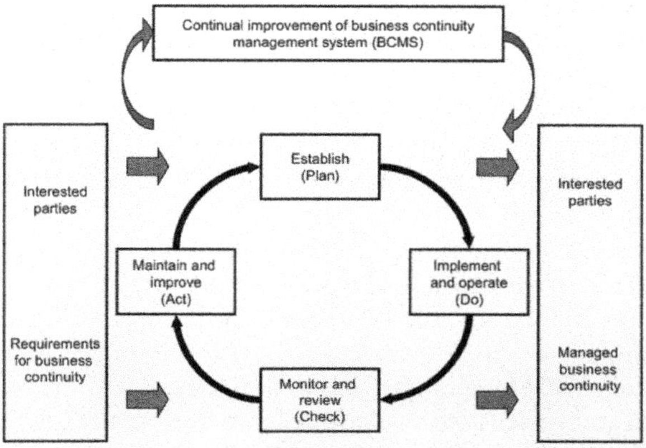

Explanation of PDCA model	
Plan (Establish)	Establish business continuity policy, objectives, targets, controls, processes, and procedures relevant to improving business continuity in order to deliver results that align with the organization's overall policies and objectives.
Do (Implement and operate)	Implement and operate the business continuity policy, controls, processes, and procedures.
Check (Monitor and review)	Monitor and review performance against business continuity policy and objectives, report the results to management for review, and determine and authorize actions for remediation and improvement.
Act (Maintain and improve)	Maintain and improve the BCMS by taking corrective action, based on the results of management review and reappraising the scope of the BCMS and business continuity policy and objectives.

Source: ISO 22301:2012 Societal security — Business continuity management systems — Requirements

When the BIA has been completed for critical relationships and activities the amount of work effort expended on due diligence and applied controls including contractual controls should be commensurate with the criticality of the activity and relationship.

This is reinforced by OCC guidance, which specifies that assessment of your third parties' business continuity planning and resilience should be "*risk-focused* and *provide oversight and controls commensurate with the level of risk.*"

The guidance goes on to say that your "assessment should include a review of the third party's disaster recovery and business resumption plans, according to criticality of services. Your third parties must have the tools, skills, resources, and processes to ensure services remain operational at all times, and can comply with minimum levels in the SLA.

"A third party's BCM plan should include backup sites, technology, and personnel for critical functions; complete documentation of business continuity processes; and a service continuity plan with a strong emphasis on power failures. It should consider dependencies on subcontractors and timing of reviews based on past incidents and experience. Participate in testing of emergency responses to a failure where possible if the third party provides highly critical services."[60]

One important consideration is where your institution fits on the third party's list of customers in the event the third party's operations are restored customer by customer. This is well worth negotiating and contracting for. You'll want assurance that your institution is at or near the top of the list.

While regulatory guidance proposes continual monitoring of business resilience throughout the lifecycle, the amount of work effort should be commensurate with the criticality of services and level of risk. When the OCC recommends participation in testing, it may also provide guidance on risk-adjusting requirements and controls. A common way to risk adjust BCM requirements is to contractually require increasing amounts of documentation and evidence on business reliance from critical third parties. This can range from attesting that they have BCM and DR plans, which are subject to testing, all the way to requiring specific certifications and/or participating in testing activities.

Program Management

Critical third parties should be identified in every relevant business segment's and business unit's RCSA. Documentary evidence of due diligence, risk assessment, and testing and monitoring activities should be part of the book of record for the relationship and for each unique engagement. The accountable executive is responsible for ensuring that documentation is complete and of acceptable quality.

Controls should make sense and be commensurate with findings from assessments and monitoring activities and be commensurate with criticality and the level of risk presented by the third party's BCM and DR practices. They should be updated over time as findings, needs, and standards change.

Solem says, "Collaboration between the business continuity staff and the third-party oversight team enables more efficient, ongoing monitoring of the critical third-party relationships."

The third-party risk management office program manager should conduct quality assurance on documentation, particularly regarding the results of testing and monitoring. The BCM function, where it exists, is responsible for developing BCM and DR lifecycle management processes and tools for use by the business and in the third-party risk management function, including risk-adjusted controls and setting risk tolerance thresholds for KRIs and KPIs.

---

[60]OCC 2013-29 Third Party Relationships Risk Management Guidance

6

Technology Risk

Technology risk encompasses the traditional domain of IT organizations: enterprise architecture and infrastructure, networks, applications, hardware, software, application development, and application development and maintenance (ADM). It also encompasses all technologies deployed across an institution.

The U.S. Federal Financial Institutions Examination Council (FFIEC) recognizes this broad scope of technology risk and the importance of effective management in its *IT Examination Handbook: Management*. "IT supports most aspects of a financial institution's business; therefore, effective ITRM [information technology risk management] is not limited to technology," it notes. "IT management is critical to the performance and success of a financial institution. ITRM involves more than containing costs and controlling operational risks and does not work in isolation."[61]

IT and IT risk management practices recognize that third-party technologies introduce a wide range of risk exposures. The impact of deficiencies and failures can include operational and service disruptions; financial losses; legal and reputational damage resulting from a failure, defect, or inadequacy; and illegal or unauthorized use of the institution's information, network, and systems.

Due to extensive outsourcing and consolidation, fintechs usually represent a significant portion of any institution's critical third parties and activities. Kicking it up a notch, fintechs invariably dominate the short list of "enterprise critical" third-party relationships. Enterprise-critical third parties are those that can instantly bring your institution to its knees if something goes seriously wrong.

While your institution's focus is on its own third-party relationships, regulators are also focused on systemic risk. As a result, the Federal Reserve, Office of the Comptroller of the Currency (OCC), and Federal Deposit Insurance Corporation (FDIC) have claimed "statutory authority to supervise third-party servicers that enter into contractual arrangements with regulated financial institutions."[62] Other federal and state banking agencies can also choose to participate in interagency examinations.

---

[61]FFIEC Information Technology Examination Handbook: Management (Nov 2015) http://ithandbook.ffiec.gov/media/210375/managementbooklet2015.pdf

[62]FFIEC: Supervision of Third Party Service Providers (TSP) IT Examination Handbook Oct 2012 http://ithandbook.ffiec.gov/ITBooklets/FFIEC_ITBooklet_SupervisionofTechnologyServiceProviders(TSP).pdf

Allocation of regulators' resources to the supervision of fintechs is helpful for their financial institution customers: If asked, regulators will provide a copy of their examination findings. Regulatory supervision of fintechs has a broad reach. Many financial institutions and their non-bank subsidiaries provide fintech products and services to other financial institutions. Depending on business mix, your institution may also be subject to targeted fintech exams.

Fintechs offer direct-to-consumer products and services that were once the exclusive domain of financial institutions. Disintermediation by fintechs means that unregulated financial services are widely available to consumers.

In March 2017, the OCC announced it was prepared to accept applications from fintechs for Special Purpose National Bank Charters.[63] The bad news for traditional financial institutions is that competition will continue to intensify. The good news is that bank charters come with explicit regulatory and capital requirements, and fintechs must look elsewhere for funding because they will not be licensed to take deposits. This is a good start towards leveling the playing field for traditional players in the heavily regulated financial services sector.

Innovation

Fintechs of all sizes bring a continuous stream of innovative technologies to market, each with a unique set of features, benefits, and risks. Driven hard by consumer preferences, competitive forces, cost pressures, and disintermediation, many financial institutions have outsourced core operations (such as MDPS—more on them to follow). Most are rapidly adopting significant new technologies such as cloud computing, application programming interfaces (API), "X as a Service" (XaaS), distributed ledger technology (blockchain), robotic process automation (RPA), and artificial intelligence (AI).

In October 2016, the OCC issued "Recommendations and Decisions for Implementing a Responsible Innovation Framework."[64] **Responsible innovation** means using new or improved financial products, services, and processes to meet the evolving needs of consumers, businesses, and communities in a manner consistent with sound risk management and aligned with the bank's overall business strategy.

The purpose of the framework is to encourage innovation and mitigate risk, while acknowledging dramatic changes in technology and service delivery. Occasionally, adoption gets well ahead of risk management.

[63]OCC: Comptroller's Licensing Manual Draft Supplement - Evaluating Charter Applications from Financial Technology Companies (March 2017) https://www.occ.treas.gov/news-issuances/news-releases/2017/nr-occ-2017-31.html

[64]OCC: Recommendations and Decisions for Implementing a Responsible Innovation Framework (Oct 16) https://www.occ.gov/topics/responsible-innovation/comments/recommendations-decisions-for-implementing-a-responsible-innovation-framework.pdf

What You Should Know

Because they dominate the list of highly critical relationships and activities in any financial institution, fintechs are of particular interest to examiners. Here are some technologies and third-party relationships that deserve special attention:

1. **Multi-regional data processing servicers** (MDPS) are usually highly critical and bring high levels of third-party risk—even more so if the firms are foreign-based—even after considering the strength of the third party's controls.

   MDPS also pose a high degree of systemic risk because of their large customer base of financial institutions. Many smaller financial institutions outsource a substantial portion of IT services to a small number of fintechs, and many financial institutions—large and small—use the same fintechs for many services. As a result, MDPS often have complex operations, delivered from many data centers, located in many different geographic regions.

   Where these relationships exist, your institution's MDPS should be identified as top tier (tier 1 or tier 2) critical relationships and activities, and closely managed and monitored.
2. **Cloud computing** can be characterized as third-party, multi-tenant technology solutions. The FFIEC defines cloud computing as "a migration from owned resources to shared resources in which client users receive information technology services on demand from third-party service providers via the Internet "cloud." In cloud environments, a client or customer relocates its resources—such as data, applications, and services—to computing facilities outside the corporate firewall, which the end user then accesses via the Internet."[65] Cloud computing relationships should be managed throughout their lifecycle in a manner consistent with other outsourcing relationships, according to their criticality and risk profile.

   Cloud computing could be characterized as a type of time-share arrangement. Cloud can mean use of shared networks, servers, storage, applications, and transaction processing. Near instantaneous provisioning, flexibility to quickly scale up and scale down, the speed and ease of implementation, and dramatic cost benefits mean that your institution and its third parties should be expected to separately and aggressively pursue "cloud first" technology strategies.

   To reduce costs and cycle time, financial institutions are cautiously implementing a wide range of cloud solutions. The risks are real. The European Network and Information Security Agency (ENISA) warns that "for cloud computing to reach the full potential promised by the technology, it must offer solid information security."[66]

   While some firms offer excellent data protection, many don't. In addition to information security concerns, many cloud providers offer little assurance that your institution's data is completely wiped upon exit from the relationship, even where the service your institution acquired is a private or multi-tenanted cloud.

   Some cloud providers have found ways to satisfy safety, security, and regulatory requirements. That was the case for Amazon Web Services. *Forbes* noted in 2014 that it had been approved "by De Nederlandsche Bank (DNB), the Netherlands' national banking regulator

---

[65]FFIEC IT Examination Handbook InfoBase http://ithandbook.ffiec.gov/glossary/cloud-computing.aspx
[66]ENISA: Cloud Computing Benefits, Risks and Recommendations for Information Security (Nov 09) https://www.enisa.europa.eu/publications/cloud-computing-risk-assessment

... for a range of banking services including websites, mobile applications, retail banking platforms, high performance computing, and credit risk analysis."[67]

Cloud computing solutions are offered in various ways, each with a different risk profile. Here are three common cloud computing service offerings:

- **Private cloud** is built for the sole use of a single institution, either hosted and managed behind your institution's firewall, or hosted externally by the third party. Private clouds typically have a significant physical footprint with commensurate investments in real estate, hardware, software, and personnel. Many of the benefits of cloud computing are lost in private cloud deployments because they need a high degree of engagement by the financial institution to implement, manage, and update.
- **Public cloud** is an unlikely choice for financial institutions because solutions are delivered over a network that is open for public use (e.g., DropBox). There is a big difference between the security, liability, and privacy of private and public cloud solutions, even when the third party owns its own infrastructure and data centers.

  Some public cloud providers such as Amazon, Microsoft, and Google offer a private connection to a peering point. In these solutions, your institution's data may be separate. Because these large third-party cloud providers are making significant investments, security is improving all the time and breaches are relatively rare. Regardless, as of now public clouds with private peering point connections are less secure than private clouds.
- **Hybrid cloud** is a strategy, not a specific cloud relationship. Deliberate hybrid cloud configurations exist when an institution deploys a combination of cloud solutions and/or hosted infrastructure with several third parties. Hybrid cloud solutions provide access to flexible scale, capacity, and computing power while maintaining your financial institution's security and business continuity standards. For example, one cloud provider may store sensitive customer information and another may perform data analytics. Yet another may provide temporary capacity when a private cloud can't, avoiding recurring costs for unused capacity.
- **Multi-cloud** is another term in everyday use. It is simply multi-sourcing of several discrete cloud solutions.

Be aware that most Web-based applications are cloud-based. As a result, you may be utilizing public cloud solutions without being aware.

3. **Application program interface (API)**

   Whether behind your institution's firewall or within your cloud computing solutions, much software is improved by application program interfaces (APIs) between other applications or data sources. APIs have become indispensable because they are an efficient way to create interoperability and user interfaces between legacy, distributed, or emerging technologies for your employees, customers, and third parties without the complexities of integration.

   The downside is that they provide another point of entry to your institution's applications, infrastructure, and information. Because APIs often have no or a very small additional cost, they may not be subject to third-party risk management controls.

[67] Tom Groenfeldt, Forbes, Some Banks Are Heading to the Cloud -- More Are Planning To (Jun 14) https://www.forbes.com/sites/tomgroenfeldt/2014/06/26/some-banks-are-heading-to-the-cloud-more-are-planning-to/#51ab22ce58c9

4. **"As a Service"** is prevalent because it offers so many advantages over outright purchase, implementation, and management. "As a Service" solutions are licensed technologies accessed within the third party's environment. This may be infrastructure, software, or (computing) platforms. Many third parties offer only "XaaS" solutions, particularly Software as a Service (SaaS).

   While cloud computing is an XaaS solution, regulators have designated cloud as a separate category of third-party risk. This is because of the higher risk profile—particularly data in the cloud that may be in constant motion, making its whereabouts extra cloudy.

5. **Blockchain** is a revolutionary technology with a profound impact on the financial services sector. It provides secure, multi-access to a single ledger of financial information, a record of transactions and events that is shared between "permissioned" parties.

   When you talk about blockchain, a discussion about Bitcoin inevitably follows. Bitcoin is a digital or cryptocurrency, a great example of blockchain technology in action. Bitcoin uses blockchain to create a record of "ownership" and the ability to transfer ownership. The "block" is "hashed" records with many independent verifications. Blocks can't be altered or erased. The "chain" is the fluid series of irrefutable transactions. Bitcoin presents a serious challenge to financial institutions and their regulators because it exists only in cyberspace, attracts no fees, and ownership is anonymous.

   Blockchain is in its infancy, but is expected to dramatically reduce costs while improving security, accuracy, and speed. Settlement transactions are instantaneous and recorded in a single, accessible ledger, all but eliminating settlement risk and fraud.

   Blockchain will have a profound effect on the financial services sector, including financial institutions, central counterparties like financial market utilities, exchanges and financial market intermediaries, and financial services customers.

   For the foreseeable future, information security, privacy, and business continuity will be top-line risks for blockchain solutions.

Robotic process automation (RPA) and artificial intelligence (AI) is top of mind everywhere, and evolving very quickly. A tremendous source of their value, and risk, is the ability to access and process huge volumes of data from internal and external sources, at very high speeds. Cycle time drops like a stone while accuracy shoots up like a rocket. The number of people accessing your institution's systems and data will drop, improving privacy, security, and exposure to fraud. But RPA is a tempting target for hackers, and the speed at which things can go very wrong is exponential.

The most significant risk is that your institution is buying "black box" technology. Underlying logic, algorithms, and models are trade secrets so it will not be possible to thoroughly assess third-party RPA risk.

RPA software often works at the "presentation layer" (user interface) of computer systems and mimics a human user. Because RPA can sit on top of the existing IT infrastructure and applications, it can be implemented without altering existing infrastructure and systems. RPA depends on minutely detailed processes to implement and high quality, structured data to execute.

Robotic process automation is different from previous iterations of process improvement, including those achieved through automation. RPA is essentially a software application that will partially or fully automate human tasks and activities. Basic RPA applications automate operational processes that are manual, repetitive, and rules-based. Embedded software "bots" manage execution of each sub-process. Bots are smaller software programs within larger applications. The combination of process automation software and bots is where the concept of RPA and AI come together.

More complex examples of RPA are occurring in finance and customer relationship management, leveraging investments in enterprise resource planning (ERP) and customer relationship management (CRM) systems. Many institutions are investigating or moving forward with Know Your Customer RPA implementations. The implementations promise a way to comply with anti-money laundering, anti-terrorist financing regulatory requirements and laws that is less manual and labor intensive. Others are using RPA in their contact centers. Some RPA applications that have natural language programming (NLP) embedded in their bots are so sophisticated that it's hard to tell when you're talking to a person and when you're talking to an application. Think Siri on steroids.

Realistically, there are few if any examples of artificial intelligence. What has been implemented to date is robotic process automation with intelligent automation. This means deploying bots to run programs and sub-processes and make "decisions," combined with machine learning and natural language programming to continuously improve the functionality of bots.

More broadly, some indicators of higher levels of third-party technology risk are:

- Complex, multi-sourced technologies and third-party relationships.
- Complex projects with inadequate implementation timelines.
- New, untested, or poorly understood technologies.
- Inexperienced third parties or shaky references.
- Technology start-ups and more established third parties that are new entrants to specific technologies.

What Your Institution Should Do

IT projects have a well-deserved reputation for taking longer than planned, running over budget, and delivering less than expected. Implementation timelines are finite. So are timelines to test for errors and vulnerabilities. Understand the risks before approving projects and break the scope into manageable pieces.

To mitigate technology implementation risk, hire good people that utilize tried and true methodologies for technology project managers, such as the Project Management Institute's (PMI) *PMBOK® Guide* (Project Management Book of Knowledge) and the PMI's global standards, including the *PMBOK® Guide* to specific types of projects. They provide easy access to many purpose-built tools to help with implementation including PMBOK's Requirements Traceability Matrix (RTM). RTM is a tool that creates a clear line of sight between requirements and deliverables, increasing the probability of achieving intended results.[68]

[68]PMI: https://www.pmi.org/pmbok-guide-standards

While technology project managers are well armed with tools, it falls on business leaders to define the business requirements. Harking back to the Johari window in Chapter 3, this is easier said than done. There are many examples of technologies being implemented before requirements have been finalized, and well before negotiating the contract. Usually this results in longer time to implement, a narrow focus, plenty of rework, and loss of negotiating power.

In many cases, exposure to third-party and operational risk is compounded because due diligence and risk assessment processes are bypassed. Hence the disconnect between the intention, the plan, the budget, the result, and risk management controls. Something needs to change.

Consider looking beyond the financial services sector for best practices in managing quality and technology risk, such as the aerospace and automotive industries. Begun in the 1940s by the U.S. military, "Failure Modes and Effects Analysis (FMEA) is a step-by-step approach for identifying all possible failures in a design, a manufacturing or assembly process, or a product or service." [69] Tools, courses, and certifications are available through ASQ, a not-for-profit global community of individuals and organizations passionate about quality.

"The purpose of the FMEA is to take actions to eliminate or reduce failures, starting with the highest-priority ones. FMEA is used during design to prevent failures. Later it's used for control, before and during ongoing operation of the process. 'Failure modes' means the ways, or modes, in which something might fail. 'Effects analysis' refers to studying the consequences of those failures. Failures are prioritized according to how serious their consequences are, how frequently they occur, and how easily they can be detected."[70]

New Technologies

Investments in new technologies are critical to your institution's long-term success. Some are "game changers," so it's important to keep your board apprised of strategies and plans to adopt new technologies like cloud solutions, RPA, IA and AI, big data analytics, and mobile banking. New entrant companies may not meet your institution's risk thresholds for "financial condition, business resilience, and IT security posture."[71]

An important thing to consider is whether anyone has assessed all the functionality embedded in third-party products and services, even when your institution is not planning to use it.

A recurring complaint from business and IT leaders is that they can't move forward with technology startups and small technology firms in a timely manner because such firms can't satisfy risk management requirements. It is likely that your institution's third-party risk management program will need to adapt requirements, controls, and oversight to enable testing and implementation of new technologies. This is a form of "risk adjustment."

[69] ASQ: Failure Mode Effects Analysis http://asq.org/learn-about-quality/process-analysis-tools/overview/fmea.html

[70] Ibid.

[71] FFIEC Information Technology Examination Handbook: Management (Nov 2015) http://ithandbook.ffiec.gov/media/210375/managementbooklet2015.pdf

Allison Sagraves, chief data officer with a large U.S. bank, offers the following advice (*which does not represent the advice of her employer):

> *One practical strategy to accelerate innovation is to lower the barriers to partnership through small-scale pilots on premises. New ideas can be tested, data can stay within your company, and proofs-of-concepts can be conducted without large investments while containing risk. Such trial periods can allow partners to demonstrate value, and identify and address issues early before big investments are made by either side. This concept of "just-in-time" risk management aligns effort and resources when and where needed. An innovation portfolio, for example, can be managed separately with more flexibility as a series of proofs-of-concepts that are managed in a risk-adjusted manner. Those with promise can be advanced and additional funding provided as value is demonstrated, at which point oversight can be expanded as the pilot scales.*

To encourage innovation, some financial institutions fund a discrete innovation investment budget, and others have an Innovation Center of Excellence. For example, Deutsche Bank has three innovation labs, in London, Berlin, and Palo Alto. They enable the bank to evaluate emerging technologies that can enhance products, services, and internal processes. The labs "further strengthen the bank's ability to innovate, while deepening its relationships with start-ups."[72]

Cloud Computing

Because third parties pursue the same benefits from cloud computing, it's important to contractually limit their use and deployment of cloud computing solutions until your institution can assess the risks, approve specific use, and implement appropriate compensating controls.

Consider limiting use of cloud solutions to third parties that provide "logical separation" of your institution's data from other clients' data. And consider requiring that your institution's data is subject to controlled replication, and that applications and processing are separated across multiple data centers in multiple geographies. Confidential data should be protected by multiple layers of encryption when it's "in transit" and "at rest." These compensating controls will improve safety and security, performance, and data recovery.

Most cloud computing contracts are "non-negotiable," so selection of the third party should be based on the services, delivery network, controls, and contract terms best suited for the intended purpose.

Compensating controls include encryption and key management, tight access and user controls, restrictions on processing and storing sensitive information, replication of data, and ongoing monitoring and testing.

When contracting, ENISA recommends, "pay attention to rights and obligations related to notifications of breaches in security, data transfers, creation of derivative works, change of control, and access to data by law enforcement entities. Because the cloud can

---

[72]Deutsche Bank website: Deutsche Bank Opens Innovation Lab in Silicon Valley (Apr 16) https://www.db.com/newsroom_news/2016/medien/deutsche-bank-opens-innovation-lab-in-silicon-valley-en-11531.htm

be used to outsource critical internal infrastructure, and the interruption of that infrastructure may have wide-ranging effects, carefully consider whether standard limitations on liability adequately represent allocations of liability, given the parties' use of the cloud, or responsibilities for infrastructure."[73] As cloud computing evolves, negotiability in contracting may evolve as cloud providers' risks decrease.

Member-driven, global organizations like Cloud Security Alliance exist to promote best practices. Members work collaboratively to create methodologies, tools, and best practices and share information for the benefit of members and beyond.[74] Encourage your risk experts' participation in organizations like this one.

Application Program Interface (API)

APIs may not be recognized as risky by business leaders, so user education will be helpful. Your institution's technology gurus and information security risk control specialists should assess and approve each API prior to implementation, introducing compensating controls as they would with any other technology solution. It's a good practice to keep an inventory of all APIs, set up a schedule to confirm they are still required, then validate that there are not changes to the risk profile.

Blockchain

Blockchain is one of those technologies that your institution needs to stay on top of, and even attempt to influence its development. Getting involved in the Hyperledger project is one way to do this.

The Hyperledger project is a self-described "open source collaborative effort created to advance cross-industry blockchain technologies. It is a global collaboration, hosted by The Linux Foundation, including leaders in finance, banking, Internet of Things, supply chains, manufacturing, and technology. Only an open source, collaborative software development approach can ensure the transparency, longevity, interoperability, and support required to bring blockchain technologies forward to mainstream commercial adoption. That is what Hyperledger is about—communities of software developers building blockchain frameworks and platforms."[75]

Robotic Process Automation, Artificial Intelligence, and Natural Language Programming

RPA relationships should be subjected to much more extensive testing than other third-party relationships, particularly those that include AI and NLP. Bots are a form of machine learning that run on algorithms and models, none of which will be available for evaluation during the selection process.

---

[73]ENISA: Cloud Computing Benefits, Risks and Recommendations for Information Security (Nov 2009), pg. 6 https://www.enisa.europa.eu/publications/cloud-computing-risk-assessment

[74]Cloud Security Alliance (CSA) https://cloudsecurityalliance.org/

[75]The Hyperledger Project https://www.hyperledger.org

Because RPA technologies are "black boxes" that change over time, it is unclear how changes made by bots and other forms of machine learning are managed, monitored, and tested by the third party. Unless you contract for and initiate testing, you won't get any visibility into testing or how things work post-implementation. Third-party relationships don't relieve your institution of its responsibilities, so your institution is 100% accountable if anything goes wrong. Your governance team should include individuals who are extremely good at developing test cases and scenarios. Testing should be done often and as thoroughly as possible.

Another consideration is pricing. It may be tempting to accept a large price decrease offered by an incumbent third party as an incentive to adopt its RPA/AI solution and extend the contract. Without doing your homework it isn't possible to know the "should cost" to evaluate the offer. Another pricing challenge is that some third-party providers price services by the bot. If your institution is willing to accept this pricing model, get ready for the feeling of being gouged.

Although there are many considerations, one that your institution should address is which party has the right to suspend operations if something seems to be or is going wrong, and how to get this done. The speed of processing means that errors will process at the same speed.

In Closing

Systemic technology concentration risk can't be easily mitigated. In some cases, it really can't be mitigated at all except by collaboration with peer institutions across the sector. For example, institutions that outsource highly critical core operations to the same fintech could mitigate systemic risk by preparing a plan to finance and take over operations in the event of a Chapter 11 event.

7 Anti-Money Laundering

You may ask yourself why the Bank Secrecy Act (BSA) and anti-money laundering are often referenced together. Here is the answer, directly from the *Bank Secrecy Act/ Anti-Money Laundering Examination Manual*:

"In 1970, Congress passed the ... 'Bank Secrecy Act,' which established requirements for recordkeeping and reporting by private individuals, banks, and other financial institutions. The BSA was designed to help identify the source, volume, and movement of currency and other monetary instruments transported or transmitted into or out of the United States or deposited in financial institutions." The manual goes on to say the BSA enables "law enforcement and regulatory agencies to pursue investigations of criminal, tax, and regulatory violations, if warranted, and provide evidence useful in prosecuting money laundering and other financial crimes."[76]

The manual defines money laundering as "the process used to [intentionally] disguise the source of money or assets derived from criminal activity. It compromises the integrity of legitimate financial systems and institutions, and gives organized crime the funds it needs to conduct further criminal activities. It is a global problem, and the techniques used are numerous and can be very sophisticated."[77]

To address the problem, the BSA was reinforced by The Money Laundering Control Act of 1986, which "precludes circumvention of the BSA requirements by imposing criminal liability on a person or financial institution that knowingly assists in the laundering of money, or that structures transactions to avoid reporting them."[78] Fraud and money laundering are often interrelated, and drug traffickers and terrorists launder money to obscure its source and protect the identity of ultimate beneficiaries.

Under the glare of tough regulations and regulatory exams, financial institutions have made huge investments in "KYC" (Know Your Customer) programs, processes, and technologies which are designed to prevent and detect money laundering. But it's increasingly difficult to stay ahead of sophisticated money launderers. Innovation and the pace of

---

[76]FFIEC Bank Secrecy Act / Anti-Money Laundering Examination Manual (2014)

[77]FINTRAC: Guidance on the Risk-Based Approach to Combating Money Laundering and Terrorist Financing (March 16, 2016) http://www.fintrac-canafe.gc.ca/publications/rba/rba-eng.asp#s4.1

[78]FFIEC Bank Secrecy Act/ Anti-Money Laundering Examination Manual (2014)

technological change, interconnected global financial markets, and new financial product developments obscure detection of this crime.

You may not immediately think of the potential for a third-party relationship to expose your institution to money laundering. But when you consider the extensive reliance by most financial institutions on outsourcing, third-party products and distribution channels, correspondent banking, customer servicing, wire transfer platforms and services, Software as a Service, and cloud-based relationships, you'll understand why anti-money laundering (AML) programs need to encompass third-party relationships.

Stuart Davis, chief anti-money laundering officer at BMO Financial Group, explains, "While the origins of money laundering are linked to criminal activity, known as 'predicate offenses,' the list of what that includes is not always obvious and keeps expanding. Some of the non-obvious predicate offenses include the avoidance of government reporting for cash-based transactions, cyber intrusions, and tax evasion. Under current regulatory requirements most financial institutions and even some non-financial institutions such as casinos, money-service businesses, dealers in precious metals and jewelry, real estate agents, lawyers, and even auto dealers may have reporting obligations. The reporting requirements depend on the nature of your institution and can be as simple as filing a form when a significant amount of cash is accepted as a form of payment, up to a full and comprehensive program of monitoring and reporting of suspicious activity or transactions."

Depending on the duration, extent, and dollars involved, the consequences of a third party laundering money under the cover of your financial institution's good reputation can be severe. An institution found to be enabling money laundering risks reputational damage, regulatory sanctions and enforcement actions, fines, financial losses, and/or legal action. Because money laundering and terrorist financing activities can be intertwined and have global reach, the involved institution's risk exposure can be global. This added dimension makes it extremely complicated. The resulting involvement by legal, police, and regulatory bodies globally can be very expensive to remediate.

Davis notes, "In recent years, fines and other penalties for failure to comply with the rules have been in the billions of dollars largely because firms were not addressing the risk of who they were doing business with."

The methods for money laundering are varied, opaque, and intricate, and are part of a three-stage process:

1. **Stage 1 - Placement:** Processes for getting "dirty money" into the financial system.
2. **Stage 2 - Layering:** Processes for converting the proceeds of crime (predominantly cash) into another financial format (e.g., a stock market transaction), then creating complex layers of transactions intended to conceal their source and obscure the audit trail.
3. **Stage 3 - Integration:** Processes for creating the appearance of legitimacy when reintroducing laundered money to the financial system.

Davis cautions:

> *Do not expect to see these stages occur in immediate sequence or even within your institution. Money launderers will often seek to separate the stages across multiple firms and parties to hide their true intentions and avoid getting caught. For example, in the*

layering stage, multiple banks, accounts, and account holders could be used to move money around that ultimately still is under the control of one party known as the beneficial owner.

Almost every country and even some states and provinces have anti-money laundering laws and regulations. For example, in the U.S. there have been three primary laws, including the Bank Secrecy Act of 1970, the Money Laundering Control Act of 1986, and the Uniting and Strengthening America by Providing Appropriate Tools Required to Intercept and Obstruct Terrorism Act of 2001, otherwise known as the USA Patriot Act. Each law will have many follow-on regulations and interpretations making the understanding quite complex, and thus it can be important to engage a local expert as the rules are continuing to change and evolve rapidly.

Money laundering and reporting requirements can be global in their reach. Do not assume that just because the activity is not occurring within the United States, it is not subject to the laws of the United States. It may still be subject to the regulatory requirements of the U.S. when the transaction involves a U.S. person or corporation, when crossing the U.S. border, and sometimes just because U.S. dollars are used in a transaction.

Increasingly, other regulatory guidelines and requirements are being included in anti-money laundering programs. These include sanctions rules, import-export restrictions, and anti-bribery and corruption rules among others. The penalties and fines can be just as severe if not more so, as seen with many of the recent sanctions violations. Unlike anti-money laundering, which may only apply to certain designated financial institutions and other firms, sanctions, import-export restrictions, and anti-bribery and corruption laws and rules are applicable to any person or any entity in a very broad sense. Consider these carefully in every third-party relationship.

With plenty of experience and expertise building and implementing KYC programs, AML risk specialists can rely on what they already know to help guide development and implementation of the AML elements in their institutions' third-party risk management programs.

What You Should Know

Many third-party risk management professionals are not aware that certain products and services that are entwined with their relationship with third-party service providers create AML risk exposure. The result is AML risk is often excluded from third-party risk management programs, contract language, and lifecycle management processes.

In the case of third-party, non-customer AML risk, identifying the nature and extent of risk exposure may be affected by a combination of vulnerabilities. "The concept of vulnerabilities as used in risk assessment comprises those things that can be exploited by the threat or that may support or facilitate its activities," notes the Financial Action Task Force.[79] Vulnerabilities may be caused by:

[79] FATF Guidance: Anti-Money Laundering and Terrorist Financing Measures and Financial Inclusion (2013)

- **A high-risk profile for the third party itself.** The third party may have been infiltrated by criminals, either as employees or trusted contractors; may have an inadequate prevention and detection program; or may have weak internal controls. Alternately, criminal elements in the third party may have infiltrated your employee base, enabling collusion necessary for an "inside job."
- **Susceptible products and services.** Some products are more likely than others to be used to facilitate money laundering. Presenting the highest risk are third-party products and services that offer greater anonymity, such as pre-paid cards, or involve high volumes of currency or currency equivalents—particularly if they can be rapidly transacted like wire transfers.
- **High-risk geographic location(s)** are often a contributing factor. Some geographies are well known as notorious havens for money-laundering activities, and may readily facilitate one or more steps that aid in layering.
- **Weak rule of law.** Differences in the relative strength of the legal system in multiple geographies may be leveraged by criminals when developing money-laundering strategies. Some countries have a reputation for tolerating corruption.
- **Susceptible delivery channels.** Using a fourth-party agent relationship, such as a money-transfer agent, to facilitate the transaction may result in control weaknesses that are exploited by criminals for money laundering.

Unquestionably, your institution faces each of these vulnerabilities because it outsources all or elements of a wide range of transaction-processing and other customer services, creating reliance on the respective third parties' internal controls. And your institution has no alternative but to rely on purpose-built third-party relationships for many types of high-volume, high-value financial transactions such as correspondent banking transactions and wire transfers. Your institution may also rely on third parties to act as your agents or servicers, at times directly interacting with your customers.

It's important to be aware of some of the higher risk third-party relationships and products where many institutions rely on use of non-customer third parties. "The bank's BSA/AML risks when dealing with a processor account are similar to risks from other activities in which the bank's customer conducts transactions through the bank on behalf of the customer's clients."[80] For example, banks may be exposed to a variety of risks when originating, receiving, or processing ACH transactions, or outsourcing to a third party.[81]

Here are some products and services that may be delivered by a third party and therefore should be subject to lifecycle management processes embedded in your institution's third-party risk management program. The list is not exhaustive, but it's part of the process of developing a good working knowledge of potential sources of exposure to third-party AML risk.

- Affinity relationships, particularly if the financial institution is the issuer (branded cards).
- Agent relationships and networks, particularly for non-face-to-face delivery channels.
- Automated clearinghouse (ACH) transaction processors (may facilitate money laundering, identity theft, fraud schemes, and illicit transactions or transactions prohibited by the Office of Foreign Assets Control (OFAC)).

---

[80]FFIEC BSA/AML Examination Manual (Jan 2014): Expanded Examination Overview and Procedures for Consolidated and Other Types of BSA/AML Compliance Program Structures

[81]OCC Bulletin 2006-39, Automated Clearing House Activities: Risk Management Guidance (Sep 2006)

- Cash-in-transit services (armored car; ATM servicing).
- Custody by a third party of customer collateral such as cash collateral and marketable securities pledged to loans (domestic and foreign).
- Correspondent banking relationships (may facilitate layering and/or mask the identity of customers).
- Distributors and sales channel relationships for your institution's products and services.
- (Pre-paid) Electronic cash product providers (digital currency, mobile payments, payroll cards, stored value cards), including where your institution is the issuer and/or the purchasers are anonymous.
- Electronic funds transfer agents (domestic and international).
- Escrow accounts established by and managed by third parties.
- Law firms (including the potential to collude with appraisers).
- Foreign exchange counterparties.
- International correspondent banking relationships.
- International private banking counterparties.
- Payment processors, particularly where they set up the accounts or provide value-added services.
- Payroll service providers.
- Peer-to-peer payment services and lending networks.
- Remittance counterparties.
- Services provided by third-party payment processors.
- Services provided to third-party payment processors (thereby assuming their AML risks).
- Third-party automated teller machines (ATM).
- Third-party custodians (financial market transactions).
- Third-party credit cards (acquirers and processors).
- Trust and asset management counterparties.
- Third-party financial product providers and sales agents (e.g., investment products, bearer bonds/shares, insurance).
- Third-party monetary instrument and counterparties (drafts and money orders).
- Trade finance counterparties.
- Wire and money transfer third-party providers.

Certain delivery channels also create an additional dimension to third-party AML risk exposure. According to FINTRAC, "A delivery channel is a medium that can be used to obtain a product or service, or through which transactions can be conducted. Delivery channels should be considered as part of the risk of the transactions. Delivery channels allowing for non-face-to-face transactions have a higher inherent risk."[82] For example, many financial institutions "rely on introducers, intermediaries or other third parties for client information-gathering and verification purposes. These include, for example, deposit and mortgage brokers and solicitors."[83] AML risk management may be compromised if the third party doesn't ensure that client identification requirements are followed.

---

[82]FINTRAC: Guidance on the Risk-Based Approach to Combating Money Laundering and Terrorist Financing (Mar 2016) http://www.fintrac-canafe.gc.ca/publications/rba/rba-eng.asp#s4.1

[83]OSFI B-8 (Dec 2008) Deterring and Detecting Money Laundering and Terrorist Financing http://www.osfi-bsif.gc.ca/Eng/Docs/b8.pdf

Davis advises, "A good rule of thumb is that everything you would have to do if you were performing the activity yourself also applies to any third parties acting on your behalf."

Clearly there is a high potential to expose your institution to money laundering and terrorist financing through your relationships with third parties. The expertise found in your institution's AML group should help protect your institution from third-party AML risk.

What Your Institution Should Do

Davis says, "Knowing who you are doing business with is common sense but it is also foundational to helping you meet the many anti-money laundering regulatory requirements. A whole industry has evolved around the concept of providing information to financial institutions so they can undertake risk assessments, collect adverse news and social media, and analyze findings to guide risk-based decision making. Essentially the same concepts found in KYC are the basis for third-party risk management: Know your third party."

The first step is to ensure that AML risk is captured in your institution's third-party management program. This element of the program needs to be documented and support the risk identification and assessment processes. AML risk specialists should provide overall leadership on due diligence, compensating controls, management, and monitoring activities, and provide oversight and governance. The Federal Financial Institutions Examination Council's *BSA/AML Examination Manual* says, "risk assessment, internal controls (e.g., suspicious activity monitoring), independent testing, or training may be managed centrally."[84]

Davis recommends, "If a third party is subject to the AML rules directly, you should conduct and evidence a review to show that they also align with your AML policies and guidelines. It is important to assess their BSA/AML policies and programs, internal controls, access rights, systems integrity and monitoring capabilities, governance and oversight, and employee screening and background checks.

"Determine whether the third party has implemented robust BSA/AML employee training and compliance attestation programs. If they haven't, consider allowing them to adopt and implement the content and rigor of your institution's programs. Effective risk management isn't a trade secret."

Using a standardized due diligence questionnaire for the third party to complete is a good approach. The questionnaire can help identify weaknesses or gaps that need to be addressed. Just because everything is not perfect does not mean that you must avoid the use of a third party's services. Rather, the approach is risk based and any deficiency should be used as an opportunity for dialogue regarding enhanced controls that benefit the entire ecosystem of AML effectiveness. Specialized questionnaires for certain industry types such as correspondent banks, money-service businesses, third-party payment processors, charities, and casinos will benefit you as well, allowing you to delve into some unique risks that may not otherwise be obvious.

Risk appetite is an essential element of your institution's BSA/AML risk management program and sets your tolerance for adverse AML events. "Your risk tolerance will have a direct impact on creating risk-reduction measures and key controls, your policies, and procedures," FINTRAC says, "and training and determining your risk tolerance is an ex-

[84]FFIEC BSA/AML Examination Manual (Jan 2014): Expanded Examination Overview and Procedures for Consolidated and Other Types of BSA/AML Compliance Program Structures

ercise that should include obtaining senior management approval."[85] Risk tolerance for BSA/AML risk should be tightly aligned with your institution's risk tolerance.

Due diligence on third parties that create AML risk should specifically assess "corporate documentation, licenses, references (including independent reporting services), and, if appropriate, documentation on principal owners and the third party's overall compliance culture," the FFIEC says.[86] Due diligence should also be conducted on the third party's beneficial owners and key management. The same approach should be used regardless of their business purpose, and therefore should include charities, non-government organizations (NGOs), other banks, and governments.

All third parties and their country of origin should be checked against the U.S. Department of the Treasury's OFAC list to ensure that their corporate officers and the third-party firm itself—and its operating jurisdictions—are not on the sanctions list.[87]

After the prospective third party passes the initial qualification process, the next step is to assess its BSA/AML policies and programs, internal controls, access rights, systems integrity and monitoring capabilities, governance and oversight, and employee screening and background checks.

Material fourth parties should also be assessed if they deliver services to the third party that directly support their relationship with your institution. Site visits, including at selective material fourth parties, may be in order, particularly if the third party or material fourth parties are in geographies with weak rule of law or are known "hot spots" for money laundering.

Some things to consider for due diligence processes and assessment of the third party's internal controls:

- Can funds be transferred to or from an unknown third party?
- Is verification of cardholder identity done entirely remotely by third-party or fourth-party program managers, processors, or distributors?
- Can cardholders access third-party prepaid products, ACH, wire transfers, and credit and debit cards internationally, thus avoiding border restrictions and reporting requirements applicable to cash and monetary instruments?
- Is specific holder activity transacted through pooled accounts? Is that data managed by a fourth party?
- Is the marketing of third-party payment products and onboarding of new customers primarily handled by third parties separate from the issuing bank?
- Is the source of payroll funding through an intermediary banking relationship transparent?

Once you assess the AML risk for third parties and material fourth parties your institution is doing business with, you can decide whether it is appropriate to impose re-

[85]FINTRAC: Guidance on the Risk-Based Approach to Combating Money Laundering and Terrorist Financing (Mar 2016) http://www.fintrac-canafe.gc.ca/publications/rba/rba-eng.asp#s4.1

[86]FFIEC BSA/AML Examination Manual (Jan 2014): Expanded Examination Overview and Procedures for Consolidated and Other Types of BSA/AML Compliance Program Structures

[87]Office of Foreign Assets Control Sanctions List: https://www.treasury.gov/resource-center/sanctions/SDN-List/Pages/consolidated.aspx

strictions on their products and services, or the countries in which they operate on your behalf.

Your AML function can help determine appropriate due diligence requirements and controls assessment processes, and may lead the AML controls assessment process during any site visits. It should also determine standard compensating controls, risk adjusted for criticality.

Contracts should specifically include BSA/AML, OFAC, terrorist financing and compliance requirements, and internal control requirements, risk adjusted as appropriate. Contractual terms may also include provisions that allow for exit of the relationship should there be material AML or sanctions risks or failure to comply with requirements. Where the third party is delivering all or any aspect of services from a foreign location, consider additional controls designed to address deficiencies in the rule of law and the willingness to enforce international standards for anti-money laundering and terrorist financing.

Regulators have the right to access and assess any third party performing a service for a financial institution. This may occur in the form of examinations where specific information is requested and deadlines are critical. Contract provisions that include turnaround time for AML-related information requests should be specified in applicable third-party contracts.

Monitoring activities should be specified, including frequency and required documentary evidence. Activities may include confirming the third party's key officers and beneficial ownership information is up to date; reviewing evidence that the third party conducts annual compliance training for all employees; requiring notification and providing appropriate evidence of due diligence and third-party management over material fourth parties; and conducting periodic onsite assessments and reviews.

Stuart Davis reminds us that "oversight and monitoring of third-party relationships which perform AML activities on your behalf is absolutely critical. You must have the same level of oversight as if you were doing the activity yourself and be able to demonstrate that on an ongoing basis. This usually takes the form of monitoring and quality assurance reports from the third party that you assess on a routine basis. Transaction testing can be used to evidence that acceptable standards are being met."

Transaction testing is an important aspect of monitoring for effective BSA/AML risk management. Your institution's AML function should be in an advantageous position to define compensating controls, monitoring, and testing requirements. They've had a lot of practice.

Some institutions may exit or choose not to pursue specific third-party relationships due to risk exposure and compliance costs. For example, a June 2016 International Monetary Fund report noted that individual banks were deciding to withdraw from correspondent banking relationships—also known as "de-risking"—due to "more rigorous prudential requirements, economic and trade sanctions, anti-money laundering, and combating the financing of terrorism (AML/CFT) and tax transparency." [88]

---

[88]IMF Staff Discussion Note (June 2016): The Withdrawal of Correspondent Banking Relationships: A Case for Policy Action https://www.imf.org/external/pubs/ft/sdn/2016/sdn1606.pdf

8

Model Risk

The financial services sector was founded on taking calculated risks to make a profit. "Risk connotates the possibility of harm, so financial theory is intimately bound up with the mathematical theory of probability," says noted quantitative analyst and businessman Emanuel Derman in *Models. Behaving. Badly.*[89] Apportioning probabilities, then, is inseparable from successful risk taking. And successful risk taking is inseparable from sound economic and financial modeling. As a result, there are many explicit and implicit risk models in use in all financial institutions. Many are third-party models. They are used for valuing portfolios and securities, for decision making, and in financial and regulatory reporting. Some models are relatively simple spreadsheets and others are highly sophisticated algorithms built into automated decision-making tools that govern millions of transactions.

This adds up to pervasive reliance on models to predict outcomes and probabilities and make informed decisions. While models are the domain of advanced finance and risk specialists, for obvious reasons models are also of keen interest to regulators.

Ashish Gupta, vice president, Model Risk Management at E*Trade Financial Corp., notes that the "use of models is intrinsic to offering financial products and services, and for managing the business. This engenders model risk."

In SR 11-7, Guidance on Model Risk, the Federal Reserve says that "model refers to a quantitative method, system, or approach that applies statistical, economic, financial, or mathematical theories, techniques, and assumptions to process input data into quantitative estimates." The guidance goes on to say that models "might be used for analyzing business strategies, informing business decisions, identifying and measuring risks, valuing exposures, instruments, or positions, conducting stress testing, assessing adequacy of capital, managing client assets, measuring compliance with internal limits, maintaining the formal control apparatus of the bank, or meeting financial or regulatory reporting requirements and issuing public disclosures."[90]

---

[89]Emanuel Derman: Models. Behaving. Badly (2015) Free Press, pg. 49

[90]FRB Guidance on Model Risk SR 11-7, pg. 1 https://www.federalreserve.gov/bankinforeg/srletters/sr1107.htm

Simply stated, "models are opinions embedded in mathematics." [91] Some models are predictive, like the probability of loan repayment, and some models are used to make informed decisions, like a pricing model. Regardless of their intended purpose, models are *imperfect representations of reality.*

Models:

- Are dependent on the skills, experience, and knowledge of their creators, good or not.
- Rely on historical data.
- May assume that history will repeat itself.
- Are limited by the quantity, quality, and suitability of input data.
- Include their creators' unconscious assumptions and biases.
- Should specify the estimated margin of error.
- Are dependent on generating "false negatives" during testing to reveal structural or coding errors.
- Are static until updated or changed.

Recognizing that there are always unknown variables, sophisticated models may include stochastic models to recognize the presence of unknown variables. These models introduce random variables (that's all "stochastic" means) to represent uncertainty.[92] There is a good example of their use on Wikipedia.

For greater clarity, an economic model enables "informed predictions" about the economic future of a country, a region, or globally. A financial model enables "informed predictions" about the financial impact of specific actions and decisions and aids informed decision making.

One example of using a model as an "informed prediction" is to assess the risk of making a loan. In this example, a model is embedded in consumer loan-decisioning software that generates an "informed prediction" of the loan being repaid. The consumer applies for the loan and provides a set of predetermined information and data which usually includes the purpose of the loan, income, assets, liabilities, and collateral. This is fed into loan-decisioning software with an embedded model that relies on this data, usually along with data from third parties. Third-party data usually includes the potential borrower's credit history and FICO score. The model itself usually includes data provided by the financial institution, such as loan-purpose portfolio limits, the institution's repayment experience with this type of loan, and the customer profile—including repayment history, other products and services the customer has acquired from the institution, etc. Lots of data. Lots of information. Lots of assumptions. And lots of opportunity for error.

A second example is real-time auto-approval models for credit card transactions and models that are intended to detect and prevent credit card fraud. Both types of models are embedded in credit card operations and technologies, and they are in constant conflict. The conflict is between ever-increasing customer expectations for personalized service—*which means seamlessly approving customer transactions*—and mounting credit

[91]Cathy O'Neil: Weapons of Math Destruction (2016). Penguin Random House UK pg. 21

[92]Hannah Christensen: Banking on Better Forecasts: the New Maths of Weather Prediction (January 2015) www.theguardian.com/science

card fraud losses. (In the U.S. fraud losses rose from 5.99 to 11.76 basis points per $100 in transactions from 2005 to 2015.[93]) In 2015, worldwide credit, debit, and prepaid card transactions fraud losses totalled $21.84 billion absorbed by financial institutions, credit card issuers, ATM acquirers, and merchants.[94] The relentless, high-stakes conflict between customer experience goals, competitive market pressures, and the bad guys means that models for automated transaction approval and fraud detection and prevention are constantly changing. All changes need to be thoroughly tested before they can be relied on, no matter how short their life will be.

In SR 11-7 the Federal Reserve acknowledges that a model may include "*quantitative approaches* whose inputs are partially or wholly qualitative or based on expert judgment, provided that the output is quantitative in nature."[95] Think back to the financial crisis and the reliance on the lethal combination of bad data and judgment that was far from "expert" or "quantitative in nature." The consequences were negative and unintentional for many, but not for all: A handful of true financial experts analyzed the models and profited from informed decision making.

"Anyone who relies on theories or models must first understand how they work and what their limits are," says Derman.[96]

Easy to say, hard to do. Economic and financial models can incorporate many assumptions, advanced theories, imperfect data, and complex algorithms. All variables can be extremely volatile.

In other words, buyer beware! "Models are not infallible," Derman warns, noting: "Forecasters rely on sophisticated mathematical models to predict the weather."[97] And we know how well that works out!

A major contributing factor to the financial crisis was creative financial engineering by a handful of enterprising investment bankers and the widespread failure to understand that the assumptions and input into the underlying financial models were faulty. One of these assumptions was that rating agencies had done their homework. Another assumption was that quantity would make up for lack of quality. But more does not always mean better. The financial instruments that drove the crisis were new, opaque, and very risky. This was contrary to what was communicated to and by the financial institutions buying, selling, and trading in these instruments.

Author and former Wall Street quant Cathy O'Neil says, "Opaque and invisible models are the rule, and clear ones very much the exception."[98] The financial instruments that led to the financial crisis were opaque. They were built with inadequate analysis and testing of underlying financial models and their assumptions. Follow-the-leader decision making, the irresistible opportunity to make big profits, and opaque insight or misinformation regarding the risks almost toppled the global financial system. The root cause of the financial crisis was faulty assumptions and inaccurate financial models,

---

[93]The Nilson Report, October 2016 www.nilsonreport.com

[94]Ibid.

[95]FRB Guidance on Model Risk SR 11-7, pg. 1 https://www.federalreserve.gov/bankinforeg/srletters/sr1107.htm

[96]Emanuel Derman: Models. Behaving. Badly (2015) Free Press

[97]Ibid.

[98]Cathy O'Neil: Weapons of Math Destruction (2016). Penguin Random House UK

fueled by easy money—regardless of whether the sellers were or were not aware of the risks.

Relationships with third parties may intentionally or unintentionally include models that are embedded in technologies and purpose-built decision making and management tools. Models are of great interest to senior management and regulators. Gupta notes, "Businesses often source models from third parties or vendors. Therefore, models acquired from third parties should be governed for model risk in the firm, just as models developed internally would." The most reliable method of capture to incorporate model risk is to include it in third-party risk management programs.

Once a model is designed or acquired through a third party, a formal approval process should be in place—prior to deployment. Approval and risk acceptance is dependent on several factors:

1. Awareness that a third-party model exists.
2. Suitability for its intended purpose.
3. Quality and completeness of the model.
4. Results from testing.
5. The expertise and experience of the decision makers.

The complexity of the model, lack of confidence in the model approver's own mathematical abilities, competing priorities and work pressures, and the potential for aggrandizing the model or modeler are some reasons why unsound and suboptimal models are approved and deployed.

The financial crisis heightened awareness that model risk is a key risk driver. As a result, many financial institutions have invested in separate model risk functions, usually as part of their enterprise risk management function. Having a model risk function creates a center of excellence. It brings a body of knowledge and expertise to the institution. A model risk function can be held responsible for designing lifecycle management processes for third-party model risk including the model risk framework, standards and policies, testing procedures and frequency, compensating controls, and model risk oversight. It also plays a key role as "challenger." Its efforts can help build a critical mass of individuals and functions with a working knowledge of third-party model risk.

The model risk function should create and maintain an inventory of all models deployed across the enterprise—to stress test the models when they are created and changed, including underlying assumptions, and to challenge the model creators and owners if models are deemed flawed or ineffective.

From the Federal Reserve's SR 11-7: "A guiding principle throughout the guidance is that managing model risk involves 'effective challenge' of models: critical analysis by objective, informed parties that can identify model limitations and produce appropriate changes. Effective challenge depends on a combination of incentives, competence, and influence."

In addition to the examples provided, there are many, many examples of models used by financial institutions. Actuaries use them to determine life expectancies, which in turn are used to price insurance premiums and capital requirements. Stress testing liquidity and capital adequacy are other examples of how models are used. Loan and securities portfolio limits are based on models, as are loan loss provisions.

What You Need to Know

Third-party model risk is inevitable for all financial institutions. In its guidance, the Fed reminds us that models are "imperfect representations of reality."[99]

As with any third-party risk, third-party model risk can expose your institution to financial losses, ill-advised or suboptimal business decisions, a poor customer experience, the loss of existing or potential customers, misstatement of external financial reporting, or damage to your institution's reputation.

Regardless of how simple or complex, models are an essential tool. How pervasively they are used, how much an institution relies on third-party models for critical activities, and their complexity are key indicators of the degree of third-party model risk. But such indicators can be hard to identify. Once they are, use of theories, complexity and appropriateness of embedded algorithms, quality and accuracy of the model itself, choice and quality of underlying data, and alignment with explicit and implicit assumptions will help determine the degree of third-party model risk exposure for your institution.

Meanwhile, institutions "outsource analysis to coders and statisticians"[100] and benefit from streamlined or automated processes, minimizing headcount requirements. Models are designed by people, tested by people, and programmed by people. People make mistakes. "Model design flaws, invisible bias in underlying assumptions, coding errors, slow reaction to external market forces, and flawed judgment about which data will be included are all sources of third-party model risk."[101]

"All models are wrong but some are useful."

—George E.P. Box

The first hurdle your institution faces is determining whether a third party presents model risk. If your institution hires a third party to create a new model, or change or test an existing model, the first hurdle is easily cleared.

If a model is embedded in third-party software or processes, the first hurdle is higher. It can be difficult to determine that the third party is using a model to support services to your institution. Awareness and education of business leaders and risk specialists is your best defense.

Once it has been determined that there is reliance on a third-party model that is embedded in software or processes, the second hurdle is much, much higher. One of the biggest challenges your institution will face when assessing and managing third-party model risk is the lack of transparency.

All third parties will fiercely protect their models, assumptions, and underlying algorithms. Their models are highly valuable intellectual property, key differentiators, and may be at the heart of their competitive advantage. Consider Google. Its Internet search

[99]FRB Guidance on Model Risk SR 11-7, page 1 https://www.federalreserve.gov/bankinforeg/srletters/sr1107.htm

[100]Cathy O'Neil: Weapons of Math Destruction (2016). Penguin Random House UK pg. 9

[101]Cathy O'Neil: Weapons of Math Destruction (2016). Penguin Random House UK pg. 21.

model PageRank and the underlying algorithms and assumptions that drive it are Google's most closely guarded secrets. PageRank is essential for Google's continued marketplace dominance.

Another risk is that models, particularly those designed by a third party, may be used incorrectly or used for an unintended purpose. Documenting the model's intended purpose, its design principles, the data selected for inclusion and the rationale for those decisions, and the model's underlying assumptions will contribute to avoiding or minimizing incidents of misuse. Harking back to the Johari window, it's almost impossible to articulate all relevant assumptions. This increases the potential for misuse.

Misusing models that are embedded in third-party software, such as loan-decisioning software, is possible but less likely than with standalone models that were custom-created for an intended purpose. When it comes to software, contractual terms and licensing restrictions—combined with participation by knowledgeable risk specialists in internal approval processes—go a long way in preventing misuse.

These barriers to misuse are much lower for cloud-based software that can be accessed through the third party's Web-based portal. In these instances, third-party risk controls; technology risk education; and a close working relationship between business leaders, IT, and risk functions may be all that stand between your institution and implementation of untested, risky models.

You should also determine whether it's important for the third party's model to scale. In other words, can the model's capacity grow along with business needs? The ability to scale is important as a future cost-avoidance technique as your business grows.

Case Study: "Model Risk Management in Action"

By Ashish Gupta

Vice President, Model Risk Management at E*Trade Financial Corp.

Let's start with an assumption that the firm has a model risk policy and a model risk management (MRM) or model risk oversight (MRO) process within an MRM organization. Let's also assume the firm has a third-party oversight or vendor management group.

In the third-party service acquisition lifecycle, the most effective way to manage model risk is by following this process:

1. Every vendor goes through the third-party oversight group or procurement process. The details of the service being procured will be reviewed.
2. Whenever a third-party relationship appears to have a tool or a model, the process should require review by the model risk management group to:
   - Opine if the tool is a model and, if so,
   - Follow the MRM requirements for model risk management throughout the life of the third-party relationship. This may include acquiring detailed documentation about the method, data used, testing evidence, support for ongoing model performance monitoring, and the ability for the business to interact with the vendor to understand market or product changes that would need model change.
   - The contract should explicitly contain all MRM/MRO requirements, as outlined above.

New technologies like robotic process automation (RPA), intelligent automation (IA), and artificial intelligence (AI) bring opportunities for dramatic cost reduction, exponential improvements in the quality of transaction processing, and greatly reduced cycle times. These latest technologies have the potential to greatly reduce risks in areas like network access controls, but they can also bring exponential levels of risk.

The pace of change is a top line risk. The third-party models, algorithms, underlying assumptions, choice and quality of data used in the model, and ever-changing external forces mean that third-party models are subject to endless changes. The complexity of a model makes it difficult to know if the changes will generate the optimal, expected outcome, and can be exceedingly difficult to thoroughly test.

Bots are integral to process automation software. Bots are the sub-applications that perform automated tasks. Bots can also be learning machines. And learning machines are a type of artificial intelligence that can make changes to models without being explicitly programmed. Imagine the possibilities. Imagine the risks.

These recent technologies can and do increase the opacity of models. They limit the institution's knowledge about the exact nature of complex models implemented by third parties and how they work. Initial due diligence, no matter how thorough, will quickly be outdated.

Add in robotic process automation (RPA), which is intentional software design that speeds up processing and reduces cycle times. The chapter on technology risk covers these and other emerging or new technologies. RPA, IA, and AI mean that when errors or unintended outputs occur, scale has a very different connotation. In these instances, scale can be a very daunting enemy. Scale, combined with rapid and highly automated processing, can have a massive impact on your institution's customers, your reputation, and the bottom line.

Switching gears, common sense and experience reduce third-party model risk. Your people often know where risk lives and what it looks like. Intuition comes into play here too. People are rarely conscious of the mental models they rely on when making decisions but most people are comfortable consciously relying on their intuition. Intuition is a mental model.

Models are not infallible. In a business setting, seasoned professionals may rely on intuition to tell them something is wrong or about to go wrong, even if they can't prove it. Also, many people are conflict averse and prefer to avoid challenging their colleagues. Making it easy to voice concerns, then investigating and taking visible action can help to minimize or avoid customer experience issues or incidents, processing errors, and financial losses.

Model risk functions are relatively new, so expect the war for top talent to be fierce. Building and constantly upgrading capabilities and effectiveness can be problematic. Like most professional disciplines, your institution is entirely dependent on hiring managers to be able to attract and retain top talent. They need an intimate understanding of the discipline, including necessary skills and capabilities that will result in "getting to strong."

In the absence of a knowledgeable leader and good governance, it will be hard to judge whether your institution's model risk function is efficient or effective.

What Your Institution Should Do

The first step in managing third-party model risk is to educate internal stakeholders, particularly front-line managers, the third-party risk management team, and IT. A surprising number of people in the financial services sector are not familiar with model risk—or, by extension, third-party model risk. Risk frameworks and assessment processes should be updated to encompass model risk.

Financial institutions "routinely use models for a broad range of activities, including underwriting credits; valuing exposures, instruments, and positions; measuring risk; managing and safeguarding client assets; determining capital and reserve adequacy; and many other activities."[102] Outside of enterprise risk management functions, the number of internal stakeholders with a working knowledge of model risk are few and far between.

Internal stakeholders can't participate in risk management activities if they don't understand what a third-party model risk is, where they are typically found, and what to do when they find them. Education leads to awareness, and awareness increases the probability that third-party model risk will be identified, assessed, managed, and controlled throughout its lifecycle.

Regardless of whether your institution has a formal model risk function, someone in enterprise risk management or senior management should be responsible for the risk framework, standards, and policies relating to third-party model risk and lifecycle management tools that enable identification, assessment, management, and control of third-party model risk. And regardless of whether processes to assess third-party model risk are still in early stages, it's important to build a complete inventory of third-party models in use across the institution. Developing a simple set of questions of key indicators that a third-party model is in use or planned is time well spent.

Some questions that could be included:

1. Whether a spreadsheet or tool that was built in whole or in part by a third party or third-party software application generates:
   a. An estimate (e.g., loan loss).
   b. A valuation (e.g., hard-to-price securities).
   c. A forecast (e.g., financial forecast).
   d. A score (e.g., creditworthiness).
   e. A decision (e.g., automated loan decisioning).
2. Whether a spreadsheet or tool that was built in whole or in part by a third party or third-party software application is used for:
   a. Detection (e.g., AML, credit card fraud).
   b. Regression analysis (e.g., capital reserve adequacy).
   c. Distribution analysis (e.g., portfolio concentration).
   d. Testing (e.g., software, validation).

If the response is "yes" to any of these, a third-party model is most likely in use.

Every third-party model must be evaluated for "*conceptual soundness*."[103] This means making the model risk specialists aware of its existence, preferably before it is deployed. Typically, the model risk team will have a defined methodology for assessing the quality

[102]OCC 2012-12a Supervisory Guidance on Model Risk Management

[103]FRB Guidance on Model Risk SR 11-7 https://www.federalreserve.gov/bankinforeg/srletters/sr1107.htm

of model design and how it was constructed. They will review supporting documentation for clarity, completeness, and alignment with its intended purpose. They will also want to understand and assess the input variables and data that were selected or rejected, and why.

In simple terms, this means that the purpose and intended use should be clearly documented, along with the underlying assumptions, relevant external and internal reference points, and which data is included in the model—including the rationale and source. Documentation should include when the model was created, how and when it was tested and the results, and resolution of any challenges.

Like with software or tool deployment, "user acceptance" testing is a crucial step prior to deployment. In complex situations, it isn't feasible to test all possible instances of use and scenarios that can ensure the model generates expected outcomes. Building good test cases or scenarios, running them through the third-party model, then comparing the results with the expected results is the best way to create confidence that the third-party model will behave as expected.

Building test cases and scenarios takes experience. This step should include subject matter experts from the business, finance, and risk functions. They will increase the probability that the test cases and scenarios cover the right bases. And their expertise should minimize the number of test cases and scenarios that will be built and tested. The rationale and assumptions should be clearly documented.

The pace of business often makes it tempting to cut corners but your institution will need to document how the third-party model was tested. This work is re-usable. Experience dictates that testing is never once-and-done. Testing can take days or weeks, so you should incorporate adequate testing time into the deployment timeline. Think about that old axiom "marry in haste, regret in leisure."

Taking a page from third-party risk management software tool deployment projects, I'm a strong advocate for creating a "control group" of data and results that can be tested within the model after it's configured or constructed. Then run the test cases or scenarios through the model prior to deployment to ensure it generates the expected result. If it doesn't, this can significantly reduce the timeline for resolution.

In regulatory parlance, testing and scenario analysis is called "outcomes analysis." "Back-testing is one form of outcomes analysis that involves the comparison of actual outcomes with model forecasts during a sample period not used in model development at a frequency that matches the model's forecast horizon or performance window," says the OCC. "Different tests have different strengths and weaknesses under different conditions. Any single test is rarely sufficient, so banks should apply a variety of tests to develop a sound model."[104]

"Without constant feedback," says O'Neil, "systems grow outdated and dumb."[105] Performing periodic reviews of third-party models according to criticality, risk, and/or policy requirements is integral to ongoing monitoring. Like other categories of third-party risk management, the model risk specialist function is in the best position to establish the frequency and processes for reassessing risk in deployed third-party models. Third-party risk management software tools have built-in workflow and reminders for when this

[104]OCC 2012-12a Supervisory Guidance on Model Risk Management

[105]Cathy O'Neil: Weapons of Math Destruction (2016). Penguin Random House UK pg. 111

work needs to be completed. Changes to third-party model risk profiles should be a trigger to involve the model risk specialists.

Models are constantly changing, as is the external environment. Change can be exponential when models are changed by bots or learning machines. Sharp changes in consumer behavior, product characteristics, markets, and the economy usually means that changes need to be reflected in financial models. At times, it means that existing models need to be replaced. The best way to stay on top of change is to periodically validate that the model is behaving as expected, and there are few unexplained anomalies in the data. Another question you might ask is the number of approved exceptions. Exceptions can be a lagging indicator that the model is not generating optimal results.

You may want to keep Simpson's Paradox, a "reversal" paradox, in mind when working with third-party model risk. Simpson's Paradox is a tested statistical theory that illustrates how data can lie. The underlying assumptions, choice of data, and causal effects in the model can generate results that are the exact opposite of reality. Something to chew on.

9 Reputation(al) Risk

An organization's reputation does not necessarily conform with social norms of "good" and "bad." It is more complex than that. Reputations are externally defined by customer expectations, social and cultural norms, and media messaging.

Reputations are built on an institution's explicit and implicit stated core values, and judged by whether its actions are perceived to be in alignment with stated values such as integrity, transparency, reliability, and social responsibility. The strength of the public's and its customers' belief that the institution will act in accordance with its core values determines reputation. There is a direct correlation between an institution's reputation and its revenues and market capitalization.

"Board attention to reputational risk has escalated in light of increased breaches, supply chain mistakes, behavior of sitting CEOs, and other issues that are instantly highlighted not just in the press, but social media," says Catherine Allen, chairman and CEO of The Santa Fe Group and corporate board director. "Most boards today have either a communications committee, reputational risk committee, or risk committee that addresses these risks, in addition to discussion with the full board. One only has to look at Target, Uber, or Pizza Hut to understand the impact this risk has on the business and stock price."

In December 2015, the Office of the Comptroller of the Currency (OCC) published updated guidance on risk assessment systems (RAS)[106] to clarify the relationship between an institution's CAMELS[107] rating—the sum of safety and soundness assessments—and its risk assessment system. In this guidance, the OCC[108] expanded strategic and reputational risk assessments to include both quantity of risk and quality of risk management. The *quantity of risk* reflects the level of risk assumed during the course of business. The *quality of risk management* assesses whether the bank's risk management systems can identify, measure, monitor, and control risk.

The Federal Reserve defines reputational risk as "the potential that negative publicity regarding an institution's business practices, whether true or not, will cause a decline in

---

[106]OCC Bulletin 2015-48 Risk Assessment System
[107]CAMEL: Capital, Assets, Management, Equity, Liabilities
[108]OCC Bulletin 2015-48 Risk Assessment System

the customer base, costly litigation, or revenue reductions."[109] An institution's ability to manage reputation risk is extremely important—it is one of six broad categories evaluated by regulators in the context of assessing safety and soundness and fiduciary and compliance risk.

Reputational risk is special. It's different from other categories of risk.

It's special because it's foundational. "While building and maintaining a solid reputation is important for all types of organizations, it is especially important for financial institutions," a Federal Reserve enforcement specialist has noted. "It could be argued that protecting a financial institution's reputation is the most significant risk management challenge that boards of directors face today."[110] Without a "good" reputation it's hard to attract and retain customers, and the bottom line suffers.

Krystelle Bilodeau, a senior business line executive in a systemically important bank, describes her view of an institution's reputation and its reputation risk this way:

> *A "good" reputation is not necessarily synonymous with our traditional view of "good" and "bad" behavior. Instead, it is linked to predictability—predictability that the organization will behave in a manner that is in alignment with its implicitly and explicitly stated values and objectives. An organization acting in a manner that contradicts what its customers have come to expect is what causes reputational damage. And the less visible and more assumed the expected behavior—the more implicit it is—the harsher the impact on the organization's reputation.*

Allen, who sits on the board of Synovus Financial Corporation, says the flip side to reputational risk is being acknowledged as an organization that prioritizes its reputation. Synovus was named *American Banker's* Most Reputable Bank in 2017. "We work hard to do the right thing at Synovus and it starts at the top, with the board and senior management not only putting policies and practices in place, but acting as role models for team members. Service leadership is a mantra at Synovus," says Allen.

When customers and key stakeholders take the financial services sector's core values as a given—core values like honesty and integrity—a serious risk event that violates that trust results in a strong and more visceral reaction. Their reaction to transaction processing errors or temporary unavailability of services pales by comparison. A risk event that shakes their trust in the institution and violates its core values will cause grave concerns about the institution's fundamental ability to deliver reliable, trustworthy services. This distrust grows exponentially if the customer is personally affected by the risk event.

Affronts to consumers' implicit expectations that financial institutions are safe and secure are difficult to mitigate. Failures are a betrayal of consumer trust, and can potentially destabilize the institution's core values. A simple processing error or poor customer service can usually be remediated quickly and effectively, but an organizational conspiracy will take a very long time to repair.

Reputational risk regarding third parties is different from other categories of third-party risk because it's the *impact* of a risk event that's embedded in most institu-

---

[109] Federal Reserve Bank: SR 95-51: Rating the Adequacy of Risk Management Processes and Internal Controls at State Member Banks and Bank Holding Companies

[110] William J. Brown, Enforcement Specialist, Philadelphia Fed: Understanding Reputational Risk: Identify, Measure, and Mitigate the Risk

tions' third-party risk assessments. While other risk categories assess the effectiveness of the third party's risk policies, practices, and controls, third-party risk management assessment tools for reputational risk attempt to quantify the external impact of a risk event.

When it comes to reputation risk, there are no specific reputation risk policies or documentary evidence that your third party can submit to your institution's risk specialists for evaluation of relative strength and overall effectiveness.

Reputational risk is also different because it's difficult to establish controls. It is extremely challenging to determine the level of risk, partly because the impact of a risk event is highly subjective and influenced by the expectations and cultural biases of customers and onlookers. And reputational risk exposure constantly changes along with ever-changing customer expectations. Only when a third-party risk event significantly destabilizes customer expectations is there a realistic opportunity to truly understand its impact.

Your institution's reputational risk exposure to a third party is always assumed to be neutral or negative. There are no controls to assess, so it's hard to determine the potential negative impact and its likelihood of occurring. Likewise, there is no process to assess a likely positive impact on your institution's reputation, either by public association with the third party or because of the expertise, innovation, and thought leadership it delivers.

In other ways, though, reputational risk is like other categories of third-party risk because it is risk centric: Not all reputation risk is created equal.

What You Should Know

Your institution's reputation, while distinct, is directly tied to the sector's overall reputation for safety and soundness. That sector-wide reputation waxes and wanes over time, according to what's in the news and how consumers view the sector and individual financial institutions' responses.

The 2014 Deloitte global survey on reputation risk noted, "As the trigger point for the global economic downturn, financial services firms have faced some of the biggest challenges in managing reputation risk and protecting the value of their brands."[111]

You may be pleasantly surprised to learn that just two years later (2016), financial institutions were rated as among the most trustworthy companies in America. Per *Forbes*, "Measures taken in the wake of the financial crisis led a high number of financial institutions to rank among the most trustworthy companies in America, according to the[ir] criteria used to build the list. The dominance of this particular industry, coupled with the unique regulatory environment in which it functions, led to the creation of a separate list of the Most Trustworthy Financial Companies."[112] Good job!

Bilodeau observes that the active remediation efforts made across the sector were in alignment with what customers expect and their values.

Your institution has a distinct reputation, built over a long period of time. It requires constant strengthening and vigilant protection. It is hard to build a great reputation, and very easy to damage it. Canada's Office of the Superintendent of Financial Institutions (OSFI) has observed that

[111]Deloitte 2014 Global Survey: Reputation@Risk https://www2.deloitte.com/content/dam/Deloitte/pl/Documents/Reports/pl_Reputation_Risk_survey_EN.pdf

[112]Kathryn Dill, Forbes: America's 50 Most Trustworthy Financial Companies [2016] http://www.forbes.com/sites/kathryndill/2015/08/03/americas-50-most-trustworthy-financial-companies-2/#329376572c2c

"all institutions must recognize that their reputation is a strategically important asset and should endeavour to strengthen their reputation risk management practices."[113]

The impact third-party relationships could have on your institution's reputation should be assessed in the context of serious risk exposures their actions could introduce and the likelihood of their occurrence.

Bilodeau proposes that "in the context of an institution's reputation, a serious event that results in widespread damage could be classified as a direct affront to the institution's explicit and implicit reputation, and should prompt a better understanding of potential sources, levels, and impact of risk events."

Reputational risk exposure should be determined, assessed, and rated in financial terms. Recalling the Fed's definition of reputational risk, the impact of a serious reputational risk event is "a decline in the customer base, costly litigation, or revenue reductions."

"Separate to being a repository of shareholder value, corporate reputation is also a means to grow it," a *World Economics Journal* article noted. "A notional 5% improvement in the strength of an extant reputation would yield a market capitalization growth of 2.5% in a company in the S&P 500.

"Reputation value analysis can reveal the most pressing value-generating or -destroying components. Moreover, by disentangling the individual drivers of reputation value it can shed light on whether the reputation issues are truly messaging problems, operational problems, or some combination of the two."[114]

There are serious deficiencies in current processes to identify, assess, manage, and control reputational risk at the enterprise level. These flow directly to your institution's ability—or lack thereof—to identify, assess, manage, and control third-party reputation risk. Current practices and programs don't meet the basic principles for effective third-party risk management: 1) compliance 2) completeness 3) risk centric 4) risk adjusted.

When it comes to assessing exposure to reputation risk from a third party, most practitioners tend to flatten out this complex topic into one or two questions. Typically, there is a question about the number of customers that would be affected by a material risk event and a question about how widespread the negative news is likely to be. These questions are usually responded to by the relationship or project manager in the first line of defense. Responses are the best guess of the person answering them, and are rarely subjected to additional scrutiny or a challenge.

These questions are typically weighted, and the responses are typically assigned a score in the matrixed calculation. The combination of weighted questions and scored responses for reputation risk determines the risk rating and overall risk tier for each third-party relationship.

---

[113]OSFI: Review of Reputation Risk Practices - Principles, Observations and Next Steps http://www.osfi-bsif.gc.ca/eng/fi-if/in-ai/Pages/rep_risk.aspx

[114]WORLD ECONOMICS Vol. 13 • No. 3: The Impact of Reputation on Market Value http://www.world-economics-journal.com

This process seems to lack rigor, particularly because reputation risk is an important risk driver at the enterprise level, and therefore should be at the risk category level for third-party risk.

All issues and incidents that affect an institution's reputation lead to financial loss. Successful mitigation relies on a quick response that is aligned with customer expectations and social and cultural norms. Regrettably, despite the potential to have a lasting effect on an institution's reputation, responses to issues and incidents can be ad hoc, defensive, or shortsighted. Highly accessible social media and a tendency for consumers to use it with few or no restraints can translate into immediate, uncontrollable media coverage. Social media inhibits consumers' ability to filter facts from fiction, and truth from falsehoods.

What Your Institution Should Do

Risk by association is a lens through which reputation risk management processes could easily be tightened. Reputation "risk by association" could be assessed and risk rated as part of your institution's "go to market" process for a new relationship or service, regardless of whether the process includes an RFP. Most financial institutions have implemented robust procurement processes for third-party "vendor" relationships. These processes are often mature and effective, when utilized as intended.

Procurement-related due diligence typically includes the company profile and market competitiveness; the range of products and services and lines of business, products, and services; data about ownership, parent company and key officers; their track record for corporate social responsibility; policies and practices for employee background checks and drug testing; their history of litigation, regulatory sanctions, and fines; current and historical financial statements; and results from checking relevant client references. This information is foundational to assessing and rating reputation "risk by association," which considers the risks and likelihood of any aspect of third-party reputation risk to manifest itself during your institution's third-party relationship.

The argument that procurement processes don't apply to non-vendor third-party relationships has proven to be unfounded. Many institutions use the same processes for all third-party relationships, with few changes needed to expand the scope to include non-vendor relationships. This was validated by third-party risk management executives during RMA's 2015 Third-Party Risk Management Survey.

Your institution could quickly and easily **tighten up risk assessment processes** by mandating collection and assessment of "risk by association" data during qualification, selection, and reviews or renewals of all third-party relationships. Using existing tools and processes found in procurement processes will minimize the time to implement.

A word of caution: An unintended consequence of using standard procurement processes and tools could be a significant misalignment between benefits and workload. Before proceeding, verify that these processes have been right sized or risk adjusted according to the criticality and complexity of the third-party relationship.

Build a better mouse trap. Today, most third-party reputation risk assessment processes consist of two input factors: 1) How many customers would be impacted if a significant failure occurs? 2) How widespread would the communication of negative news be? Over time it should be possible to assess the impact of reputation risk by considering specific, known third-party risk exposures, such as information security and privacy risks.

The metric for determining third-party reputation risk is the financial impact of a third-party risk event that causes a "decline in the customer base, costly litigation, or revenue reductions."[115] Current third-party reputation risk-assessment processes don't assess the financial impact.

For these reasons, operational and third-party risk management processes related to reputation risk must continue to evolve. The sector needs to "up its game," evolving simple risk calculators that assess and quantify complex risk exposures like reputation risk.

Third-party reputation risk should be determined in the context of your own institution's reputation: how your institution defines it, and how changes are monitored and measured—*positively and negatively*—over time.

Bilodeau strongly recommends that, because "an organization's reputation is as individual as a thumbprint, models to evaluate and measure it should also be tailor made, taking into account all relevant baselines for information."

Developing a tool or model to baseline and assess changes to the institution's reputation is aligned with the enterprise risk management, customer experience, and operational risk functions' responsibilities—not the third-party risk management function. Working closely with risk specialists, the institution should leverage the enterprise-level reputation risk assessment model to evolve third-party reputation risk management.

Given the complexities and dynamic nature of models, identifying and assessing third-party reputational risk starts with developing a deep understanding of the reputational issues that matter to your institution's customers and key stakeholders. It sounds obvious, but it's not a common practice in the financial services sector.

Once customer expectations are better understood, they can be used to establish an enterprise-level baseline of an institution's reputation. This enterprise-level reputation baseline should be used as the foundation for building a third-party reputation risk model.

The new third-party reputation risk-assessment model should include specific risk exposures that can be or are currently assessed within the existing third-party risk management program. Third-party reputation risk should also be risk adjusted according to the criticality of the activity and third-party relationship, risk exposure, and likelihood of occurrence.

Bilodeau also proposes that you determine how damaging the potential affront could be to your institution's explicit and implicit values.

For example, the impact of a reputation risk event may depend on the institution's customer base, business lines, products, and services. A retail bank has a different set of values than an investment bank. An investment bank has a different set of values than a central bank. Each customer base likewise has a different set of values and expectations according to their relationship with an institution.

This would lead to improvements in the relevance and quality of controls. The third-party relationship and customer responses could be monitored, including how they

[115]The Board of Governors of the Federal Reserve System (1995)

change over time and how your institution's brand and brand strategy evolves over time. Your institution may also want to consider how to assess and measure the potential financial impact of systemic reputational risk, and the cumulative impact of a series of smaller risk exposures and incidents.

Given that a key input to enterprise-level management and monitoring of reputation risk is third-party reputation risk, it should be possible to develop a separate and specific model to assess and quantify third-party reputation risk. Using the fundamental operational risk equation "Risk x Likelihood = Exposure," it should be possible to create a reputation risk assessment model with rigor.

Here are some ideas for quantitative and qualitative inputs for a third-party reputation risk model:

> (EXPOSURE: cost to remedy a breached customer record x the number of records the third party has access to x LIKELIHOOD: the strength of their controls = FINANCIAL IMPACT).

Here is one regarding the third party's financial condition:

> (EXPOSURE: switch costs / lost revenue per day x LIKELIHOOD: Chapter 11 during the term of the contract = FINANCIAL IMPACT).

This one combines quantitative and qualitative factors by assigning costs and values to equations:

> (EXPOSURE: cost to monitor regulatory sanctions x LIKELIHOOD: controls effectiveness = FINANCIAL IMPACT)

A quick response minimizes losses. When a third-party risk event occurs and there is a realistic potential that it will negatively impact your institution's reputation, the best defense is a good offense. Trained incident-response teams with clear accountabilities and responsibilities can quickly get on top of things. They can alert the chain of command, invoke procedures, and initiate remediation and root cause analysis. They can be expected to decrease the issue-resolution time, minimize the loss exposure, and implement controls designed to prevent similar future incidents or issues.

SECTION

Driving Best Value

10

Monitoring, and Post-Contract Management

Third-party monitoring is a "team sport." It takes many people across the enterprise lots of time and proven expertise to make third-party lifecycle and risk management processes effective and efficient. It's worth the effort. Risk is a constant, but rewards are elusive unless you're intentional about nurturing and harvesting them.

Every institution builds its third-party management program with an intent to comply with regulatory requirements, meet management's expectations, and conform with internal operating norms. A comprehensive framework, policies, procedures, and tools should integrate and operationalize this unprecedented level of matrixed activities to identify, assess, manage, and control third-party risk.

Consider that third parties support virtually every aspect of a financial institution's operations, and are embedded in delivery of every product, service, and critical activity. The stakes are high if things go wrong.

When everything is going well, the rewards can extend far beyond regulatory compliance. Not only can third parties deliver what you contracted, your institution has a great opportunity for much more. Close relationships with top-tier critical third parties open the door to their expertise, technologies, subject matter experts, and investments in innovation.

But they also open the door to increased operational risk, defined as "the risk arising from the execution of an institution's business functions."[116] Since third parties experience their own operational risk—and since that risk is substantially outside the direct control of their financial institution clients—such relationships amplify the clients' operational risk.

Operational excellence has a better chance of being realized if performance and risk management expectations are clear, pragmatic metrics and measures are put in place, and your institution "inspects what you expect." When it comes to critical third-party relationships, this means actively managing what can be managed, and proactively monitoring third parties for changes to their risk profile that may positively or negatively affect your institution's operations, customers, and reputation.

---

[116]RMA: Operational Risk Management http://www.rmahq.org/operational-risk/

Many people across your institution need to have a solid working knowledge of operational risk management fundamentals, the third-party risk management program, their role and the roles of other key stakeholders, the critical activities and relationships in their line of sight, and how it all comes together to deliver services and protect the institution.

The biggest population of internal resources in every third-party risk management program are the relationship managers in the first line of defense. But third-party relationship management may not be their core competency, and only the largest relationships have dedicated resources. In its 2013 Guidance on Managing Outsourcing Risk, the Federal Reserve says, "Financial institutions should ensure personnel with oversight and management responsibilities for service providers have the appropriate level of expertise and stature to manage the outsourcing arrangement." [117]

The second line of defense consists of operational risk management functions with specialized expertise. Risk specialists may be in operational risk, technology, legal, procurement, or embedded in the first line of defense. Regardless of the function that they report to, they need education and training in third-party risk management. Third-party risk management is a new dimension to what they already know, so they can be expected to quickly acquire competence.

Once assessments and selection of a critical third party are complete, the real work begins. Monitoring is the most important aspect of third-party risk management, and that importance has certainly gained the attention of regulators. "Performing ongoing monitoring of the third-party relationship once the contract is in place is essential to the banks' ability to manage risk of the third-party relationship," the Office of the Comptroller of the Currency notes in its own third-party guidance. "More comprehensive monitoring is necessary when the third-party relationship involves critical activities."[118]

The Federal Financial Institutions Examinations Council (FFIEC) says, "Monitoring should encompass:

- Key service level agreements (SLAs) and contract provisions;
- Financial condition of the service provider;
- General control environment of the service provider through the receipt and review of audit reports and other internal control reviews; and
- Potential changes due to external environment." [119]

Monitoring Financial Viability

The frequency of all monitoring activities should be risk adjusted according to criticality and risk. There are certain risk monitoring activities that regulators expect. One is monitoring the financial stability of each institution's population of critical third parties, something they seem to expect will be done every year.

---

[117]FRB Supervisory Letter SR 13-19 Guidance on Managing Outsourcing Risk https://www.federalreserve.gov/bankinforeg/srletters/sr1319a1.pdf

[118]OCC Bulletin 2013-29 Risk Management Guidance for Third Party Relationships https://www.occ.gov/news-issuances/bulletins/2013/bulletin-2013-29.html

[119]FFIEC Outsourcing Technology Services (Jun 2004) http://ithandbook.ffiec.gov/ITBooklets/FFIEC_ITBooklet_OutsourcingTechnologyServices.pdf

Financial services regulators are highly sensitized to the impact the financial instability of critical third parties can have. This is likely due to the grave systemic and individual institutional risks of failure during the last major economic downturn.

Because FFIEC guidance specifically instructs financial institutions on this topic, you can expect your institution's examiners to follow suit. "To fulfill its fiduciary responsibility, an institution involved in an outsourcing arrangement should determine the financial viability of its provider(s) on an annual basis. However, if the financial condition of the provider is declining or unstable, more frequent financial reviews are warranted," the FFIEC says in its "Outsourcing Technology Services Booklet" for examiners.[120]

Monitoring Incentive Compensation

Incentive compensation can be hidden in pricing agreements and service level agreements in your critical third-party contracts. For example, if a third-party collection agency is compensated on the basis of collections realized with no controls over how many times your customer is contacted each day, with no differentiation between high-net-worth customers and those that are chronically overdue, the pricing agreement is a form of incentive compensation that may be contrary to your institution's principles and goals.

The Federal Reserve's Supervisory Letter SR 13-19 provides the most specific guidance in incentive compensation: "Financial institutions should also ensure that an effective process is in place to review and approve any incentive compensation that may be embedded in service provider contracts, including a review of whether existing governance and controls are adequate in light of risks arising from incentive compensation arrangements."[121] The Fed's primary focus is on third-party relationships where the third party sells a financial institution's products and services directly to consumers on the institution's behalf, and whether compensation incents the third party to take inappropriate risks or encourages the sale of inappropriate products to consumers.

Most institutions have not yet put processes in place to monitor incentive compensation. This raises some important questions, says a former head of third-party risk management at a large U.S. bank: "How could your institution ensure that its third parties are not wrongly incentivized? How would you establish the monitoring and subsequent testing to ensure no discriminatory or predatory practices are being performed?"

This subject matter expert advises that your institution should:

1. *Flag all third-party relationships where such behavior is possible. The best time to do this is at the contracting stage.*
2. *Establish descriptions, limits, and thresholds for what is or is not acceptable.*
3. *Acquire periodic attestations from your critical third parties confirming that they remain within established limits and risk tolerance.*
4. *Mandate that the first line of defense complies with regulations and laws, undertakes sampling, and documents evidence of sampling and monitoring activities.*

---

[120]FFIEC Outsourcing Technology Services (Jun 2004) http://ithandbook.ffiec.gov/ITBooklets/FFIEC_IT-Booklet_OutsourcingTechnologyServices.pdf

[121]FRB Supervisory Letter SR 13-19 Guidance on Managing Outsourcing Risk https://www.federalreserve.gov/bankinforeg/srletters/sr1319a1.pdf

5. *On a predefined frequency, as a part of your institution's compliance management systems, the regulatory compliance team should review what the first line of defense has done in terms of sampling, monitoring, and documenting its activities. This also supports effective challenge and the review of regulatory requirements.*
6. *If results of the review do not meet expectations, appropriate action plans are needed. Action plans should specify who is accountable for each action, and target a completion date. Once closed, there may be a need to update the residual risk rating of the relationship.*
7. *All of this needs to get baked into your residual risk calculations and ratings.*

Monitoring SSAE 16 and SOC Reports

While they are not a "silver bullet," the third party may have SSEAE 16, Type 2, and SOC 2 reports available for review. Alternatively, for "enterprise critical" relationships, your institution may decide to share in the expense of conducting a third party SSAE Type 2 or SOC 2 audit that is specific to services acquired.

Accredited independent auditors' reports can help your institution determine the adequacy of a third party's control environment. A "clean" independent audit of the third party's internal controls can reduce work effort during the monitoring phase. If the third party's control environment is sound, and the scope of the audit and the third party's internal controls align with your institution's requirements, these reports may be relied on as an acceptable substitute for some or many of the monitoring activities your institution might otherwise need to do.

SSAE 16 and SOC[122] reports require significant commitments of time and money, and provide different information. "Type 1" reports are designed to audit the effectiveness of controls design, but don't test controls design. "Type 2" signifies that the auditor opined on the suitability of the controls design as of a specific date *and* audited the effectiveness of controls over a specific time frame: six to 12 months. These reports are typically acquired under non-disclosure agreements. SOC 3 reports are publicly available.

SOC 2 reports are said to be superior to SSAE16, Type 2 reports because the auditor, not management, determines the scope of audit. FFIEC Technology Service Provider examination reports (on significant fintechs) also provide reliable information about the third party's control environment.

Independent Monitoring Services

The FFIEC recommends that the financial services sector work together to create independent user groups, saying, "Independent user groups can monitor and influence a service provider better than its individual clients."[123]

---

[122]American Institute of Certified Public Accountants' Service Organization Control [SOC] report www.AICPA.org

[123]FFIEC Outsourcing Technology Services (Jun 2004) http://ithandbook.ffiec.gov/ITBooklets/FFIEC_IT-Booklet_OutsourcingTechnologyServices.pdf

Many attempts are underway, but there are few if any independent financial services user groups in existence today. Instead, your institution may decide to engage a reputable third-party monitoring service provider.

Residual Risk Ratings

Once your institution's third-party risk management program has been operationalized, take some time to learn from experience. Rushing into rating residual risk when you're unsure if processes will generate sound and defensible residual risk ratings is problematic.

Faulty or questionable residual risk processes will generate questionable risk ratings. This will impede your institution's ability to actually manage third-party risk. And you may lose the hearts and minds of key stakeholders, impeding adoption and compliance. Any possibility of rewards will be well out of reach.

Resource Allocation

Regulators expect every institution, and its critical third parties, to make appropriate investments in processes, people, and technology commensurate with the size and complexity of operations, services, and third-party relationships.

According to the FFIEC, "management should periodically rank service provider relationships according to risk to determine which service providers require closer monitoring. **Management should base the [risk] rankings on the residual risk....**"[124] For many institutions, residual risk ratings are currently aspirational. This is due to the size of the population of third-party relationships; nascent due diligence and risk assessment processes; weak or no service level agreements and key performance indicators (KPIs), and unfamiliarity with what constitutes an effective, partially effective, or ineffective control.

Inadequate resourcing is an impediment to effective third-party management. It is difficult to see beyond day-to-day operational management to focus on actively managing third-party risk—particularly if performance, cost, and risk and management activities are highly decentralized. Human resources can be engaged to assess headcount requirements based on workload estimates and required skills.

Effective and efficient third-party management may be out of reach if your institution has been slow to invest. It takes time, money, and expertise to build an effective program. Your institution needs capable third-party relationship managers; a risk-adjusted program; and change-management skills to drive adoption, user training, and technology that manages workflows, sends notifications when tasks are due, distributes and stores due diligence assessments, data, and evaluations, generates reports for management, and enables trend analysis.

---

[124]FFIEC Outsourcing Technology Services (Jun 2004) http://ithandbook.ffiec.gov/ITBooklets/FFIEC_IT-Booklet_OutsourcingTechnologyServices.pdf

What Your Institution Should Know

In most financial institutions, post-contract management and monitoring are the most underdeveloped aspects of the third-party risk management program. This is because the first line of defense has always been the final decision maker for which third-party relationships will support their business; risks they are willing to take; and who and how they will manage the relationship, performance, risks, and costs. Prior to intensified regulatory requirements, post-contract monitoring for changes to the risk profile was virtually non-existent. And prior to updated regulatory guidance, the second line of defense had no real authority to challenge decisions or practices, even where the third-party relationship was high risk or unnecessarily increased the number of third parties the institution was contracting.

According to the OCC, "Performing ongoing monitoring of the third-party relationship once the contract is in place is essential to the bank's ability to manage risk of the third-party relationship. Ongoing monitoring for the duration of the third-party relationship is an essential component of the bank's risk management process."[125]

Allison Sagraves, chief data officer at a large U.S. bank, offers the following personal comments (*which do not represent the views of her employer):

> *Having well-established operational governance protocols is a key component of risk management. Establishing regular SLA review sessions with senior managers, tracking issues and resolution, and escalating issues promptly are all fundamental aspects of day-to-day oversight.*
>
> *Anticipating what could go wrong and having contingency plans in place is also important. Fully incorporating vendors into your own disaster recovery planning and testing is essential.*
>
> *The cost and skills required to effectively manage relationships are often underestimated. Effective oversight requires time and trained staff. Managing partnerships remotely is not easy. It requires professional staff who are able to think proactively, anticipate and remediate risks when possible, and recognize early warning signs of problems.*
>
> *Connecting dots such as sudden attrition, dips in SLAs, lost business, or management changes are just some of the potential indicators that enhanced oversight and risk mitigation strategies may require.*
>
> *There is an art and science to effective relationship management. The best SLAs do not always tell the whole story; and even the most comprehensive terms and conditions do not cover potential reputational risk if service suffers.*

Your institution is relying on its critical third parties to deliver high quality, predictable products and services at an agreed-on price. Quality includes accuracy and availability and predictability includes timeliness and availability, all of which should be part of the contractual agreement. Pricing and incentives should be fair to both parties, and should be sufficiently clear in the contract or pricing agreement so that invoices, expenses, or revenue sharing can be easily deciphered and audited for accuracy.

---

[125]OCC Bulletin 2013-29 Risk Management Guidance for Third Party Relationships https://www.occ.gov/news-issuances/bulletins/2013/bulletin-2013-29.html

Decentralized ownership, and a limited (or no) policy about who, how, what, and when to monitor and manage critical third parties, performance, costs, and operational risk naturally resulted in significant variation within each business function, across the institution and the sector. More prescriptive regulatory guidance means there is a need for clear, consistent policies, processes, and practices.

Communication Tips

The balance of power between buyer and seller has shifted in the past few years. Third parties are increasingly selective about which RFPs they will respond to, and the value of each customer relationship. In the same way that financial institutions exit or decline customer relationships that don't meet their risk tolerance or revenue goals, third parties are doing the same thing. Being a good customer is important, and gets your institution more value than if you're difficult, demanding, and unreasonable. The only time this may not be entirely true is if your institution is among the "Top 10" in the industry, a group that can sometimes get away with bad behavior with few or no consequences. According to Sagraves:

> *There is real value in being a good customer and approaching a third-party relationship with a win-win perspective. For those partners who are deeply integrated into your processes, treating them as an extension of your team helps promote engagement, and can lead to better performance and willingness to go the extra mile. Including your partner in team calls, recognition programs, updates on company developments, and strategies helps promote a "one team" culture. Being a good customer also can help with retention as well as attract the top talent to your team. People want to work for customers who value and recognize their work, and customers with good internal reputations can command top resources.*
>
> *Understanding your vendor's business model and cost structure can help you negotiate better terms and conditions. If you can work in partnership to optimize resources such as improving seat utilization, sharing of resources with proper terms to address risk, and moving toward unit or outcome pricing that rewards innovation and better performance, both parties gain. Creative deal structures that align incentives and allow both parties to benefit can lead to successful long-term partnerships, which in effect reduces risk.*
>
> *Simple things such as being a referenceable client can be beneficial, as this is a no-cost way to provide value to your vendor and can help promote good service.*
>
> *Just like being a good customer can yield benefits, being a bad one can result in risks. Heavy-handed negotiations that reduce margins may well result in your vendor paying less attention to your account, staffing with lower quality resources, and underinvesting in the relationship. These behaviors may increase operational risk. The cost of a relationship can be more than the fees paid if service suffers and risk increases.*

Many people seem to believe that their institution's relationship with the third party is more important to the third party than it is to the financial institution. How many times have you heard "but we're such and such institution, and they benefit from having us as their customer"? Maybe, maybe not. An interesting question you can ask is what the third party wants from the relationship besides the revenue.

Most relationships are strengthened with regular, positive communication. When it comes to third-party relationships, the old adage "the squeaky wheel gets the grease" is particularly true.

Risk Management Never Ends

The old days of "once and done" for risk assessments and due diligence are well behind us. "The OCC expects the bank's ongoing monitoring of third-party relationships to cover the due diligence activities discussed earlier," the OCC says in its third-party risk management guidelines.[126] This requirement is the primary reason for treating management and monitoring as separate activities.

In smaller institutions, 100% of the responsibility for managing third-party relationships, refreshing due diligence, and monitoring risk usually resides in the first line of defense. In larger ones, these activities may be completed by either the first or second lines. For example, it is unlikely that the first line of defense is qualified to assess information security risk, but it is usually responsible for managing and monitoring business continuity risk.

Monitoring versus Management

In regulatory guidance, management and monitoring are treated as interchangeable terms. For some institutions, management and monitoring are performed by the same people, making separation a moot point. In other institutions, separation of duties recognizes that that these are separate activities.

Managing and monitoring are complementary activities, but they are not the same. Monitoring is a relatively passive activity, consisting of checking, verifying, and overseeing. Management is an active endeavor, consisting of conducting, controlling, and directing operations, performance, and risk.

Management activities are typically associated with ongoing business operations. Monitoring activities are typically associated with oversight, including activities which are infrequent and periodic. As a result, most institutions treat management and monitoring as different activities, assigned to different internal functions.

Management of Critical Third Parties

Managing in-scope service provider relationships is performed by the contract owner and/or relationship manager, with ultimate accountability at the department or group executive level. Within the first line of defense, relationship managers and accountable executives may number in the hundreds or even in the thousands. It will be a challenge communicating, training, and accrediting them to perform their responsibilities and accountabilities in a satisfactory and timely manner.

To overcome this challenge, in larger organizations, complex and critical third-party relationships supporting large functions like IT or operations may be managed by a spe-

[126]OCC Bulletin 2013-29 Risk Management Guidance for Third Party Relationships https://www.occ.gov/news-issuances/bulletins/2013/bulletin-2013-29.html

cialized governance team within that group. In others, relationship management tasks are centralized for groups and departments with few third-party relationships, which inhibits the learning process.

How, what, when, and who is responsible for the wide range of activities needed to effectively manage critical third parties shouldn't be left to chance or vague requirements in your institution's third-party management policy and procedures. One institution's policy consisted of a three-page laundry list of activities, liberally sprinkled with the word "continuous." Consistency is unattainable, and the value equation is questionable at best.

Managing critical third-party relationships should consist of concisely described activities and tasks, including frequency, timing, and whether they are mandatory or recommended, and be supported by a RACI matrix (see Page 124).

Scope of Activities

Depending on the size and complexity of the third-party relationship, the relationship manager may lead a team of managers and analysts. From a day-to-day perspective, relationship managers, and their team where applicable, manage service delivery, quality, and operational performance.

Relationship managers rely on a series of agreements, tools, and processes, all of which should be documented:

- Service descriptions
- Service level agreements (SLA)
- Operating level agreements (OLA)
- Key performance indicators (KPIs)
- Transition and implementation project plans
- Financial and budget management practices
- Pricing tables
- Invoice review/audit procedures
- Project plans and commitments
- Automation and process improvement plans
- Change-management processes and logs
- Issue and incident management processes
- Communication plans and tools
- Dispute-resolution processes
- Escalation protocols
- User-satisfaction surveys
- Contract-management tools
- Business continuity plans
- Disaster recovery and contingency plans
- Management reporting

To improve efficiency and reliability, an emerging practice is to centralize routine monitoring tasks and activities. This improves efficiency and promotes consistency, while ensuring activities are completed in a timely manner. Tasks such as insurance verification, reassessing financial stability, scheduling business reviews, and monitoring critical relationships for adverse news can be standardized and centralized.

In some institutions, all third-party risk specialists are centralized in one function. They are responsible for conducting due diligence and refresh activities, then presenting results and recommendations to the first line of defense for risk acceptance. Centralizing operational and performance management into a team outside the business owner's department or team is not advisable. Services, delivery, performance, and risks are owned by the accountable executive, so relationship management is most effective when under the direct control of that same accountable executive.

A relatively new aspect of third-party risk management is producing documentary evidence of your institution's proven abilities for consistent risk identification, controls assessments, management, and oversight. To ease the burden of proof, many institutions have invested in a purpose-built technology solution or a centralized repository to store and access documentary evidence of assessments and activities throughout the lifecycle of the relationship.

If your institution is assessing technology solutions, ensure the selection team verifies that the number of levels and degree of flexibility in the hierarchy of relationships is what is needed, and that they understand any restrictions on custom fields that your institution may want to add.

The primary advantages of a technology solution are the sound architecture to store and retrieve data and documents, embedded workflow, automated notifications, and ease of generating management reporting.

Monitoring Critical Third Parties

The OCC's list of expectations for monitoring third parties is a long one. According to the OCC, monitoring activities include "assessing changes to the third party's:

- business strategy (including acquisitions, divestitures, joint ventures) and reputation (including litigation) that may pose conflicting interests and impact its ability to meet contractual obligations and service level agreements.
- compliance with legal and regulatory requirements.
- financial condition.
- insurance coverage.
- key personnel and ability to retain essential knowledge in support of the activities.
- ability to effectively manage risk by identifying and addressing issues before they are cited in audit reports.
- process for adjusting policies, procedures, and controls in response to changing threats, new vulnerabilities, and material breaches or other serious incidents.
- information technology used or the management of information systems.
- ability to respond to and recover from service disruptions or degradations and meet business resilience expectations.
- reliance on, exposure to, or performance of subcontractors; location of subcontractors; and the ongoing monitoring and control testing of subcontractors.
- agreements with other entities that may pose a conflict of interest or introduce reputation, operational, or other risks to the bank.
- ability to maintain the confidentiality and integrity of the bank's information and systems.

- volume, nature, and trends of consumer complaints, in particular those that indicate compliance or risk management problems.
- ability to appropriately remediate customer complaints."[127]

Monitoring includes systematically verifying controls and testing for changes, and can serve as an early warning system for your institution.

Monitoring includes periodic and ongoing activities. Depending on the size and organization structure of the financial institution, some monitoring activities may be completed by risk specialists in the second line of defense. Repeating specific activities completed during the selection phase, updated risk assessments, analysis, testing controls, and rating risks are common forms of periodic monitoring. Regardless of who undertakes these activities, they are subject to risk acceptance by the first line of defense.

Other monitoring activities are continuous, and may be completed by the relationship manager or a shared services organization. The first line of defense identifies or is made aware of issues, concerns, and material changes, and is responsible for acting.

Scope of Activities

Effective third-party risk management includes monitoring your third parties throughout the lifecycle of the relationship, so you know if something has changed. Monitoring typically includes periodic business reviews, intentionally refreshing due diligence that was undertaken during the selection phase of the relationship, updating risk assessments and risk ratings, and responding to any findings.

The frequency of refreshing due diligence and risk assessments should be established according to the criticality of the activity or relationship, exposure to certain types and levels of risk, and as a reaction to serious issues or concerns. The "refresh" process typically consists of verification that the information the third party provided about its control environment is unchanged.

Many institutions refresh risk assessments on a one-, two-, and three-year cycle, aligned with the risk tier of the relationship or engagement. Monitoring activities can always be intensified on an exception basis, or accelerated if warranted.

Because third-party risk management practices are still evolving, the refresh process can be at least as labor intensive as the initial due diligence and risk assessment processes. This is because risk assessments and risk rating tools are prone to change due to regulatory, legal, or environmental changes, and the growing experience of risk specialists.

Monitoring also means continuously keeping abreast of news about critical third parties, positive and negative; significant management changes; and changes to business operations, products, and services.

Talent Management

Krystelle Bilodeau, senior business line executive in a systemically important bank, observes, "Relationship managers are the most important line of defense in managing third-party risk. To do this well, it's critical that relationship managers have the right skills

[127]OCC Bulletin 2013-29 Risk Management Guidance for Third Party Relationships https://www.occ.gov/news-issuances/bulletins/2013/bulletin-2013-29.html

and capabilities. Today there's no source for financial institutions to determine which 'soft skills' are necessary and which are most effective."

Bilodeau notes that to optimize results, the relationship needs to work for both parties: the financial institution and the third party.

> *Both parties need to invest time and energy into building trust and ascertaining how each party prefers to receive communication. One way to determine optimal relationship management skills is to consult with existing third parties and internal relationship managers where the relationships have proven to be effective, responsive, and grown in strategic impact over time.*
>
> *Establishing a few ground rules can be very helpful. As a long-term judge for the Outsourcing Excellence Awards, I had the opportunity to gain insight into what it takes to have an award-winning relationship.*
>
> *In one case, two relationship managers—one from the buy side and one from the sell side—started their award-winning relationship by agreeing on five leadership behaviors. The one that really stood out was their agreement that they would always escalate issues to executive management in both firms together, and for both relationship managers to be present in all ensuing discussions.*
>
> *Sometimes relationships that were once very troubled but are now very successful provide the best insight. Thinking back on the Outsourcing Excellence Awards, one award-winning relationship hit a wall during transition. The buy side had grossly underestimated the scope, volume, and work effort and the sell side had agreed to a fixed-price contract. Transforming this train wreck into an award-winning relationship required exceptional communication, truthfulness, exceptional relationship-management skills, and a willingness by all stakeholders to collaborate on the best path forward.*
>
> *Sophisticated third parties are incented to invest in relationship-management training for their customer-facing employees. While training may not specifically focus on risk management, successful third parties have honed their recruitment and selection processes over many years of trial and error.*

In Bilodeau's experience, systemic and silent third-party risks persist despite best efforts to implement comprehensive risk management frameworks and processes. The key to uncovering and addressing them is collaboration with experienced internal relationship managers, risk specialists, and critical third parties. The power of collaboration can increase the potential to identify important systemic and silent risks, and develop effective mitigation strategies and controls.

Bilodeau notes that monitoring cannot be static, and will be subject to change due to changing environmental and strategic forces. Relationship managers, accountable executives, and the second line of defense must be nimble to have any chance to identify new or escalating "silent" or systemic third-party risks to prevent failures or other unexpected negative consequences.

Workload Management

Most institutions underestimate the execution workload when designing their third-party risk management program. A common mistake is failing to understand the institution's capacity and readiness to execute mandatory tasks and activities, particularly during early days.

Appropriate and effective monitoring creates a heavy workload. Here are some workload reduction ideas:

- For lower tier risk-rated relationships, due diligence may be refreshed upon contract renewal, with a cap on maximum elapsed time.
- For lower tier relationships, consider implementing minimal monitoring requirements. For example, insurance verification and an annual contract review may be sufficient for many low-risk relationships.
- Refresh due diligence and risk assessments on the contract anniversary date. This can help spread the workload throughout the year—except for December anniversary dates when workload will be heaviest.
- Each third-party relationship may include more than one engagement in the form of a separate agreement, statement of work, or sub-agreement. Adding an expiry date to each assessment, and checking for reusability for each engagement associated with the third party, can reduce the workload by eliminating redundancy.
- Consider subscribing to an auto-alert service from a rating agency. Subscription services can notify your institution about significant deterioration in a critical third party's financial condition.
- For highly critical third-party relationships, consider subscribing to in-depth monitoring services (company news, credit ratings, company officers / corporate profile, information security, legal actions, etc.). Monitoring is a growth industry, and there are many high-quality services available.
- Implement APIs (application program interfaces), where possible, to receive monitoring data. This significantly reduces the manual aspect of some monitoring tasks.
- Consider establishing approved exceptions to due diligence refresh policies for large, stable, publicly traded third parties. For example, conducting annual due diligence assessments on their audited financial statements may have limited value.

The frequency of monitoring activities should consider the projected workload, availability of resources, and feasibility of timely completion. Despite advice to the contrary, some third-party risk managers believe that increasing the frequency of monitoring activities in excess of industry norms is a conservative risk management practice.

In reality, the result is diametrically opposed to the intention. High frequency typically causes institutions to fall further and further behind, particularly for information security risk assessments, putting the credibility of the program at risk. You may want to consider whether high frequency monitoring is creating an unmanageable workload, with limited value and plenty of "noise."

What Your Institution Should Do

Effort and workload to monitor and manage your institution's critical third parties should vary according to the criticality of activities and the relationship, the risk profile, and risk rating. Efficient and effective monitoring processes are contingent on establishing a sound risk identification process, controls and risk ratings that are appropriate for the situation, and risk-adjusting requirements. One size does not fit all!

You may find it helpful to build a RACI or RASCI matrix, concurrent with the development of management and monitoring standards. Or document your institution's informal matrix. This activity usually results in rich conversations about who, what, when and how, helping to avoid surprises, deficiencies, and duplication of work.

Document a RACI or RASCI Matrix

Good governance includes separation of duties, and that means assigning activities to individuals or functions. Role clarity is a critical success factor. Many companies, regardless of industry or location, build a RACI matrix to align people and processes. Regulators like RACIs and will likely ask to see yours.

RACI is an acronym for a matrix that documents which functions or individuals are Responsible, Accountable, Consulted, or Informed of every activity or task in a process.

RASCI is an expanded version of a RACI, adding "Support" to the matrix.

For clarity, only one party is **R**esponsible for tasks or activities, but more than one individual or function can be designated as **A**ccountable, **S**upport, **C**onsulted, or **I**nformed. This is a reliable way to ensure work gets done, while minimizing gaps and duplication of effort. To further explain the concept:

- **R**esponsible functions or individuals do the work or perform the task or activity.
- **A**ccountable functions or individuals oversee the work, task, or activity, often in their capacity as immediate managers and/or approvers.
- **S**upport functions or individuals are assigned to work with the project team or will provide resources to support tasks and activities performed by others. In third-party risk management, a support function may include IT, communications, HR, credit, legal, etc.
- **C**onsulted functions or individuals are typically stakeholders or subject matter experts who need to be consulted on some or all tasks or activities. They may influence the approval process, and can identify concerns and smooth the way to approval.
- **I**nformed functions or individuals typically have an interest in a given task or activity, including progress reports. They may also have an indirect stake in process execution, or a direct stake in an upstream or downstream process or project.

Here is a sample matrix:[128]

RACI / RASCI matrix

Task or Activity	Relationship Manager	Business Leader	Information Security	Business Continuity	Credit	AML	Fraud	Model Risk	Insurance
Business Requirements	A	R							
Identify Inherent Risks	A	R	C	C	C	C	C	C	I
Description									
Description									
Description									
Description									
Description									

Accountable **R**esponsible **S**upport **C**onsult **I**nform

[128]Source: Linda Tuck Chapman, Ontala Performance Solutions Ltd. (2017)

Key Players in the First Line of Defense

With hundreds or thousands of third-party relationships woven into every aspect of your institution's operations, products, and services, it stands to reason that most of the work, responsibility, and accountability lies with the first line of defense. It owns third-party relationships and the risks. The second line is available to provide expertise, support, management, and monitoring; perform governance activities; and challenge when appropriate.

Every critical third-party relationship needs to have a designated "owner"—the relationship manager—and an accountable executive. A record of these individuals must be complete and current. That is not an easy task in institutions prone to frequent reorganization, with average or higher employee turnover, and a large population of millennials with a predisposition to frequent job changes.

In larger institutions, the degree of difficulty in keeping this list current increases exponentially if there isn't a technology solution with embedded workflow that bumps up against HR records. Where a technology has been deployed, the departure of an employee responsible for a specific third party or parties can be reported to the program administrator on a daily basis, and therefore can be addressed in a timely manner.

Maintaining a current list of accountable employees and executives is both important and a regulatory requirement, and is made easier with technology. Among the many responsibilities they have for third-party management, accountable employees and executives are required to respond to periodic attestations and verifications, which are also most easily managed through automated distribution and notifications.

If the third-party relationship is aligned with a single line of business or corporate function, identifying the accountable executive (AE) and relationship manager is easy. If the third party supports multiple business units, often under separate agreements or statements of work, identifying the relationship manager is usually straightforward, but identifying the AE may not be so easy.

Many institutions solve this dilemma by assigning responsibility for specific engagements to the AE with the highest stakes. The overall third-party relationship is then assigned to one AE, with support by engagement-level AEs. The easiest way to manage this complexity is in a purpose-built, third-party risk management solution.

Depending on the size and complexity of the third-party relationship and your operating norms, the contract owner, operational manager, and relationship manager may be the same person. For multi-business unit third-party relationships, these roles may be separated between different people who may be in different departments. Regardless, the higher the risk rating and level of criticality, the more time, effort, and resources your institution will need to invest in managing and monitoring throughout the lifecycle.

1. Accountable Executives

Ownership of the relationship and risks is a first-line-of-defense responsibility. In the same way that accountability can't be outsourced, accountability for each third-party relationship's costs, performance, and risks belongs to an accountable executive.

AEs are responsible for establishing the business strategy and strategic direction, and whether a third party will be engaged. They approve selection and the contract, and accept the risks and maintain overall accountability for the third-party relationship, products and services, compliance, quality, and reliability. They approve key decisions such as required controls, business continuity and contingency plans, and resolution of escalated issues and incidents.

If the third party's performance is unacceptable—or there are serious irregularities or a growing history of issues, incidents, or serious concerns—the AE may decide to exercise the institution's right to audit. This right should be in every critical third-party agreement. Audit, in the third line of defense, may be called on to help with the decision or planning, and may lead the audit.

2. Contract and Relationship Managers

The role of the **contract manager** is to ensure contract terms and conditions are kept current and all parties are meeting their contractual obligations. Many third-party managers keep close tabs on whether the third party is meeting obligations, but overlook whether your institution is meeting its.

A useful process is an analysis of the "wills and shalls" in the written agreement. This consists of extracting all clauses containing the words "will" and "shall" from the contract and pasting them into a spreadsheet, along with which party made the commitment. The next step is testing for compliance.

Inevitably, there are a few surprises, which will lead to discussions, planning, and occasionally a contract amendment. If your relationship with the third party is strained or broken, a "wills and shalls" analysis can be a revealing part of root cause analysis.

The responsibilities of the relationship manager are extensive, and the role of the relationship manager may be separate from or combined with the responsibilities of the operational manager.

The **operational manager** is typically responsible for day-to-day oversight of service delivery and committed project plans, and acting as the point person for escalating and monitoring progress on addressing issues and during incidents and outages.

Primary responsibilities as a **relationship manager** typically include risk, performance, and cost management. At the intersection of these primary responsibilities is where value can be found.

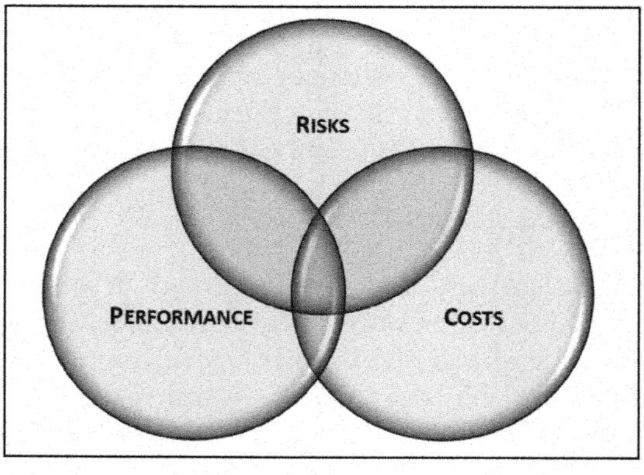

To deliver expectations, relationship managers are responsible for communication between the institution and the third party, resource and change management, quality control, and management reporting.

Depending on the size and complexity of the relationship and degree of centralization, some or all of these activities and tasks may be performed by a relationship management team. Relationship managers are often designated as the "single point of contact" for the third party.

Performance Management

Predictability, reliability, and quality rely on a clear description of services—an operating level agreement (OLA)—backed up by one or more service level agreements. These tools take time to craft but are the foundation for building healthy working relationships with critical third parties.

Service Level Agreements

"Outline the institution's predetermined requirements for the service and establish incentives to meet, or penalties for failure to meet, the requirements," the FFIEC instructs.[129] Service level agreements usually describe minimum acceptable levels of quality, availability, and timeliness, regardless of the product or service acquired from the third party. SLAs are not an arm's length management tool for your institution; they are living documents that transform expectations into commitments. They are a useful tool for your institution's third parties, because they establish clear boundaries around what they have agreed to do.

SLAs consist of critical success factors or specific performance standards, and for each standard a description that clarifies what's expected, a metric, and a measurement period. SLAs are one of the most effective tools available for the chain of command in your institution to "inspect what they expect."

It's easy to negotiate "watermelon" SLAs. You may have experienced one of these. It's an SLA that's green (the color of gains) on the outside but red (losses) on the inside. Watermelon SLAs exist because poorly crafted SLAs are very common.

Here are a few tips for crafting good SLAs:

- Keep the number of metrics down to a manageable number. Ten or fewer is a reasonable number.
- If the third party is providing multiple or highly complex services, craft separate SLAs for each. The information is more quickly actioned than if you have a single, lengthy SLA to manage against.
- Where possible, craft metrics that measure more than one thing. For example, measuring uptime and response time as a single metric paints a clearer picture of performance than if you measured them separately.
- Negotiate an agreement in your contract to review and refresh SLAs on a scheduled basis. Depending on the complexity of service, this could be semi-annually or annually but should not be more frequent than that.

---

[129]FFIEC Outsourcing Technology Services (Jun 2004) http://ithandbook.ffiec.gov/ITBooklets/FFIEC_IT-Booklet_OutsourcingTechnologyServices.pdf

- Before negotiating changes to SLAs, first conduct an environmental scan to ensure existing SLAs are relevant and to determine whether new or different content or metrics should be negotiated. The scan should include business units reliant on quality and service levels, and risk control specialists who want changes in the control environment.
- Do the math on the metrics before you agree to them. Sometimes you'll need a discrete number as a metric and other times it will be an average. Averaging can mask serious problems. Sometimes you'll need to specify maximums and minimums. And the measurement period counts. The longer the period, the easier it is to mask serious problems.

Escalation

Contracts and operating procedures should make it crystal clear what happens when there's a serious incident. This includes a predefined notification period according to the severity of the issue or incident; a communication hierarchy ensuring that individuals with similar levels of authority are communicating with one another; frequency of updates; timing for root cause analysis; and agreement to present findings and any preventative measures within a reasonable time frame.

Risk-Adjusted Effort

Depending on the services acquired from third parties, relationship managers may be in periodic or constant contact with a third party. Daily, weekly, monthly, quarterly, semi-annual, and annual performance meetings are all in common practice.

Performance reporting is typically provided by the third party and reviewed by the relationship manager, with findings and results reported to the AE. In multi-business unit third-party relationships, consolidated information can provide insight into opportunities and risks. User satisfaction surveys can be bilateral, which can help reveal any concerns the third party has with the relationship.

Managers universally agree that performance standards and goals, metrics, and performance reviews are a best practice for managing employees. Surely the same is true for critical third-party relationships. A review of critical third-party relationships may reveal that your institution does not require agreements to include an SLA. This is a poor business practice, and contrary to regulatory expectations.

Cost Management

Spend is not a risk driver, but spend matters. Third-party relationships constitute a substantial proportion of budgets, and one-third or more of the institution's total annual expenses. Most institutions devote insufficient time to negotiating cost transparency and how expenses will be presented on invoices. At times, costs can be quite opaque.

The risk of higher than contracted, duplicate, or excessive costs is exacerbated by a common practice of assigning invoice verification to individuals without sufficient time, expertise, or experience to verify their accuracy. A periodic audit of invoices against contracted pricing and usage can mitigate this risk.

These sources of value come neatly together to form an information-rich, third-party "portfolio management" strategy. With robust capabilities and risk reporting, your business leaders will have insight into relative strengths and weaknesses in each key third party's internal control environment, true and comparative costs, and performance against negotiated SLAs or contractual terms.

Program Development Roadmap

Some institutions create a multi-year roadmap to guide program evolution and expansion. A well-constructed roadmap should be iterative, and structured in a manner that enables and measures progress.

The roadmap can address program deficiencies and improvements. One important element of the roadmap is to plan for risk-adjusting controls and requirements. For example, risk adjusting the frequency of specific due diligence based on experience will improve the efficiency and therefore the effectiveness of your institution's third-party risk management program. Another example is to risk adjust contract controls, making it faster and easier to negotiate contracts by not overreaching what is actually required.

At a minimum, the roadmap and timeline should be approved by enterprise risk management and your institution's third-party governance committee. Assuming the scope and timeline are deemed reasonable and project plan milestones hit their timeline, this may be acceptable to all stakeholders.

Change Management

As noted at the start of this chapter, third-party risk management is a "team sport," with the team consisting of a vast number of people in the first and second lines of defense. In larger institutions, the team can number in the thousands, most with many other things to do every day. The number of critical third parties supporting your institution's critical activities will also number in the hundreds or thousands. Implementing a program of this magnitude deserves some thoughtful investments in change management. Making changes to the program will become less onerous over time, but still requires skillful change management.

A guru of change management is John Kotter, a Harvard University professor who developed an eight-step process more than 40 years ago. Some things improve with age, and his process is one of them. Dr. Kotter's groundbreaking book, *Leading Change*, is a useful tool to learn about the fundamentals.

Change management consists of vision, planning, communication, leadership, training and follow-up. Human resources, corporate communication, and training resources may be available to craft and support change management efforts. A documented plan and a timeline can be useful tools.

Training and Attestations

Issuing a policy and procedures is the least effective way to lead change, and does not constitute training.

Lecture-format training is common, and a good start when you're training a large population. All stakeholders in your institution's third-party risk management program will need to have a basic working knowledge of operational risk management, and an understanding of the context for change. This form of training leans towards a risk management education.

Training for third-party risk management fundamentals typically encompasses:

- An overview of regulatory requirements.
- A third-party risk management framework.
- Alignment with enterprise risk management and operational risk management frameworks.
- Key risk drivers, risk indicators, and potential impact.
- RACI/RASCI.
- Introduction to risk specialists in the second line of defense.
- Tools and processes.
- Systems training, as required.

Adults learn best from doing, so it's best to ensure there are follow-up test cases they can play with and help-desk support available. Depending on which theory you subscribe to, it takes anywhere from 21 to 66 days to form a habit. And much longer if the task or activity is infrequent.

Evidence of participation in training should be maintained, and recorded in your third-party risk management technology solution, if you have one. All new contract, operational, and relationship managers, and accountable executives, should be required to complete training within a specific time frame after assuming responsibility for critical third-party relationships if they haven't taken the training. Risk specialists in the second line of defense will require training: a subset of the full suite at a minimum.

Annual compliance training and attestation are coming into common practice. Some institutions have developed compliance training for critical third-party relationships. Training must be completed by all new employees in any role interfacing with any aspect of services provided, and annually by all employees assigned to the engagement.

11

Relationship Management in the Age of Millennials

You may be asking what do millennials have to do with third-party lifecycle and risk management? The answer has to do with the fact that, in the "people, process, technology" axiom, there's a reason why "people come first." You can have the best processes and technology ever, but third-party lifecycle and risk management starts with people. Because of this, the best next question is how do millennials differ at home and at work from the generations before them?

Some key findings from research I conducted with this chapter's "co-authors"—Krystelle Bilodeau, a business segment executive in a systemically important financial institution, and Cynthia Bilodeau, a professor of counseling and psychotherapy at Saint Paul University in Ottawa—are that millennials:

- Are better educated than previous generations.
- Had nurturing parents who valued their opinions and preferences.
- Grew up in relative safety.
- Received frequent positive feedback that built confidence and self-efficacy.
- Grew up with access to technology, the Internet, and social media.

Impact on Third-Party Lifecycle and Relationship Management

We were unable to locate specific research linking key characteristics of millennials to their impact on operational risk. Instead, we developed the following "problem statements" related to third-party lifecycle and risk management, analyzed these as contributing factors to three ubiquitous risks related to millennials, and later proposed some risk mitigation strategies.

Problem Statements:

1. Employee turnover at all levels has dramatically accelerated, eroding "institutional knowledge" and the relative depth and breadth of skills and expertise.
2. Each time someone from a critical third-party relationship management team leaves, they take their relationships, knowledge, and experience with them. Fre-

quent turnover diminishes our capabilities for managing critical activities and third-party relationships, and they never have a chance to fully recover.

3. Employee disengagement is driving new and higher risks into our business, resulting in inconsistent business practices, lifecycle and risk management, and results.
4. The use of text and instant messaging as communication preferences makes it hard to build meaningful professional relationships and trust.

Context for Action

Millennials are the children of boomers and older Generation Xers. According to the U.S. Census Bureau, millennials are currently between 18 and 34, the first wave having been born in the 1980s. Millennials number more than 70 million-strong in the U.S. today. They are the largest generational population in North America, and are on the cusp of being the largest employee cohort group in the North American workforce.[130]

The following chart, taken from a research report published by the Pew Research Center's "fact tank" that provides information on social issues, public opinion, and demographic trends, illustrates these points in a graph. Here is what the data from their study said:

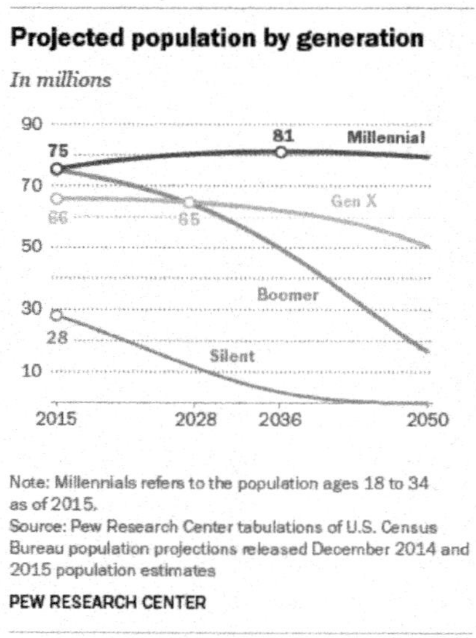

Much has been done to analyze the needs and wants of millennials, and the impact of some of the conclusions and their impact on third-party management will continue to be addressed. Less talked about is the post-millennial generation, sometimes referred to as Generation Z, an even larger generation than the millennials. They are the most educated and tech-savvy generation to ever enter the workforce, and the first wave has arrived.

130PEW Research Center Report (2016): Millennials Overtake Baby Boomers as America's Largest Generation http://www.pewresearch.org/fact-tank/2016/04/25/millennials-overtake-baby-boomers/

Back to millennials. Because they are the generation that dominates today's workforce, and they bring perceived differences in values and real differences in workstyle, millennials are inseparable from your institution's reputation and its promise to your customers.

Significant differences in personal values, workstyles, communication preferences, and career goals means that millennials, Gen Xers, and boomers have been on a collision course for several years. Some of the differences have a positive influence on operational risk, and specifically on third-party lifecycle and risk management. Others, not so much.

Three ubiquitous, related risks are examined here to determine whether they are the root causes of these problems:

Risk # 1: Millennials Are Job-Hoppers

Critical third-party relationships are "mini-operational and cultural ecosystems" unto themselves. Each one is a compilation of your institution, the third party, fourth parties, and the markets you all operate in. The uniqueness of each "mini-ecosystem" is intensified by its unique operations, and reliance by your institution on its third parties and fourth parties.

These mini-ecosystems and each critical third-party and fourth-party relationship are the responsibility of many players in your institution—staff, managers, and executives in the first and second lines of defense—mirrored by those employed by your critical third and fourth parties. This complex relationship equation multiplies the number of individuals involved in making it work smoothly, evolve, and improve over time. And each company in each mini-ecosystem is experiencing rapid employee turnover.

A 2014 research study commissioned by CareerBuilder[131] found that "the majority of employers (55%) said that they've hired someone they'd categorize as a job-hopper. Of those employers:

- 34% said the job-hopper left after a short period of time.
- 40% said the job-hopper stayed for at least two years.
- 17% said the job-hopper stayed for at least three years."

An article published in the *Plos One* journal noted, "Employees' retention is becoming one of the key issues for many organizations that are striving to retain talented employees in order to be competitive in today's economic market....The costs of losing an employee range from 1/2 to five times that employee's annual salary." [132]

---

[131]Harris Poll on behalf of CareerBuilder (2014): Nearly One-Third of Employers Expect Workers to Job-Hop http://www.careerbuilder.com/share/aboutus/pressreleasesdetail.aspx?sd=5%2F15%2F2014&id=pr824&ed=12%2F31%2F2014

[132]US National Library of Medicine, National Institutes of Health: Employees' Organizational Identification and Affective Organizational Commitment: An Integrative Approach (2015) https://www.ncbi.nlm.nih.gov/pmc/articles/PMC4395289/

For employees with complex roles and relationships, costs are likely to be at the higher end of the range. And the cost equation ignores lost expertise, knowledge, institutional knowledge, relationships, and opportunities. It is hard to say if you can ever get traction: It can take 12 to 18 months before the manager and the institution realize a positive return on investment for new hires, but increasingly employees' tenure is getting shorter.

The following includes key facts and myths related to millennials in your workforce, how they impact third-party lifecycle and risk management, and conclusions as food for thought.

Fact or Myth?

In the 1980s, when boomers dominated the workforce and the first millennials were just being born, employee tenure looked much different that it does today. "Among workers aged 35 to 44 in January 1983, more than one-third had been with the same employer for 10 years or more, and among workers 45 and over, nearly one-third had been at their jobs for at least 20 years," according to the U.S. Bureau of Labor Statistics.[133]

Tenure looks very different today. Millennials are less likely to be attached to individual institutions and their traditions. Millennials currently change jobs more often than other generations, looking for more stability, greater job satisfaction, or additional rewards.

Difficulties finding good-paying work that's commensurate with their investments in post-secondary education, fewer permanent roles, and the exorbitant cost of health care are a few reasons why the employee retention picture for millennials looks different than for older workers.

Citing a survey, a CNBC.com article noted that nearly 90% of millennials would stay with the same employer for a decade if it meant annual raises and upward mobility. The article also said "77% would be willing to take a salary cut in exchange for long-term job security."[134]

The Pew Research Center published a fact-based report on employee tenure. Here is what U.S. Census data told them: [135]

---

[133]Monthly Labor Review, Bureau of Labor Statistics, U.S. Department of Labor: Occupational Mobility and Job Tenure in 1983 https://www.bls.gov/opub/mlr/1984/10/art2full.pdf

[134]CNBC: Millennial Employees Are a Lot More Loyal than their Job-hopping Stereotype (2017) http://www.cnbc.com/2017/05/10/90-of-millennials-will-stay-in-a-job-for-10-years-if-two-needs-met.html

[135]PEW Research Center Report (2017) Millennials Aren't Job-hopping any Faster than Generation X Did http://www.pewresearch.org/fact-tank/2017/04/19/millennials-arent-job-hopping-any-faster-than-generation-x-did/ft_17-04-17_millennialjobtenure/

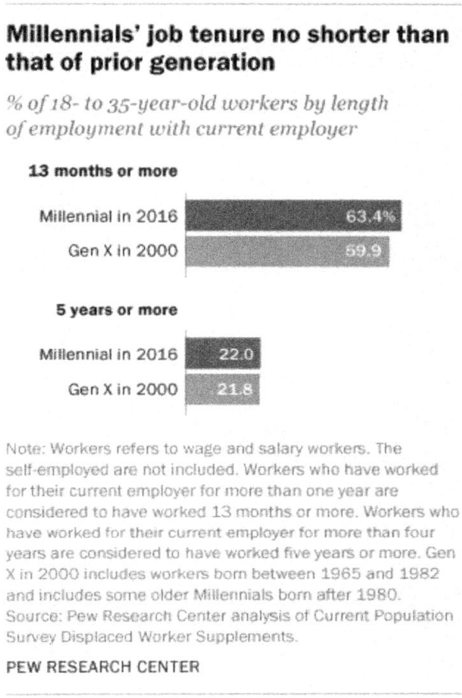

http://www.pewresearch.org/fact-tank/2017/04/19/millennials-arent-job-hopping-any-faster-than-generation-x-did/ft_17-04-17_millennialjobtenure/

These statistics should cause us to question our assumptions about millennials and expand our thinking to the workforce at large.

The Impact on Third-Party Lifecycle and Risk Management

Third-party programs and critical third-party relationships are characterized by complexity; the potential to generate a wealth of new opportunities to innovate, improve quality, and reduce costs and heavy workloads; and the need to comply with stringent regulations and produce documentary evidence to prove it.

Great employees easily master the technical aspects of their roles. Their value skyrockets when they embrace the context for their work, understand their impact on the institution and its customers, and form strong working relationships. Because relationships need time and common experiences, they take time to jell, and even longer to build trust.

The upside to job-hoppers is that they bring a wide range of experience and expertise. They may have been job-hopping for "legitimate" reasons, looking for more money or a challenge, or a better opportunity to learn, grow, and make a real difference. If you can satisfy their needs while respecting their values, will they break the pattern and stay?

The downsides of rapid turnover are many:

- Finding the right employees, then orienting, educating, and training them is costly and time consuming.
- The complexity of critical third-party relationships, many of which are multi-sourced and have co-dependent operations, means that there is a steep learning curve. And millennials aren't lauded for perseverance.
- When the talent walks out the door, it must be replaced and must be fully assimilated.
- It takes time for relationships to form and even more time to build trust.
- It's hard to add value until the technical aspects of the role have been mastered and relationships have been formed to smooth out issues and mine opportunities.

A possible solution is to stop relying on outdated management theory. Stop trying to retain employees. Instead, try to look differently at how you could effectively address the "institutional," technical, and relationship risks.

We currently treat employees as vessels of knowledge. What if we developed more natural ways to embed knowledge transfer within our routines, processes, practices, and norms of how we manage our teams and organization?

It would require the identification of where critical knowledge exists, where and how key decisions are actually being made, how problems are identified and resolved, and what information was used as the source data that was incorporated into decision making and problem resolution.

Having more brains applied to how and why decisions were and are made builds resilience through more widely shared understanding and knowledge. Finding ways to embed this naturally in your organization requires more thoughtful communication and an understanding of what knowledge is really critical so we don't paralyze the system.

Then you'll need to develop new strategies and tactics to transfer this knowledge to a larger critical mass to surround the relationship and its key decision points.

A specific tactic you may wish to consider is utilizing social media style technologies that may be available internally to capture institutional, technical, and relationship knowledge. For example, when deploying a third-party risk management program in a large bank, one design team recorded and inserted videos describing each step, each no longer than three minutes. This "just in time" knowledge transfer helped to drive adoption and compliance, while recording rationale at the time of initial design. This technology could be made available to relationship managers to capture relationship knowledge and history, making it easily accessible to those who assume their role over time.

Conclusions:

Rapid employee turnover is endemic, and is not confined to millennials. The revolving door for top performers and hot skills never stops turning, in every economy. If we can't count on long-tenured employees, maybe it's time to build better business resilience strategies.

Critical third-party relationships are complex, and take experience and expertise to manage effectively. If you're still mastering the fundamentals, it's hard to find the bandwidth and insight that leads to innovation, improvements, and enhancements—and even harder to find the time to build the kind of trust that brings your institution safely through serious issues and incidents.

Rapid employee turnover in the relationship management team for critical third and fourth parties is a "top line" risk. And the more reliant your institution is on each critical activity mini-ecosystem, and the more complex the ecosystem and critical activity, the higher the risk.

Acknowledge that old ways of doing things don't always work over time. Learn and try out new management strategies and tactics. Expand the critical mass of the team that manages critical third-party relationships. Sharing knowledge helps to maintain and sustain it.

Risk #2: Millennials Are Disengaged Employees

An academic term for employee engagement is affective commitment (AC), which "refers to employees' perceptions of their emotional attachment to or identification with their organization."[136] To most people, engaged employees are committed to their work and their employer, actively contributing to its success.

It's easy to understand why high levels of employee engagement are highly desirable. Statistics show that companies with a highly engaged workforce are more productive, produce higher quality work, and are more innovative and more profitable. Engaged employees are more inclined to stay, often turning down "better" offers.

Millennials are reported to have different values than older workers, and some of these may look like disengagement on the surface. The stereotypical millennial is defined by casual workplace attire, telecommuting versus life in a cubicle, an unrelenting pursuit of work/life balance, demands for longer maternity or paternity leave, texts versus calls, a keen sense of entitlement, and unwillingness to work hard.

In their research, Krystelle and Cynthia Bilodeau have found that that millennials hold many of the same values as prior generations, but they also have new values. They offer the following observation: Millennials have a preoccupation with social responsibility and highly value constant communication and feedback. Prior generations were not focused on saving the environment. Most millennials grew up with that goal, creating a generational shared value. Millennials grew up alongside rapid technological changes. Access to powerful technologies is an integral part of their lives. It may therefore be much more acceptable for millennials to sleep with their phone under their pillow.

The Bilodeaus believe that these new values shape how millennials express themselves through their behaviors, which in turn impacts how millennials are perceived in the workplace.

For example, constant informal communication and interaction with technology can be interpreted as antisocial or over-reliant behavior. But it may just be a "new norm," and an indication of how much millennials value communication and feedback. Remember that millennials grew up with parents who valued their opinions, and placed their emphasis on providing them with feedback designed to build self-esteem.

136Williams, J.: Sloan Work and Family Encyclopedia (2004). Job Satisfaction and Organizational Commitment http://wfnetwork.bc.edu/encyclopedia_entry.php?id=244&area=academics

Meanwhile, the penchant to watch cat videos at the office could be interpreted as slacking off. Instead it may simply be a form of shared experience and mental release, equivalent to a boomer going for a walk with a colleague at lunch time.

Personal experience and unconscious bias are key when it comes to interpreting differences in values and behavior. Millennials do not necessarily have different values than those before them. But they may hold new ones that older generations may not have internalized in the same way, and they do behave differently. Understanding such differences may be a good thing, as it may open your thinking to leveraging varied skills and abilities across a diverse workforce. Try shifting your focus to how these different behaviors can send you along a path of solutions to mitigate silent or creeping risks. Risk mitigation isn't always about changing how the other party does things. It also means changing how we manage our business and third-party relationships.

A behavioral study found that 29% of millennials are "engaged," meaning they are emotionally and behaviorally connected to their job and company. While this number sounds low, it is actually higher than other demographic groups. You may believe that millennials simply want more and more, or lack the ability to make a commitment. In fact, most millennials just want a job that uses their skills and expertise, and makes them feel like they're making a difference.

Fact or Myth?

Despite popular opinion, research has shown that millennials have the same dreams as those before them. Writing in the *Harvard Business Review* about the long-term career goals of millennials, Generation Xers and baby boomers, KPMG partner Bruce N. Pfau noted that "a group of researchers from George Washington University and the Department of Defense analyzed more than 20 published and unpublished studies examining generational differences and concluded that meaningful differences among generations probably do not exist in the workplace. The small differences that do appear are likely attributable to factors such as stage of life more than generational membership."[137]

Some differences are easy to spot, others are "below the water line."

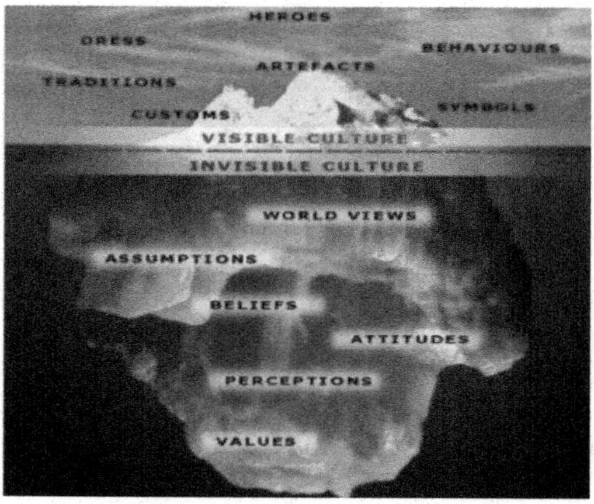

[137] Bruce N. Pfau, Harvard Business Review (2016): What Do Millennials Really Want at Work – The Same Things as the Rest of Us Do https://hbr.org/2016/04/what-do-millennials-really-want-at-work

For example, millennials have few expectations about job security. Nor, perhaps, should they. According to a 2015 report published by the U.S. Government Accountability Office, "contingent workers comprised 35.3% of employed workers in 2006 and 40.4% in 2010."[138] With self-managed 401K plans, flexible workforce policies, and easy access to jobs and contract work, it's hard for them to get excited about job security.

Millennials are connected and acutely aware of the world around them. Most are tech-savvy and comfortable with technology. Because of this, they learn to use innovative technologies quickly and may use more functionality than older users. Millennials may also be indifferent to data privacy and data security. Perhaps because their own confidential data is the "currency" that gives them access to social media, or because data privacy breaches are so common, or because they are at a time of life when they have limited assets, they perceive there is little personal risk.

Millennials have more education than most older workers, and most attained it at a younger age. Many have a post-secondary education and specialized training and/or advanced degrees, which accords them critical thinking, problem solving, and technical skills. They want to use them.

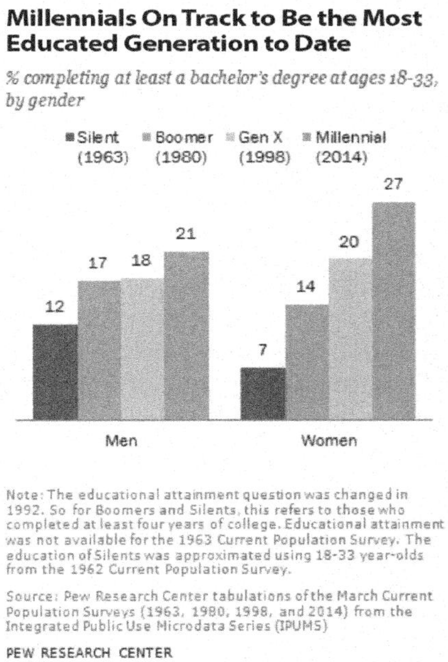

Source: Pew Research Center [139]

---

[138]U.S. Government Accountability Office – Contingent Workforce Size, Characteristics, Earnings and Benefits (April 2015) http://www.gao.gov/assets/670/669899.pdf

[139]PEW Research Report: How Millennials Compare with Their Grandparents 50 Years Ago (2015) http://www.pewresearch.org/fact-tank/2015/03/19/how-millennials-compare-with-their-grandparents/ft_millennials-education_031715/

Millennials openly care about the environment, and many demonstrate this value through employment and lifestyle choices. Corporate social responsibility, reducing the carbon footprint, community involvement, and responsible sourcing matter to them. They are attracted to managers and companies that share their values and provide them the opportunity to contribute.

Millennials want to make a difference in the world.

The Impact on Third-Party Lifecycle and Risk Management

Outsourcing has been around for a long time, and so has the failure of these relationships to meet expectations. These days, third-party mini-ecosystems are far more complex. The technical aspects of individual roles and responsibilities within these ecosystems can be quite challenging. If the workforce responsible for managing and governing these critical third-party relationships is not fully engaged, it won't take long before the number of issues and incidents begins to rise. Customers will notice.

Things can go very bad, very quickly in complex operations and relationships. Then heads will roll, the organization will need to throw lots of time and energy at the problems, costs to recover may be significant, and your customers may walk.

Potentially compounding employee disengagement and apathy is millennials' aforementioned disregard for cyber and data privacy. This propensity means that there is an ongoing need to increase investments in training and awareness for all stakeholder groups in your institution's critical third-party relationships and your complex mini-ecosystems. There may also be an increased risk of information or data breaches that could damage your institution's reputation and potentially attract fines or unwanted regulatory attention.

On the upside, the post-secondary education common to millennials emphasizes problem solving and critical thinking. These skills and a more tech-savvy workforce can flatten out learning curves, increasing the speed to competency. In turn, they may create more opportunities for improving operations, quality, and results. Harnessing a deeply rooted desire in the workforce, particularly with millennials, to make a difference can bring tangible benefits to these complex third-party relationships and mini-ecosystems.

This means that employees within or close to each mini-ecosystem can be given specific opportunities to make a difference through innovation, improving a process, eliminating redundant work, or seeking new CSR solutions. Or by working in teams from multiple mini-ecosystems to solve systemic issues and look for broader opportunities.

Tech-savvy employees, well educated in critical thinking and with a bent for innovation, bring a fresh approach to problem solving. Here's a simple "case study" provided by Krystelle and Cynthia Bilodeau to illustrate this point:

Problem	Pens don't work in outer space due to ink failures, zero gravity, and irregular temperatures
Commercial Solution	Invest $$$$$ to develop a space-friendly pen
Soviet Solution	

This example is provided as an example of reframing the problem versus solving the problem. The Americans problem-solved, and their solution was expensive and complex. The Soviets reframed the problem and in doing so, found a simple solution.

Although pencils were later supplanted by the Fisher Space Pen (still used by the Americans and Russians today), this case study illustrates how fresh thinking helps reframe problems. Reframing the problem can lead to optimal, fit-for-purpose solutions.

Diversity is a natural byproduct of a multi-generational workforce. There is strength in diversity, and diversity means diversity of thought, experience, and expertise.

Tech-savvy millennials have very different communication expectations and those expectations have influenced communication practices across the entire workforce. Their communication tends to come in bite-sized pieces that are efficient and focused on the immediate. Being "always on" means they tend to answer questions quickly. Dialogue is crisp and to the point. Responsiveness is valued much more than proper spelling and grammar. The downside is that such communication can be superficial, leaving no opportunity for the deeper, richer conversations that build relationships, help to uncover new opportunities, and address systemic issues.

One senior executive accountable for an "enterprise critical" third-party relationship said that over time, weekly status meetings with the third party were all but eliminated. To counter any superficiality, an "untouchable" line item in the budget is the quarterly full-day offsite meeting between the internal and third-party team. The morning is all business and the afternoon is all fun. This format bridged business needs and relationship building.

Conclusions:

Companies struggle to engage their entire workforce; the risk of disengagement is not specific to millennials. This is an old problem, but one that has worsened.

Low levels of employee engagement mean less commitment to critical third-party relationships. A disengaged workforce is likely to result in suboptimal third-party relationships, increasing the potential for damage to your institution's operations and reputation and more lost opportunities.

Generational differences are manifested as behavioral differences. Behavioral differences can cause friction and lack of respect between and for individuals who are crucial to the success of critical third-party relationships. Generational and individual biases may also interfere with the individual ability to form productive relationships that leverage diversity.

The workforce, particularly millennials, uses technology differently than prior generations. They prefer texts to e-mails and phone calls. In the example above, technology rendered face-to-face and phone meetings less useful, so they were often canceled. They were replaced by the "quick touch"—a text.

E-mail is perceived as requiring more formality, but e-mails are getting shorter and shorter. Skype texts are bite-sized and agile, but their superficiality removes the opportunity for depth, and perhaps for breadth. The acquisition of knowledge and therefore making decisions is fragmented by how we use technology. Opportunities to exercise critical thinking skills, and the low value placed on informed analysis and deep learning, are making these things of the past.

Data is not knowledge. Data is the capture of discrete activities. Information is data with context. Knowledge is the ability to use data and information for informed decision making.

Risk #3: Millennials Don't Know How Things Are Done Around Here

The following are commonly held beliefs among older workers: millennials have a short attention span; an inflated opinion of their abilities; disdain for older workers with long tenure and depth in a specific role or function; an unwillingness to invest in learning more than what is absolutely necessary to get the job done; won't read more than a couple of hundred words at a time; need endless positive feedback; and respond poorly to under- and over-communication.

These traits converge into substantial loss of "institutional knowledge." Institutional knowledge is the what, who, how, and why the scope, structure, requirements, operations, and risk controls are what they are in complex third-party relationships. These are critical activities and relationships. Institutional knowledge provides tangible value.

Fact or Myth?

"The average attention span for the notoriously ill-focused goldfish is nine seconds, but according to a new study from Microsoft Corp., people now generally lose concentration after eight seconds, highlighting the effects of an increasingly digitalized lifestyle on the brain," a Time.com article noted. "On the positive side, the report says our ability to multi-task has drastically improved in the mobile age."[140] Please note that this study is about "people"—not just millennials.

Lots of education; limited job security; access to affordable, powerful technology and information; loyalty to themselves and their friends and not to the companies that employ them are facts, not fiction, when it comes to millennials. The impact of these facts on generational differences in the workplace are summarized in the following chart.

ORGANIZATIONAL GENERATIONAL CLASH POINTS

Clash Point	Traditionalists	Boomers	Xers	Millennials
Work/career goal	To build a legacy	To build a stellar career	To build a portable career	To build parallel careers
Reward system	Satisfaction of a job well done	Money, title, recognition	Freedom is the ultimate reward	Meaningful work
Feedback	No news is good news	Once a year is enough	"How am I doing?"	Comes at the push of a button
Changing jobs ...	Carries a stigma	Puts your career behind	Is necessary	Is part of my daily routine
Retirement is ...	A reward	Time to retool	Time off to renew	Recycling
Training	"I learned it the hard way; you can too."	"Train 'em too much and they'll take the new skills and leave."	"The more they learn, the more they stay."	Continuous learning is a way of life.

Source: CHA USA.org Terrence F. Cahill, Ed.D., FACHE and Mona Sedrak, Ph.D.: Age-Related Conflicts: The Generational Divide (July – August 2011)

140Kevin McSpadden, Time.com (May 14, 2015): http://time.com/3858309/attention-spans-goldfish/

If you haven't consciously changed how you engage and manage your multi-generational workforce, it's time to start.

The Impact on Third-Party Lifecycle and Risk Management

To fulfill their responsibilities for third-party risk management reviews, the Office of the Comptroller of the Currency specifies that examiners will:

- "Determine whether there is appropriate staffing and expertise involved in due diligence activities.
- Determine if the bank has enough staff with adequate experience and expertise to properly oversee third-party relationships and the bank's third-party risk management process.
- Determine whether management has dedicated sufficient staff with the necessary expertise, authority, and accountability to oversee and monitor the third party in a manner commensurate with the level of risk and complexity of the relationship.

"Personnel are the bank staff and managers who execute or oversee processes. Personnel should be qualified and competent, have clearly defined responsibilities, and be held accountable for their actions. They should understand the bank's mission, risk appetite, core values, policies, and processes. Banks should design compensation programs to attract and retain qualified personnel, align with strategy, and appropriately balance risk-taking and reward."[141]

This guidance is sound advice, but is increasingly more difficult to do.

Each critical third party and each mini-ecosystem has its own operational and technical uniqueness, and history of operations and services, often over a long horizon. Frontline workers, middle and senior managers, and senior management at every level in your institution and within your critical third and fourth parties are cycling through jobs faster than ever before.

Edmund Burke, politician, author, orator, and philosopher said, "Those who don't learn history are doomed to repeat it."

In the case of third-party lifecycle and risk management programs and the complex relationships that exist within them, learning about history is quickly becoming an abstract concept. If knowledge is key, then we need a better approach and tools for knowledge management.

Current due diligence, risk assessments, and risk monitoring processes typically examine the third parties' policies, practices, and senior management. Rarely, if ever, do any financial institutions evaluate the quality and expertise of the operations team, back office, and the third party's risk control personnel.

"When you look at high-level employees transitioning within a company, research indicates they feel they add value by about six months," says Michael Watkins, a professor of

---

[141] OCC (2017) Supplemental Examination Procedures for Risk Management of Third-Party Relationships [2013-29] https://www.occ.gov/publications/publications-by-type/comptrollers-handbook/pub-third-party-exam-supplemental-procedures.pdf

Leadership and Organizational Change at the IMD business school. "But if you're coming into a challenging job from outside the company, it may take a year."

Performance management consultant Dick Grote[142] agrees. "Onboarding time is a function of the job," he says, and the idea of a new employee hitting the ground running is a farce. Says Watkins, "Often the people who get the least attention are those making internal moves," but even those transitions "can be terribly challenging." [143]

This means that incumbents in key roles within each company will never have the time on the job necessary to acquire the depth and breadth necessary to fully understand the complexities of the critical activity, third-party relationship, and/or the mini-ecosystem they function within.

Thinking about current realities and current practices and their relative effectiveness could lead you to different approaches to onboarding and transferring "institutional" knowledge.

If you agree that the workforce has dramatically changed, and practices haven't kept pace…

And if you agree that each critical third-party relationship is important to the long-term health of your institution...

And if you agree that each critical third-party relationship is a micro culture, parts of which you will never see, such as the third party's back office and risk personnel…

And if you agree that collectively these increase the risk to your institution…

- Are you willing to change your management style?
- Can you change the way things are done?
- Would you do what it takes to reach that "critical mass" of employees needed to manage those critical third-party relationships over the long term?
- Can you prioritize change to deliver positive returns, in terms of employee engagement and better business outcomes?

Be a better leader. Stop complaining about lackluster employee engagement, high turnover, millennials, and boomers and take positive action. Identify every employee who demonstrates the ability or the potential to make a difference and make them part of your circle of "critical mass." Take the time to explain key decisions and rationale, from day one.

- Think about all the people responsible for critical third-party lifecycle and risk management within your span of control as a "critical mass."
- Consider how to increase the "mass." For example, consider if and how you could concentrate third-party relationship management within your group or an enterprise-level, purpose-built function. Some financial institutions have already taken this step and centralized the non-operational elements of risk assessments, risk monitoring, performance reporting, contract reviews, and financial and resource management. Specialized teams have the benefit of larger critical mass, reducing turnover risk. Like any function, they can be expected to create efficiencies and best practices over time.

---

142 Dick Grote, performance management consultant and author of How to Be Good at Performance Appraisals

143 Sara Stibitz, Harvard Business Review (May 2015): How to Get a New Employee Up to Speed https://hbr.org/2015/05/how-to-get-a-new-employee-up-to-speed

- Increasing "critical mass" may simply mean increasing the number of people in the first line of defense who play an active role. Problem solving and driving innovation could become common themes to build and maintain employee engagement.
- If you go this route, be specific about expectations for collaboration and information sharing within the "critical mass" for critical third-party relationship teams, holding them accountable for specific contributions and the quality of cooperation and collaboration.
- Each time a key player leaves, re-evaluate relationship risk for your most critical relationships. Theoretically your institution could be dealing with a "new" relationship, on an unpredictable rotation.
  - Determine who is key to operational, performance, and risk management; has critical knowledge or expertise; or is a key player—including those in risk management roles (e.g., third party's CISO, CTO, or subject matter experts).
  - Re-evaluate operational management and third-party risk exposure.
  - Develop action plan to address increased risks.

Develop contemporary ways to record and transfer process, technical, relationship, and institutional knowledge. Evolve your management style from capturing just the "what" to be done. Capture the "how" and "why." Process maps should be transformed into process, decision-making, and problem-solving guidance, complete with integrated questions and decisions points. Job shadowing and skills transfer should focus on these as well.

Conclusions:

Millennials are a rare, seminal generation. They've had a profound effect on work norms and the workforce at large. They've driven the change, and successfully influenced the same or similar changes among boomers and Gen Xers, including workforce composition, cultural norms, work habits, and communication. Your institution is dealing with these changes, as are your critical third parties.

A changed workforce means changes in practices, corporate culture, how work gets done, and how people learn.

New Strategies

Deliberate strategies will help you and your institution address changing needs, expectations, and challenges. Our recommendations should be treated as "a work in progress" but Krystelle, Cynthia, and I are pleased to have this opportunity to share what we have learned so far.

1. Accept that this is day-to-day reality and consciously supplement what you already know how to do with new ways of doing things. Seek to understand how business norms have changed, AND focus on what this means in the context of third-party lifecycle and relationship management. If you agree that employees' fundamental values haven't really changed but today's employees have changed the way you do business, take ownership of the relationship and the risks—don't leave them in the hands of others.
2. Create more opportunities for relationships between your folks and the third-party relationship/operations team to form, so they can mutually build trust. Trust between individuals

and across the critical mass within the relationship reduces risk, improves outcomes, and increases its value.

3. Create more critical mass by expanding the teams responsible for the critical third-party relationship.
4. Identify strategies to interact on a more personal level.
5. Make sure the teams are periodically face-to-face when trying to solve systemic issues or chasing innovation. In Krystelle's words, understanding "why is just as important as what."
6. Deliberately communicate a broad problem statement that provides an opportunity to reframe the issue. (See the space pencil example.) Shared experiences, solving problems, and finding new solutions will strengthen the relationship and create opportunities to improve operations or reduce costs (innovation, productivity, quality). Throughout their post-secondary education, millennials acquired problem-solving and critical thinking skills. You may wish to leverage them to help frame problem statements. And you also may find that they have developed many skills that are necessary to successfully innovate.
7. Be purposeful about engaging the whole relationship team at the social/work level.
8. People, process, knowledge: A three-pronged strategy is the best approach to mitigating third-party risk.
   - Extensive research by behavioral scientists confirms that "work experiences
     (a) indicating that the organization treats its employees favorably and
     (b) enhancing employees' sense of personal importance and competence are very likely to induce an emotional attachment to the organization."[144]
   - "Focus on the individual. Managing a multigenerational workforce entails seeing people as individuals, not generational stereotypes."[145]
   - Be careful what you wish for. Higher levels of employee engagement may not generate the rewards you're expecting. Being engaged does not necessarily translate into productivity. Be intentional when setting goals.
9. Remember that one size never fits all.
10. Subject matter experts with extensive depth and breadth retire or change roles. Similar changes take place within the third party's operations. This gives rise to concerns about retention of institutional knowledge for the benefit of our customers, the relationship, and the company.

Over time, status meetings with the third party's relationship management team are often replaced by frequent "issue specific" texts that can be decisioned and responded to quickly.

Bite-sized communication becomes more and more efficient, and broader communication less and less common. Operational efficiency benefits, but bite-sized communication presents contextual risk. Texts also presents few opportunities to build knowledge and no opportunities to explore a larger conversation.

---

[144]US National Library of Medicine, National Institutes of Health: Employees' Organizational Identification and Affective Organizational Commitment: An Integrative Approach (2015) https://www.ncbi.nlm.nih.gov/pmc/articles/PMC4395289/

[145]IBM Institute for Business Value: Myths, Exaggerations, and Uncomfortable truths – The Real Story of Millennials in the Workplace (2015) https://public.dhe.ibm.com/common/ssi/ecm/gb/en/gbe03637usen/GBE03637USEN.PDF

To address these risks, consider:

- Changing the content and focus of weekly status updates with direct reports. Instead of tactical reports about activities and results, focus on how they approached issue identification, analysis, and problem solving.
- Creating an accessible record and involving more people to build more critical mass of people who spend time on in-depth discussions and problem solving. This increases collaboration and builds institutional knowledge. It also strengthens operational resilience, thereby reducing risk.
- Allocating budget dollars for quarterly offsite meetings between the internal team, critical mass relationship managers, and those from the critical third party. Dedicate the first half of the day to business, the second half to play. The intent is to strengthen communication and the overall relationship, both in the business meeting and by creating memorable shared experiences.

11. Learn new ways of doing old (tactical) things:
    - Lack of flexibility in job grades and titles can demotivate employees interested in rapid career progression and varied experiences.
    - By establishing a job band across several job grades, you can promote individuals within their current role, giving them more responsibility and authority.
    - Another way to do this is to have more than one title for the same role. You can recognize individuals by promoting their title, not their job grade.
12. Learn new ways of doing old (strategic) things:
    - Periodically take the combined team offsite to solve "hairy problems," leveraging tools like Blue Ocean Strategy,[146] developed by preeminent management thinkers Chan Kim and Renée Mauborgne. According to its authors, "Blue Ocean Strategy challenges everything you thought you knew about strategic success and provides a systematic approach to making the competition irrelevant." Once everyone learns how to use tools like this one, the tools can become a reusable approach to problem solving and the foundation for shared experiences.
    - Create a different type of critical mass by introducing enterprise-level Tiger Teams responsible for higher level third-party lifecycle and relationship management. Tiger Teams are a Six Sigma tool. In the case of third-party management, Tiger Teams would not be involved in day-to-day operations, but would develop and bring transferable skills in relationship management or lead teams in problem solving.

      Tiger Teams have been described as "groups of experts who investigate and solve technical or systemic problems in an organization. These professionals possess certain skills and qualities that make them capable of performing the duties assigned to them. With their qualifications, they can be considered technical specialists who can track possible sources of problems or failures.

146Professors W. Chan Kim and Renée Mauborgne; Blue Ocean Strategy https://www.blueoceanstrategy.com/global-institutes/

"In an organization, specialized groups like Tiger Teams are required for certain tasks or projects. They are often tasked to help with projects or on process improvements. Vital projects of this kind should only be executed by individuals with the right capabilities. For this reason, organizations train and grow their own pool of talents that can perform duties effortlessly and efficiently." [147]

- Invest in new techniques in meta learning like story boarding and institutional storytelling. Visual and audio recordings can be short, and are accessible and easy to consume. They can be used to explain the decisions we made and how we got there—and to capture institutional knowledge or link problem solving with current operations and outcomes.
- Increase employee engagement by seeking to build understanding between co-workers and across generations. Invest in opportunities to increase emotional intelligence in your team, which leads to greater self-awareness and empathy.

These tactics, techniques, and strategies take time to learn, and time to execute. This also means that that you'll need to invest in yourself to become a better leader. The good news is that you can count on a good return on investment: better business outcomes, better personal performance, and better professional relationships.

[147]Aveta Business Institute Six Sigma Online: The Importance of Six Sigma Tools: Tiger Teams http://www.sixsigmaonline.org/six-sigma-training-certification-information/the-importance-of-six-sigma-tools-tiger-teams/

12

Risk Oversight and Governance

The Federal Reserve Board defines operational risk as "the risk resulting from inadequate or failed internal processes, people, and systems or from external events,"[148] a definition that conforms with the Basel Committee on Banking Supervision. Third parties are an important source of operational risk if they employ inadequate or failed processes or engage in questionable activities, thereby compounding risks to institutions from external events. It stands to reason that specific governance structures, practices, and protocols should be implemented for critical third-party relationships due to incremental operational risk.

Governance over third-party processes, systems, and activities is different than governance over internal operations because control is arm's length—and greater than arm's length for material subcontractors, commonly referred to as fourth parties. This significant difference in an institution's ability to implement controls should be reflected in third-party management governance principles and practices.

A source of guidance is *Principles for Sound Management of Operational Risk* (2011),[149] published and maintained by the Basel Committee. The principles are universal in describing the responsibilities of the board of directors and senior management for ensuring a strong operational risk management culture, framework, governance structure, policies, processes, and systems that must come together to govern all activities in alignment with an institution's risk appetite and tolerances.

Risk Governance Structure

According to the Federal Financial Institutions Examination Council (FFIEC), "The governance structure specifies the responsibilities for the board of directors, managers, auditors, and other stakeholders and specifies the level of authority and accountability for decision making. Governance also includes mechanisms for monitoring actions and decisions enterprise-wide."[150]

---

[148] FRB Supervisory Letter 1611a1: Supervisory Guidance for Assessing Risk Management at Supervised Institutions with Total Consolidated Assets Less than $50 Billion https://www.federalreserve.gov/supervisionreg/srletters/sr1611a1.pdf

[149] Basel Committee on Banking Supervision (Bank for International Settlements): Principles for Sound Management of Operational Risk (2011) http://www.bis.org/publ/bcbs195.pdf

[150] FFIEC IT Examination Handbook Infobase http://ithandbook.ffiec.gov/it-booklets/management/i-governance.aspx

Risk Governance Structure

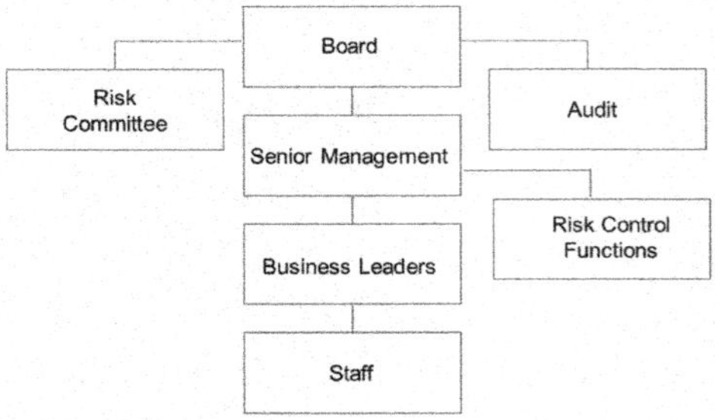

©2018 Linda Tuck Chapman

Two stakeholder groups are responsible for driving effective risk governance into and throughout the institution: the board and senior management. The Federal Reserve succinctly describes their responsibilities relating to risk governance:

- The "**board of directors** has the responsibility for establishing the level of risk that the institution should take.
- **Senior management** is responsible for implementing strategies set by the board of directors in a manner that controls risks and that complies with laws, rules, regulations, or other supervisory requirements on both a long-term and day-to-day basis. Senior management develops and implements the institution's risk management policies and procedures that address the types of risks arising from its activities."[151]

In its *Principles*, Basel says "sound internal governance forms the foundation of an effective operational risk management framework. Although internal governance issues related to the management of operational risk are not unlike those encountered in the management of credit or market risk, operational risk management challenges may differ from those in other risk areas."[152]

Like all operational risk control functions within a financial institution, third-party risk governance is a third tier in the institution's hierarchy of risk frameworks and governance:

Risk Framework Hierarchy

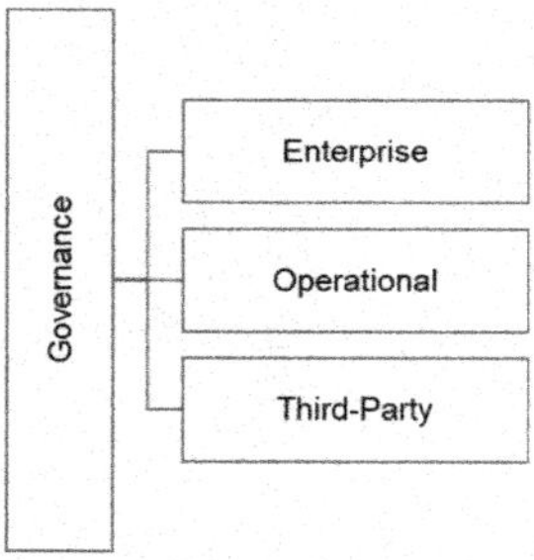

©2018 Linda Tuck Chapman

[151]FRB Supervisory Letter 1611a1: Supervisory Guidance for Assessing Risk Management at Supervised Institutions with Total Consolidated Assets Less than $50 Billion https://www.federalreserve.gov/supervisionreg/srletters/sr1611a1.pdf

[152]Basel Committee on Banking Supervision (Bank for International Settlements): Principles for Sound Management of Operational Risk (2011) http://www.bis.org/publ/bcbs195.pdf

Implementation

Per the Federal Reserve, a "sound risk management system" includes:

- Board and senior management oversight (including the equivalent governing body of the U.S. operations of foreign banking organizations).
- Policies, procedures, and limits.
- Risk monitoring and management information systems.
- Internal controls.[153]

"Once the risks are properly identified, the institution's policies and procedures should provide guidance for the day-to-day implementation of business strategies, including limits designed to prevent excessive and imprudent risks."[154]

The second line of defense, an institution's risk control specialists, are charged with developing third-party risk policies and procedures within their area of expertise. They must align their policies and procedures with the enterprise risk framework, risk appetite and tolerances, and other risk-related policies and procedures. An essential element in risk governance is consistent risk taxonomy. This improves context and comprehension, aiding adoption and consistent execution.

Both the first and second line of defense are responsible for execution of various elements of third-party lifecycle and risk management, according to their role and within the parameters of approved policies and procedures. Responsibilities and accountabilities are easily communicated by a RACI (responsible, accountable, consulted, and informed) or RASCI (responsible, accountable, supportive, consulted, and informed) chart.

Risk Monitoring

The OCC says its examination procedures "evaluate separately the quantity of risk and the quality of risk management. The quantity of risk reflects the level of risk assumed in the course of doing business. The quality of risk management assesses whether the bank's risk management systems are capable of identifying, measuring, monitoring and controlling that amount of risk."[155]

The most senior levels—the board, senior management, and group heads—must ensure critical third-party activities and relationships are proactively managed and there are actionable processes and systems in place that provide visibility into all material third-party risks, including concentrations and instances where risk exceeds the institution's risk appetite tolerances. This is what enables appropriate monitoring of an institution's exposure to risk, material loss exposure, and risk events.

---

[153]FRB Supervisory Letter 1611a1: Supervisory Guidance for Assessing Risk Management at Supervised Institutions with Total Consolidated Assets Less than $50 Billion https://www.federalreserve.gov/supervisionreg/srletters/sr1611a1.pdf

[154]Ibid.

[155]OCC Bulletin 2015-48 Risk Assessment System (RAS) https://www.occ.treas.gov/news-issuances/bulletins/2015/bulletin-2015-48.html

What You Should Know

"Governance" is an over-used term, and is frequently used interchangeably with "management." The FFIEC makes the term "governance" clear in its guidance: "**Governance refers to how financial institutions manage and control their institution.** Governance provides the structure through which an institution sets and pursues objectives while taking into account the regulatory and market environment and culture of the institution."[156]

Reinforcing concepts found in the chapter on risk culture, governance of third-party risk needs to conform with accepted doctrines that underpin the fiduciary responsibility for safety and soundness in financial institutions, specifically:

- "The board's and management's authority and responsibilities for governing operations and risks.
- Comprehensive, integrated enterprise risk management.
- An enterprise-wide risk governance framework as a means to manage risks.
- Risk culture and risk appetite.
- Risk management systems, including the three lines of defense."[157]

Ideally, says Basel, "Banks should have a strong control environment that utilizes policies, processes and systems; appropriate internal controls; and appropriate risk mitigation and/or transfer strategies."[158]

Financial institutions have a long history of building strong control environments and appropriate risk mitigation strategies. The pace and extent of outsourcing and building other complex third-party relationships is on the rise. This means an increase in the transfer of operational execution to third parties. In doing so, financial institutions attempt to transfer operational risk. This strategy will have limited success because customers, regulators, and lawmakers hold the financial institution accountable. Third-party and operational risk flows back to the institution. History demonstrates that it is not possible to transfer or outsource accountability.

"*Big G*" and "*small g*" Governance

Unquestionably, everyone in a financial institution bears some responsibility for risk oversight and governance. "Big G" risk governance is the domain of senior management and the board, who appropriately delegate activities and management responsibilities—"small g" risk governance is the responsibility of everyone else.

"Big G" risk governance—big picture, strategic risk governance—is the responsibility of:

- **The board,** for prudent stewardship and general oversight; and
- **Senior management,** for implementing the board's decisions, approving required resources, and ensuring controls effectiveness and day-to-day operational and risk oversight.

[156]FFIEC IT Examination Handbook Infobase http://ithandbook.ffiec.gov/it-booklets/management/i-governance.aspx

[157]Source: OCC: Comptroller's Handbook M-CRG (Safety and Soundness) Corporate and Risk Governance (Jul 2016) https://www.occ.treas.gov/publications/publications-by-type/comptrollers-handbook/pub-ch-crg.pdf

[158]Basel Committee on Banking Supervision (Bank for International Settlements): Principles for Sound Management of Operational Risk (2011) http://www.bis.org/publ/bcbs195.pdf

"Big G" risk governance shouldn't be confused with center-led risk management activities like program development of the framework, policies and processes for third-party risk and lifecycle management, and execution of related activities and tasks. These are management activities and tasks, delegated by the board and senior management.

"Small g" governance entails design, management, and execution of approved risk management strategies and controls. This is the responsibility of:

- **Risk functions and risk committees,** for defining risk appetite and measuring risk alignment;
- **Business leaders** in the first line of defense, for risk alignment and operational and third-party risk management in their business; and
- **Risk specialist functions** such as finance, legal, compliance, human resources, risk officers in the first and second lines of defense, and risk specialist functions in the second line of defense for defining third-party management strategies, processes and tools, and supporting execution as appropriate.
- **Internal audit** is an independent governance function, responsible for "bringing a systematic, disciplined approach to evaluate and improve the effectiveness of risk management, control, and governance processes."[159]

Each of these domains designs programs and practices; issues policies and procedures; leads execution; facilitates decisions regarding exceptions; provides training and education; and oversees resolution of issues, exceptions, and incidents. Collectively, they are responsible for operational management and risk oversight for internal and external delivery systems and the third parties that support the institution. Ideally, they also determine how to optimize this complex ecosystem, aligning it with the institution and business segment's risk appetite.

To generate actionable risk-related insight and information, financial institutions must invest in capable people, flexible information systems, thoughtful risk management processes, tools, communication, and training.

To effectively perform management and oversight responsibilities, business leaders, risk control functions, senior management, and the board of directors are highly reliant on receiving timely, consolidated, and discrete information about relevant and emerging third-party strategies, risks, costs, and performance. The keystone holding together the institution's third-party risk management structure is its risk appetite and tolerance.

Risk Appetite and Risk Tolerance

The Basel Committee says, "The board of directors should approve and review a risk appetite and tolerance statement for operational risk that articulates the nature, types, and levels of operational risk that the bank is willing to assume."[160] Easy to say, hard to do.

Capabilities for articulating an institution's risk appetite for operational risk are still somewhat immature, particularly in comparison with finely tuned risk appetite state-

[159]Institute of Internal Auditors. Definition of Internal Auditing http://www.theiia.org/guidance/standards-and-guidance/ippf/definition-of-internal-auditing/?search%C2%BCdefinition

[160]Basel Committee on Banking Supervision (Bank for International Settlements): Principles for Sound Management of Operational Risk (2011) http://www.bis.org/publ/bcbs195.pdf

ments for credit and market risk. At the next level, defining third-party risk appetite at a detailed level for the nature, types, and levels of acceptable risk for the institution and its many business segments is "aspirational."

The immaturity of third-party risk management practices and a steep learning curve for defining risk appetite for third-party relationships are likely root causes for the misalignment between resource allocation and workload, and commensurate benefits from effective third-party risk management.

"Enterprise critical" third-party relationships, those that would have a catastrophic impact on the institution if they fail or falter badly, are managed at the individual-relationship level in all institutions. Risk assessments, management, and monitoring processes continue to evolve, but are rarely consistent today.

Third-party relationships are rarely managed as portfolios, and are therefore not currently benefitting from the insight that portfolio management can deliver at the enterprise and business segment level. Leveraging what we have learned from mature credit and market risk management practices, you may agree that with easy access to information and historical data, third-party risk can be managed today at the relationship level for those critical third-party relationships that present the most significant risk exposure.

Over time, institutions should be able to cluster all third-party relationships into portfolios and manage the portfolios accordingly, dealing with problematic relationships on an exception basis.

In response to tough regulatory expectations, institutions expend tremendous effort on 100% compliance with due diligence, risk controls, and risk monitoring requirements and are therefore left without defensible checks and balances during regulatory exams and internal audits. Any deficiency between approved processes and execution is determined to be cause for concern, which ignores the concept of risk tolerances and a portfolio of third-party risks that collectively may be within the appetite of the business segment and enterprise.

There may be a limited return for pursuing or addressing all control deficiencies. It may be that the risks presented by a third party are acceptable in the context of business segment or the institution's risk appetite. Perhaps addressing or closing specific deficiencies will bring the third-party relationship into alignment.

Third-party risk oversight is facilitated by the visibility and insight afforded by:

"Small g" Risk Governance

"Small g" governance is the responsibility of third-party relationship managers, execution and support functions, and front-line staff. Their responsibilities may be more accurately described as responsibility for management, and accountability for "if you see something, say something."

"The board of directors and senior management should establish a corporate culture that is guided by strong risk management," Basel's *Principles for Sound Management of Operational Risk* say. "Clear expectations and accountabilities ensure that bank staff understand their roles and responsibilities for risk, as well as their authority to act."[161]

Tactical execution of effective risk governance is more complex than it sounds.

---

[161]Basel Committee on Banking Supervision (Bank for International Settlements): Principles for Sound Management of Operational Risk (2011) http://www.bis.org/publ/bcbs195.pdf

Risk Oversight

Depending on the size and complexity of your financial institution, information about third-party risks may be communicated to the board or a committee of the board after being presented to and screened by successive risk oversight committees. In larger institutions, third-party risk reports may be presented by the operational risk committee as a component of a summary report on all operational risks across the enterprise. In some institutions, the head of third-party risk may present this information directly to the board.

Regardless of who presents to the board, financial institutions typically have multiple layers of risk committees according to their size, complexity, and structure.

For example, in a large, systemically important financial institution (SIFI), third-party risk reports are presented to 14 risk committees before reaching the parent company board, with reporting frequency to these committees varying from monthly to annually.

What Your Institution Should Do

People, Processes, and Tools

Complex outsourcing relationships have long been recognized as one type of critical third-party relationships that requires a defined management structure and stakeholders' responsibilities. Taken from the website of ISACA,[162] an independent, non-profit association formed to develop and encourage adoption of industry-leading knowledge and practices for information systems, this diagram illustrates some of the complexities of outsourcing contract governance from an operational lens in the first line of defense.

Despite depicting many stakeholders performing a wide range of activities, it does not include risk specialists or governance stakeholders.

Figure 1—Outsourcing Governance Stakeholders

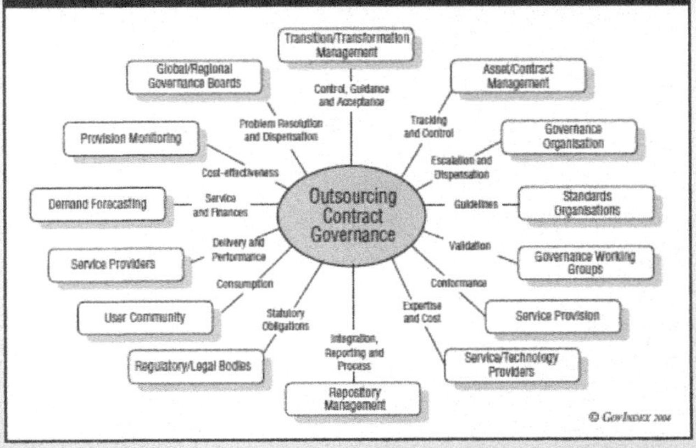

Source: ISACA.org IT Governance Institute: IT Governance Domain Practices and Competencies / Governance of Outsourcing http://www.isaca.org/Knowledge-Center/Research/Documents/Governance-of-Outsourcing_res_Eng_0105.pdf

---

162ISACA.org IT Governance Institute: IT Governance Domain Practices and Competencies / Governance of Outsourcing http://www.isaca.org/Knowledge-Center/Research/Documents/Governance-of-Outsourcing_res_Eng_0105.pdf

Note: The previous image is titled "Outsourcing *Governance* Stakeholders." But based on risk management taxonomy in common use by regulators in the financial services sector, this image describes "Outsourcing *Management* Stakeholders."

There are many stakeholders involved in managing and governing complex, critical third-party relationships. These many stakeholders in the business, the first line of defense, in risk control functions, the second line of defense, and in senior management governance roles need to know what they are accountable for. The path to success is making the right investments in the right people, processes, and tools for the job.

Selecting the right people for third-party lifecycle and risk management is a challenge. Few, if any, reliable benchmarks exist that describe optimal management and technical competencies, personal attributes, and cognitive skills to guide the selection process. Compounding the challenge of "getting the right people on the bus" is the universal, rapidly accelerating turnover in executive and employee ranks. This challenge is discussed in the chapter "Relationship Management in the Age of Millennials."

But developing the right frameworks and tools is getting easier because of a growing record of successful practices for effective third-party lifecycle and risk management. There are also a wide range of proven tools and frameworks that are transferable and can be leveraged here. Many of these are included in this book. For example, the COSO framework illustrated below can be leveraged for development and evolution of your institution's third-party program, processes, and activities.

Source: COSO.org Leveraging COSO Across the Three Lines of Defense https://www.coso.org/Documents/COSO-2015-3LOD.pdf

Risk Taxonomy

Making sense of risk management policies and processes is made easier by implementing a common risk taxonomy across the enterprise. According to the Treasury Board of Canada, "A risk taxonomy is a comprehensive, common, and stable set of risk categories that is used within an organization.

- By providing a *comprehensive* set of risk categories, it encourages those involved in **risk identification** to consider all types of risks that could affect the organization's objectives.

- By providing a *common* set of risk categories, it facilitates the **aggregation of risks** from across the organization.
- By providing a *stable* set of risk categories, it facilitates **comparative analysis** of an organization's risks **over time**."[163]

People are busy, so making it easier to deliver on their accountabilities improves adoption and compliance. Disorganized risk taxonomy makes it hard for users to comprehend risk.

One financial institution, before standardizing third-party risk management across the enterprise, had each business segment implement its own version of third-party risk tiering. The number of tiers ranged from three to seven, each with a different definition of what the risk tiers meant. User confusion was exacerbated by different risk taxonomy deployed by risk specialist functions. Before standardization across the enterprise, users needed a Rosetta Stone to figure it out!

Adoption starts with comprehension. Effective third-party governance simply can't happen with inconsistent adoption and execution.

Lifecycle and Governance Frameworks

A simple but complete target operating model makes it easy for users and those in governance roles to understand what needs to be done, and where they fit. A third-party lifecycle management framework has two components. One is the operating model that depicts key activities throughout the lifecycle of the third-party relationship, and how those activities relate to the operational and enterprise risk management frameworks.

The second component is the third-party governance framework. This framework depicts the risk management hierarchy, policies, processes, and tools supporting third-party management activities.

More information can be found in the lifecycle management chapter.

Policies and Procedures

Senior management should oversee translation of the approved operational risk management framework into specific policies and procedures for third-party management. These are implemented across the institution, and are subject to governance activities and internal audit.

Policies should be prescriptive only when required. Making policies unnecessarily detailed or onerous doesn't allow for acceptable variations in practices, interferes with proven practices within the first line of defense, and practically guarantees many unsatisfactory audits and regulatory exams.

Senior management should ensure that authority, responsibility, and reporting relationships are clear, maintain accountability, and ensure that sufficient resources and information are available to maintain third-party risks within the bank's risk appetite and tolerance.

---

[163]Government of Canada/Treasury Board: Guide to Risk Taxonomies https://www.canada.ca/en/treasury-board-secretariat/corporate/risk-management/taxonomies.html

Risk Assessments

Risk assessments are conducted at the third-party, engagement, and risk function levels. They should be designed to determine inherent risk (risks in the absence of controls) and residual risks (exposure to specific and systemic third-party risks that have not been satisfactorily addressed by controls or compensating controls).

In the absence of reasonable risk-related information, there is no assurance that management and governance activities are targeted at the right things.

Due Diligence

Due diligence is not a governance activity, but findings should generate actionable insight and information that enables effective governance.

Risk Rating/Tiering

Risk ratings align third-party relationships with predetermined tiers of risk. Risk ratings and tiers allow your institution, business segments, and risk specialist functions to cluster third-party relationships and risk exposure into portfolios by their risk tier and more granular risk ratings (e.g., by risk control function, by financial viability, by compliance with "mandatory" contract terms, etc.)

Portfolio management can be an efficient and effective way to ensure third-party lifecycle management is risk centric and risk adjusted, and enable effective governance over a large population of critical, complex relationships.

Controls

Risk controls contribute to effective governance. Typically, partially ineffective controls and serious controls deficiencies for critical third-party relationships are subject to independent challenge and require higher approval levels, senior-level risk reporting, and/or are escalated to senior management when serious issues and incidents occur.

Information Systems

Incomplete, inaccurate, or inaccessible information translates into ineffective governance. Manual processes, home-grown systems, and static databases ensure your people are consumed by low-value activities.

Meanwhile, structured, consistent processes and tools; configured workflow; automated notifications and escalations; and an auditable repository are the foundation for a reliable "source of truth" that is needed for effective governance.

Independent Challenge

Senior management is responsible for establishing the culture, delegating authority, and appropriate actions that enable an effective independent challenge process. When individuals don't feel empowered or unresolved challenges go unanswered by senior management, an important governance tool is lost.

Quality Control and Quality Assurance

Quality control is the responsibility of the first line of defense. Quality assurance is the responsibility of the second line of defense, and is typically conducted by the team responsible for driving execution or providing oversight for the third-party risk management program. These are important "small g" activities that enable "Big G" governance activities.

Training

Third-party risk management policies and procedures are usually communicated through a combination of classroom and/or online training and education, and subject to annual compliance attestation and/or training. Third-party risk management specialists can provide support to the first line of defense in execution of their duties, increasing the probability of successful third-party lifecycle and risk management, and clean regulatory exams and audits.

Everyone involved in third-party lifecycle and risk management needs to have the right prerequisite experience, relevant technical capabilities, and access to effective tools and sufficient resources. Training should reflect the seniority, roles, and responsibilities of the individuals.

Senior management enables training with investments, and the institution must keep records of all stakeholders that have completed required training. Training is usually conducted when individuals take on specific roles or responsibilities, and annually. In some cases, stakeholders may include third-party employees who are required to complete specific compliance training, according to specific regulatory requirements and/or in specific jurisdictions.

Communication

Don't leave communication to chance. Change management experts will tell you that underinvesting in communication, particularly during periods of rapid change, is a false economy. Suffice it to say that people are busy, and third-party lifecycle management isn't likely their primary responsibility. Once is not enough. Maybe 20 times is not enough.

Embedding expectations into performance criteria and compensation reinforces messages, in a very tangible way.

Reporting and Trend Analysis

Getting the right information at the right time is the lifeblood of effective governance. Looking back to OCEG's "Future State" model, reporting and trend analysis is where it all comes together for senior management.

Third-Party Governance Committee

The pace and complexity of business, and massive volumes of information, get in the way of effective governance. An empowered, senior-level third-party governance committee with a wide mix of expertise and experience and delegated authority can greatly improve third-party governance.

Over time, building broad-based institutional knowledge about your institution's critical third parties, involvement in exception and issue management, mediating challenges, and filtering the information to ensure what goes to senior management is appropriate will improve the efficiency and effectiveness of third-party governance.

13

Final Words

Greg Carmichael, president and CEO, Fifth Third Bank[164] cautions that the years of "go-go growth at any cost are well behind us." In his words, "Senior leadership needs to have a mindset of being strong through every cycle—strong in good times, and strong under adverse economic conditions."

Take a long-term view of the opportunities and impact that critical third-party relationships present throughout their lifecycle. This can make the difference between whether your company is intentional about why, what, when, who, and how to drive best value for money, protect your reputation, and improve the customer experience—or whether you're simply complying with regulatory guidance and laws.

Krystelle Bilodeau, a senior business line leader at a systemically important financial institution, reminds us that "an organization's reputation is as individual as a thumbprint. A serious event that results in widespread damage to its reputation could be classified as a direct affront to the institution's explicit and implicit values. It is of utmost importance that you have a clear understanding of the potential sources, levels, and impact of risk events."

Recently I've been asked by both financial institutions and third parties whether, in my professional opinion, third-party risk management regulatory guidance will be rolled back. It seems unlikely because third-party management capabilities are assessed as part of financial institutions' safety and soundness exam, an essential element of the "M"—management capabilities—in their CAMELS rating. More likely to change are the criteria used to determine which institutions are subject to "heightened expectations." Another possibility is there will be changes in expectations regarding how regulatory guidance is applied in community banks.

Regardless of regulatory guidance, it is up to each financial institution to determine its goals and intentions for third-party management. The best-run companies constantly look for opportunities to be the best they can be at the things that really count. Does your institution believe that third-party management is something that really counts?

164Fifth Third Bank is a U.S. "super-regional" bank, headquartered in Cincinnati, OH, with $142 billion in assets. Fifth Third provides commercial and retail banking, consumer lending, and wealth and asset management services through 1,191 branches. Fifth Third is a principal subsidiary of Fifth Third Bancorp. https://www.53.com

Mark Holladay, executive vice president and chief risk officer, Synovus,[165] says, "Just about everyone needs to know about third-party risk. Effective third-party management makes an important contribution to how the bank is managed. Without a strong third-party management program, you may be making decisions based on information that may not be appropriate for its intended purpose."

In June 2017 Synovus was named "Most Reputable Bank" in the U.S. in the annual Survey of Bank Reputations conducted by the Reputation Institute and published by *American Banker*. Synovus' overall score was the highest in survey history and nearly 10 points above the 2017 industry average.

"The most reputable banks in 2017 recognize that perceptions of good governance—inclusive of ethics, openness, honesty, and fairness—carry the most weight of importance," said Stephen Hahn-Griffiths, vice president and U.S. consulting director for the Reputation Institute.[166]

Being intentional means being thoughtful and taking time to determine whether your goal is simply to comply with regulatory guidance and laws or to transform third-party relationships into tangible assets that can make your company more competitive, more reliable, more transparent, and a better corporate citizen of the world.

Efficient, effective, risk-centric, and risk-adjusted third-party lifecycle and risk management is a new and distinct way of doing business. How your company approaches any major change like this one is up to senior leadership.

"Whether you think you can or you think you can't, you're right."

—*Henry Ford*

Senior management sets the strategic direction through tone at the top; how it communicates expectations; and how it describes purpose, goals, and expected results. Senior management controls the resources, and so decides when and how much to invest in people, tools, and technology. It also decides how much time it, the board, and governance bodies will invest in oversight and governance activities.

Senior management also needs to empower people to act, and to lend visible support to appropriate independent challenges and requirements for risk controls, management, and monitoring, while denying unfounded requests for exceptions to risk appetite and tolerance levels. Senior management needs to give people the authority they need to do their jobs.

Joyce Brocaglia, CEO of the Alta Associates[167] executive search firm specializing in information security, IT risk management, and privacy, says it well: "In a world of 'people, process, technology,' there's a reason why people come first."

Third parties need to up their game. Too many of them consider more rigorous risk controls and internal governance a client requirement, not a new way of doing business.

---

[165]Synovus Financial Corp is based in Columbus, Georgia, with approximately $31 billion in assets. Synovus provides commercial and retail banking, investment, and mortgage services through 248 branches. https://www.synovus.com/

[166]Reputation Institute https://www.reputationinstitute.com/us-banking-reptrak

[167]Alta Associates www.altaassociates.com

Worse, they simply don't understand what is needed to keep clients safe and secure and protect their reputation while doing it. "Larry's Laptop," a mini-case study that Mark Silver, vice president, Third-Party Risk, Whitney Bank, contributed to the chapter on information and cybersecurity, is a great example of ignorance on the part of the third party—ignorance to the point of negligence.

Fortunately, there are many third parties that "get it." Fintech Black Knight Financial Services[168] takes risk management as seriously as its financial services clients. Peter Hill, chief risk officer, says, "There is an old adage that is still very true: 'You can't outsource risk.' This is why vendor risk management is a mission-critical activity that must be effective in the identification and management of vendor risk and be adopted by every employee in the company." To those who say you can't outsource risk, Hill says, "Amen." Third-party lifecycle management means deliberately managing costs, proactively driving best value for money, and data-driven performance management. It's also about receiving the quality and responsiveness you negotiated so hard for during contract negotiations, and nurturing innovation to get the very best from the relationship.

Effective third-party management is much more than a compliance program. It is about effectively managing a complex ecosystem of activities and inter-reliant relationships.

"Any road will get you there if you don't know where you're going."

—*Attributed to Lewis Carroll*

Linnea Solem, vice president and chief privacy officer, Deluxe Corp.,[169] knows that "the skill sets for monitoring and assessing third-party risk continue to evolve as our ecosystem and industry have changed. Stronger governance, a focus on regulatory compliance, and cyber risk have raised the bar from vendor management to vendor risk management."

Allison Sagraves, chief data officer at a large U.S. bank, observes, "A risk that is often not considered is the risk of loss of internal capabilities and internal knowledge when processes are outsourced. This can be mitigated by retaining some expertise onsite. You still own and are responsible for what is outsourced, so ensuring that knowledge remains in the company both through managing key-person risk and keeping proper documentation on procedures is vital."

Sagraves speaks from experience. "There is an art and science to effective relationship management," she says. "The best SLAs do not always tell the whole story; and even the most comprehensive terms and conditions do not cover potential reputational risk if service suffers."

---

[168]Black Knight Financial Services is the mortgage and finance industries' leading provider of integrated technology, data and analytics solutions that facilitate and automate many of the business processes across the entire loan lifecycle. www.bkfs.com

[169]Deluxe Corp., founded in 1915, provides website development and hosting, email marketing, social media, search engine optimization and logo design, in addition to industry-leading checks and forms www.deluxe.com

In institutions with mature third-party risk programs responsibility for risk management belongs to everyone. Deborah Manos-McHenry, senior vice president and chief sourcing officer at Huntington National Bank, says, "At Huntington, we all own risk. Once due diligence is complete and subject experts have assisted the business in assessing the controls environment of a supplier, the contract is routed for approval with controls-assessment ratings and deviations from critical clauses documented and captured in the contracts repository. Approvers include the business owner and the operations or IT function acting on their behalf."

Not only does your company need to sharpen its third-party lifecycle and risk management capabilities, it needs to constantly improve its risk management capabilities in a rapidly changing threat landscape. Charlie Miller, senior vice president, Shared Assessments Program[170] and a former financial services executive, observes, "Information risk has two faces. For consumers, it's all about privacy. For companies, it's all about information security."

Of particular concern to consumers, companies, regulators, and the legal community is the exponential increase in the number and severity of information security and privacy breaches, and the fallout from successful denial-of-service, malware, and ransomware attacks.

When it comes to critical third-party relationships, it's no longer "hire and forget." A chief risk officer for information technology at a government sponsored entity (GSE) recently noted, "Our chief risk officer and the board want more specific information and conversations about third-party risk." At that level, the discussion is not about compliance. It's about the relationship, concentration risk, performance, costs, and risks.

Critical activities and critical third parties aren't distinct and separate. Third parties are integral to the reliability, predictability, quality, timeliness, and accuracy of products, services, and records. They are also integral to reports on critical activities that deliver products and services to customers and employees—and information to shareholders and regulators. Third parties can have a profound impact on your company's reputation, profitability, and long-term health.

Your critical third parties can be managed as a portfolio of valuable assets. Alternatively, third-party lifecycle and risk management may simply be an expensive exercise in regulatory compliance.

It's up to you.

---

[170]Shared Assessments Program is a division of Sante Fe Group http://sharedassessments.org/about/

References

AML/BSA

1. FFIEC BSA/AML Examination Manual (January 2014) Expanded Examination Overview and Procedures for Consolidated and Other Types of BSA/AML Compliance Program Structures
2. UK Government: Illustration of a Third Party Payment https://www.gov.uk/government/uploads/system/uploads/attachment_data/file/372273/third-party-payments.pdf
3. FINTRAC: Guidance on the Risk-Based Approach to Combatting Money Laundering and Terrorist Financing (March 16, 2016) http://www.fintrac-canafe.gc.ca/publications/rba/rba-eng.asp#s4.1
4. FFIEC: Bank Secrecy Act/ Anti-Money Laundering Examination Manual (2014) https://www.ffiec.gov/bsa_aml_infobase/documents/bsa_aml_man_2014.pdf
5. FATF Guidance: Anti-Money Laundering and Terrorist Financing Measures and Financial Inclusion
6. http://www.fatfgafi.org/media/fatf/documents/reports/AML_CFT_Measures_and_Financial_Inclusion_2013.pdf
7. Office of Foreign Assets Control Sanctions List: https://www.treasury.gov/resource-center/sanctions/SDN-List/Pages/consolidated.aspx
8. IMF Staff Discussion Note (June 2016): The Withdrawal of Correspondent Banking Relationships: A Case for Policy Action https://www.imf.org/external/pubs/ft/sdn/2016/sdn1606.pdf
9. OSFI B-8 (Dec 2008) Deterring and Detecting Money Laundering and Terrorist Financing http://www.osfi-bsif.gc.ca/Eng/Docs/b8.pdf

Business Resilience

1. www.BCM-institute.org
2. Singapore Standards 540
3. BCI Institute: HorizonScan 2017 http://www.bcifiles.com/HorizonScan2017.pdf
4. http://ithandbook.ffiec.gov/ITBooklets/FFIEC_ITBooklet_OutsourcingTechnologyServices.pdf
5. http://ithandbook.ffiec.gov/it-booklets/business-continuity-planning/appendix-j-strengthening-the-resilience-of-outsourced-technology-services.aspx
6. https://ior-institute.org/public/100310RiskControlSelfAssessment.pdf
7. http://www.iso.org
8. https://www.occ.gov/news-issuances/bulletins/2013/bulletin-2013-29.html
9. www.cloudtweaks.com

10. MICRODIS: Integrated Health, Social and Economic Impacts of Extreme Events: Evidence, Methods and Tools Combined Literature Review (Social, Health and Economic Literature Reviews) RESEARCH INSTITUTE FOR MINDANAO CULTURE (RIMCU),XAVIER UNIVERSITY Prepared by Ramonnetto S. Gervacio Maria Teresa Sharon Linog,MD
11. Singapore Standards SS540
12. OCEG.org https://www.oceg.org/resources/business-impact-analysis-playbook/

Final Words

1. Lewis Carroll
2. Mark Holladay, EVP and CRO, Synovus
3. Synovus Financial Corp is based in Columbus, Georgia, with approximately $31 billion in assets. Synovus provides commercial and retail banking, investment, and mortgage services through 248 branches. https://www.synovus.com/
4. Reputation Institute https://www.reputationinstitute.com/us-banking-reptrak
5. Black Knight Financial Services is the mortgage and finance industries' leading provider of integrated technology, data and analytics solutions that facilitate and automate many of the business processes across the entire loan lifecycle. www.bkfs.com
6. Shared Assessments Program, a division of Sante Fe Group http://sharedassessments.org/about/
7. Deluxe Corp., founded in 1915, provides website development and hosting, e-mail marketing, social media, search engine optimization and logo design, in addition to industry-leading checks and forms offering www.deluxe.com
8. Freddie Mac http://www.freddiemac.com/

Governance

1. FRB Supervisory Letter 1611a1: Supervisory Guidance for Assessing Risk Management at Supervised Institutions with Total Consolidated Assets Less than $50 Billion https://www.federalreserve.gov/supervisionreg/srletters/sr1611a1.pdf
2. Institute of Internal Auditors. Definition of Internal Auditing http://www.theiia.org/guidance/standards-and-guidance/ippf/definition-of-internal-auditing/?-search%C2%BCdefinition
3. COSO.org Leveraging COSO Across the Three Lines of Defense https://www.coso.org/Documents/COSO-2015-3LOD.pdf
4. Basel Committee for Banking Supervision (Bank for International Settlements): Principles for Sound Management of Operational Risk (2011) http://www.bis.org/publ/bcbs195.pdf
5. FFIEC IT Examination Handbook Infobase http://ithandbook.ffiec.gov/it-booklets/management/i-governance.aspx
6. OCC Bulletin 2015-48 Risk Assessment System (RAS) https://www.occ.treas.gov/news-issuances/bulletins/2015/bulletin-2015-48.html
7. ISACA.org IT Governance Institute: IT Governance Domain Practices and Competencies / Governance of Outsourcing http://www.isaca.org/Knowledge-Center/Research/Documents/Governance-of-Outsourcing_res_Eng_0105.pdf
8. OCEG.org https://www.oceg.org/

9. Carole Switzer, President and CEO, OCEG
10. Government of Canada/Treasury Board: Guide to Risk Taxonomies https://www.canada.ca/en/treasury-board-secretariat/corporate/risk-management/taxonomies.html
11. OCEG: Best Practices for Tracking Third Party Risk https://www.oceg.org/

InfoSec, Cyber

1. https://www.coso.org
2. https://www.nist.gov
3. http://www-03.ibm.com/security/data-breach/
4. https://corporate.target.com/article/2014/04/updates-on-target-s-security-and-technology-enhanc
5. FFIEC information Technology Examination Handbook: Information Security 2016 https://www.ffiec.gov/press/PDF/FFIEC_IT_Handbook_Information_Security_Booklet.pdf
6. BCI Institute HorizonScan 2017 http://www.bcifiles.com/HorizonScan2017.pdf
7. NIST Special Publication 800-184 Guide for Cybersecurity Event Recovery http://nvlpubs.nist.gov/nistpubs/SpecialPublications/NIST.SP.800-184.pdf
8. COSO (Committee of Sponsoring Organizations of the Treadway Commission): COSO in the Cyber Age. January 2015 https://www.coso.org/documents/COSO%20in%20the%20Cyber%20Age_FULL_r11.pdf
9. National Institute of Standards and Technology (NIST), US Department of Commerce: NIST IR7298 Revision 2 Glossary of Key Information Security Terms
10. The Anatomy of the Target Data Breach http://www.zdnet.com/article/anatomy-of-the-target-data-breach-missed-opportunities-and-lessons-learned/
11. Ponemon Institute Research Report (sponsored by IBM) 2016 Cost of Data Breach Study: United States https://www.ibm.com/security/data-breach/
12. Ponemon Institute https://www.ponemon.org/
13. NIST Special Publication 800-183 Networks of 'Things' Computer Security http://nvlpubs.nist.gov/nistpubs/SpecialPublications/NIST.SP.800-183.pdf
14. Gramm-Leach-Bliley Act: Summary S-900 106th Congress https://www.congress.gov/bill/106th-congress/senate-bill/900
15. Office of the Privacy Commissioner of Canada https://www.priv.gc.ca/en/privacy-topics/privacy-laws-in-canada/02_05_d_15/
16. Harvard Business Review Analytics Department: Cloud Computing Comes of Age (sponsored by Oracle) https://www.oracle.com/webfolder/s/delivery_production/docs/FY15h1/doc16/HBR-Oracle-Report-webview.pdf
17. Executive Women's Forum http://www.ewf-usa.com/
18. Joyce Brocaglia, Alta Associates http://www.altaassociates.com/
19. Mark Silver, Hancock Whitney Bank https://www.hancockwhitney.com/

Insurance

1. Terrorist Risk Insurance: https://www.treasury.gov/resource-center/fin-mkts/Pages/program.aspx

Introduction: Third-Party Management: Asset Management or Compliance Exercise?

1. CGMA Tools: "Three Approaches to Valuing Intangible Assets" (Jan 2012) https://www.cgma.org/content/dam/cgma/resources/tools/downloadabledocuments/valuing-intangible-assets.pdf
2. FASB Summary of Statement 142 (2014) "Goodwill and Other Intangible Assets" http://www.fasb.org/summary/stsum142.shtml
3. OCC A-LPM (April 1998) Loan Portfolio Management Comptrollers Handbook https://www.occ.gov/publications/publications-by-type/comptrollers-handbook/lpm.pdf
4. Risk Management Association (RMA) www.rmahq.org
5. David Stanton, Enterprise Chief Risk Officer, TMX Group
6. EY: "Shifting Toward Maturity" 2016 Financial Services Third-Party Risk Management Survey http://www.ey.com/us/en/services/advisory/ey-2016-financial-services-shifting-toward-maturity

Lifecycle Management

1. FFIEC IT Examination Handbook InfoBase http://ithandbook.ffiec.gov/glossary/compensating-control.aspx
2. Institute of Operational Risk - Operational Risk Sound Practice Guidance - Risk Control Self Assessment (Mar 10) https://iorinstitute.org/public/100310RiskControlSelfAssessment.pdf
3. Institute on Governance http://iog.ca/defining-governance/
4. OCC - Supplemental Examination Procedures for Risk Management of Third-Party Relationships (Jan 17) https://www.occ.gov/publications/publications-by-type/comptrollers-handbook/pub-third-party-exam-supplemental-procedures.pdf
5. Peter Hill, Chief Risk Officer, Black Knight Financial Services
6. Black Knight Financial Services http://www.bkfs.com
7. Deborah Manos-McHenry, SVP and Chief Sourcing Officer, Huntington National Bank
8. Huntington National Bank www.huntington.com
9. The Sante Fe Group: Shared Assessments https://sharedassessments.org/
10. Catherine Allen, President & CEO, The Santa Fe Group & Shared Assessments
11. www.oceg.org

Millennials

1. PEW Research Center Report (2016): Millennials Overtake Baby Boomers as America's Largest Generation http://www.pewresearch.org/fact-tank/2016/04/25/millennials-overtake-baby-boomers/
2. OCC (2017) Supplemental Examination Procedures for Risk Management of Third-Party Relationships [2013-29] https://www.occ.gov/publications/publications-by-type/comptrollers-handbook/pub-third-party-exam-supplemental-procedures.pdf CNBC: Millennial Employees are a Lot More Loyal than their Job-hopping Stereotype (2017) http://www.cnbc.com/2017/05/10/90-of-millennials-will-stay-in-a-job-for-10-years-if-two-needs-met.html

3. PEW Research Center Report (2017) "Millennials Aren't Job-hopping Any Faster Than Generation X Did" http://www.pewresearch.org/fact-tank/2017/04/19/millennials-arent-job-hopping-any-faster-than-generation-x-did/ft_17-04-17_millennial-jobtenure/
4. Monthly Labor Review, Bureau of Labor Statistics, U.S . Department of Labor: "Occupational mobility and job tenure in 1983" https://www.bls.gov/opub/mlr/1984/10/art2full.pdf
5. US National Library of Medicine, National Institutes of Health: Employees' Organizational Identification and Affective Organizational Commitment: An Integrative Approach (2015) https://www.ncbi.nlm.nih.gov/pmc/articles/PMC4395289/
6. Williams, J.: Sloan Work and Family Encyclopedia (2004). Job Satisfaction and Organizational Commitment http://wfnetwork.bc.edu/encyclopedia_entry.php?id=244&area=academics
7. Josh Bersin, Forbes (Mar 2014): "Why Companies Fail To Engage Today's Workforce: The Overwhelmed Employee" https://www.forbes.com/sites/joshbersin/2014/03/15/why-companies-fail-to-engage-todays-workforce-the-overwhelmed-employee/#3bdd233d4726
8. Bersin by Deloitte: Global Human Capital Trends 2014 http://marketing.bersin.com/deloitte-global-human-capital-trends-2014.html
9. Ryan Fuller and Nina Shikalof, Harvard Business Review (2017) "Being Engaged at Work Is Not the Same as Being Productive" https://hbr.org/2017/02/being-engaged-at-work-is-not-the-same-as-being-productive
10. Sean Graber, Harvard Business Review (Dec 2015) "The Two Sides of Employee Engagement" https://hbr.org/2015/12/the-two-sides-of-employee-engagement?referral=03759&cm_vc=rr_item_page.bottom
11. U.S. Government Accountability Office – Contingent Workforce Size, Characteristics, Earnings and Benefits (April 2015) http://www.gao.gov/assets/670/669899.pdf
12. PEW Research Report: How Millennials Compare with Their Grandparents 50 Years Ago (2015) http://www.pewresearch.org/fact-tank/2015/03/19/how-millennials-compare-with-their-grandparents/ft_millennials-education_031715/
13. Bruce N.Pfau, Harvard Business Review (2016): What Do Millennials Really Want at Work – The Same Things as the Rest of Us Do https://hbr.org/2016/04/what-do-millennials-really-want-at-work
14. IBM Institute for Business Value: Myths, Exaggerations, and Uncomfortable Truths - The Real Story of Millennials in the Workplace (2015) https://public.dhe.ibm.com/common/ssi/ecm/gb/en/gbe03637usen/GBE03637USEN.PDF
15. Krystelle Bilodeau, Special Assistant to the COO, Bank of Canada
16. Harris Poll on behalf of CareerBuilder (2014): Nearly One-Third of Employers Expect Workers to Job-Hop http://www.careerbuilder.com/share/aboutus/pressreleasesdetail.aspx?sd=5%2F15%2F2014&id=pr824&ed=12%2F31%2F2014
17. Sara Stibitz, Harvard Business Review (May 2015): "How to Get a New Employee Up to Speed" https://hbr.org/2015/05/how-to-get-a-new-employee-up-to-speed
18. Dick Grote, performance management consultant and author of *How to Be Good at Performance Appraisals*
19. Michael Watkins, author of the bestselling book, *The First 90 Days*

20. Kevin McSpadden, Time Health (May 2015). You Now Have a Shorter Attention Span Than a Goldfish http://time.com/3858309/attention-spans-goldfish/
21. CHA USA.org Terrence F. Cahill, Ed.D., FACHE and Mona Sedrak, Ph.D.: Age-Related Conflicts: The Generational Divide (July – August 2011) https://www.chausa.org/publications/health-progress/article/july-august-2011/age-related-conflicts-the-generational-divide
22. Professors W. Chan Kim and Renée Mauborgne; Blue Ocean Strategy https://www.blueoceanstrategy.com/global-institutes/
23. Aveta Business Institute Six Sigma Online: The Importance of Six Sigma Tools: Tiger Teams http://www.sixsigmaonline.org/six-sigma-training-certification-information/the-importance-of-six-sigma-tools-tiger-teams/

Model Risk

1. Free Press, A Division of Simon & Schuster Inc. New York. Emanuel Derman. Models. Behaving. Badly 2011
2. The Nilson Report, October 2016; www.nilsonreport.com
3. FRB Guidance on Model Risk SR 11-7 https://www.federalreserve.gov/bankinforeg/srletters/sr1107.htm
4. Cathy O'Neil, Weapons of Math Destruction (2016). Penguin Random House UK pg 21
5. OCC 2012-12 Supervisory Guidance on Model Risk Management https://www.occ.treas.gov/news-issuances/bulletins/2011/bulletin-2011-12a.pdf
6. https://www.federalreserve.gov/bankinforeg/srletters/sr1519.htm
7. https://www.federalreserve.gov/bankinforeg/srletters/sr1518.htm
8. Hannah Christensen: Banking on Better Forecasts: The New Maths of Weather Prediction (January 2015) www.theguardian.com/science
9. Ashish Gupta, VP Model Risk Management, E*Trade Financial Corporation
10. E*Trade Financial Corporation www.etrade.com

Monitoring

1. RMA: Operational Risk Management http://www.rmahq.org/operational-risk/
2. OCC Bulletin 2013-29 Risk Management Guidance for Third Party Relationships https://www.occ.gov/news-issuances/bulletins/2013/bulletin-2013-29.html
3. FFIEC Outsourcing Technology Services (Jun 2004) http://ithandbook.ffiec.gov/IT-Booklets/FFIEC_ITBooklet_OutsourcingTechnologyServices.pdf
4. FRB Supervisory Letter SR 13-19 Guidance on Managing Outsourcing Risk https://www.federalreserve.gov/bankinforeg/srletters/sr1319a1.pdf
5. American Institute of Certified Public Accountants' Service Organization Control [SOC] report www.AICPA.org

Regulatory

1. FDIC Guidance for Managing Third Party Risk https://www.fdic.gov/news/news/financial/2008/fil08044a.html

2. SR 95-51 Federal Reserve Bank: SR 95-51: Rating the Adequacy of Risk Management Processes and Internal Controls at State Member Banks and Bank Holding Companies https://www.federalreserve.gov/boarddocs/srletters/1995/SR9551.htm

Reputation Risk

1. William J. Brown, Enforcement Specialist, Philadelphia FED: "Understanding Reputational Risk: Identify, Measure, and Mitigate the Risk" https://www.philadelphiafed.org/bank-resources/publications/src-insights/2007/fourth-quarter/q4si1_07)
2. Kathryn Dill, Forbes: America's 50 Most Trustworthy Financial Companies [2016] http://www.forbes.com/sites/kathryndill/2015/08/03/americas-50-most-trustworthy-financial-companies-2/#329376572c2c
3. Matt Eagan, CNN Money Oct 24, 2016: Wells Fargo's Reputation Is Tanking, Survey Finds http://money.cnn.com/2016/10/24/investing/wells-fargo-fake-accounts-angry-customers/
4. OSFI: Review of Reputation Risk Practices - Principles, Observations and Next Steps http://www.osfi-bsif.gc.ca/eng/fi-if/in-ai/Pages/rep_risk.aspx
5. WORLD ECONOMICS Vol. 13 • No. 3: The Impact of Reputation on Market Value pg. 64, 68 http://www.world-economics-journal.com
6. Deloitte 2014 Global Survey: Reputation@Risk https://www2.deloitte.com/content/dam/Deloitte/pl/Documents/Reports/pl_Reputation_Risk_survey_EN.pdf
7. Krystelle Bilodeau, Special Assistant to the COO, Bank of Canada

Technology Risk

1. FFIEC: Supervision of Third Party Service Providers (TSP) IT Examination Handbook Oct 2012 http://ithandbook.ffiec.gov/ITBooklets/FFIEC_ITBooklet_SupervisionofTechnologyServiceProviders(TSP).pdf
2. ASQ: Failure Mode Effects Analysis http://asq.org/learn-about-quality/process-analysis-tools/overview/fmea.html
3. OCC: Comptroller's Licensing Manual Draft Supplement - Evaluating Charter Applications From Financial Technology Companies (March 2017) https://www.occ.treas.gov/news-issuances/news-releases/2017/nr-occ-2017-31.html
4. EINSA: Cloud Computing Benefits, Risks and Recommendations for Information Security (Nov 2009) https://www.enisa.europa.eu/publications/cloud-computing-risk-assessment
5. https://www.forbes.com/sites/tomgroenfeldt/2014/06/26/some-banks-are-heading-to-the-cloud-more-are-planning-to/#51ab22ce58c9
6. FFIEC IT Examination Handbook Infobase http://ithandbook.ffiec.gov/glossary/cloud-computing.aspx
7. FFIEC Information Technology Examination Handbook Management (Nov 2015) http://ithandbook.ffiec.gov/media/210375/managementbooklet2015.pdf
8. Deutsche Bank website: Deutsche Bank Opens Innovation Lab in Silicon Valley (Apr 16) https://www.db.com/newsroom_news/2016/medien/deutsche-bank-opens-innovation-lab-in-silicon-valley-en-11531.htm
9. Cloud Security Alliance (CSA) https://cloudsecurityalliance.org/

10. PMI: https://www.pmi.org/pmbok-guide-standards
11. OCC - Recommendations and Decisions for Implementing a Responsible Innovation Framework (Oct 16) https://www.occ.gov/topics/responsible-innovation/comments/recommendations-decisions-for-implementing-a-responsible-innovation-framework.pdf
12. The Hyperledger Project https://www.hyperledger.org
13. Peter Hill, Chief Risk Officer, Black Knight Financial Services
14. Black Knight Financial Services http://www.bkfs.com
15. Allison Sagraves, Chief Data Security Officer, large U.S. bank

Tone at the Top

1. The Economist (May 2017) http://www.economist.com/news/finance-and-economics/21602273-federal-reserve-contemplates-sliding-scale-bureaucracy-banks-too-small
2. FFIEC Press Release (March 2017) Banking Agencies Issue Joint Report to Congress Under the Economic Growth and Regulatory Paperwork Reduction Act of 1996 https://www.ffiec.gov/press/pr032117.htm
3. OCC: Corporate Governance and the Community Bank: A Regulatory Perspective (Jun 2005) https://www.occ.gov/static/past-conferences-and-seminars/cgts-final-exec-summary.pdf
4. American Accounting Association: Behavioral Research in Accounting http://www.aaajournals.org/loi/bria
5. SEC Enforcement Actions: FCPA Cases https://www.sec.gov/spotlight/fcpa/fcpa-cases.shtml
6. SEC Press Release: SEC Charges Software Company With FCPA Violations (Feb 16) https://www.sec.gov/news/pressrelease/2016-17.html
7. IIA Position Paper on the Three Lines Of Defense in Effective Risk Management and Control (Jan 2013) https://na.theiia.org/standards-guidance/Public%20Documents/PP%20The%20Three%20Lines%20of%20Defense%20in%20Effective%20Risk%20Management%20and%20Control.pdf
8. Financial report of the Consumer Financial Protection Bureau Fiscal Year 2015 http://files.consumerfinance.gov/f/201511_cfpb_report_fiscal-year-2015.pdf
9. OSFI Operational Risk Management Guideline E-21: Sound Business and Financial Practices (Jun 2016) http://www.osfi-bsif.gc.ca/Eng/fi-if/rg-ro/gdn-ort/gl-ld/Pages/e21.aspx
10. RMA: Operational Risk Management Framework http://www.rmahq.org/operational-risk-management-framework/
11. RMA: Enterprise Risk Management file:///C:/Users/New%20Desktop/Downloads/ERM-Framework-poster-042015.pdf
12. Standard & Poor's Ratings Direct: Evaluating The Enterprise Risk Management Practices of Insurance Companies file:///C:/Users/New%20Desktop/Downloads/insurancecriteria.pdf
13. FRB Supervisory Letter SR 13-19 Guidance on Managing Outsourcing Risk https://www.federalreserve.gov/bankinforeg/srletters/sr1319a1.pdf

14. OCC Bulletin 2013-29 Risk Management Guidance for Third Party Relationships https://www.occ.gov/news-issuances/bulletins/2013/bulletin-2013-29.html
15. OCC: Supplemental Examination Procedures for Risk Management of Third-Party Relationships (Jan 2017) https://www.occ.gov/publications/publications-by-type/comptrollers-handbook/pub-third-party-exam-supplemental-procedures.pdf
16. The Power of Collaboration (Linda Tuck Chapman), RMA Journal (Jul 2016)
17. SEC Statement on the Aggregate Impact of Financial Services Regulations (Mar 2015) https://www.sec.gov/news/statement/aggregate-impact-of-financial-services-regulation.html
18. OCC: Comptroller's Handbook M-CRG (Safety and Soundness) Corporate and Risk Governance (Jul 2016) https://www.occ.treas.gov/publications/publications-by-type/comptrollers-handbook/pub-ch-crg.pdf
19. Greg Carmichael, President and CEO, Fifth Third Bancorp
20. Fifth Third Bank www.53.com

About the Author

Linda Tuck Chapman is a recognized subject matter expert, trusted advisor, educator, and popular speaker. She is pragmatic and strategic, continuously mining her deep expertise and broad experience to drive enterprise value.

Career highlights:

- President, Ontala Performance Solutions Ltd.
- Chief Procurement Officer, BMO Financial Group
- President & CEO, Ontario Education Collaborative Marketplace
- Chief Procurement Officer, Fifth Third Bank
- Chief Procurement Officer & Executive Officer, Shared Services, Scotiabank Group
- Banking executive (retail and commercial)

Professional Profile:

Linda is Chair, Sourcing Industry Group Thought Leaders Council; member, Shared Assessments Group advisory board; long-serving judge for Outsourcing Center's Global Outsourcing Excellence Awards; and lecturer, Centre for Outsourcing Research and Education. Linda is an ICB Fellow and Medalist, and holds an MBA (Magna Cum Laude) from Dalhousie School of Business.

Linda's thought leadership is frequently profiled in industry-leading publications such as *The RMA Journal*, *The Wall Street Journal*, and *Outsource*, and strengthened by her engagement in executive networks and professional associations. Linda is passionate about making business better.